CW00968710

Rock Climbing Guide to Europe

To Charlie,

With thanks for
all the time
spent hanging
around together

[signature]

Feb '05

ROCK CLIMBING GUIDE TO EUROPE

DAVID JONES

The Mountaineers

© David Jones 1991

First Published in Great Britain in 1991 by The Crowood Press Ltd.
Gipsy Lane, Swindon, Wiltshire SN2 6DQ

Published in the USA by The Mountaineers
Founded 1906 "... to explore, study, preserve and enjoy the natural
beauty of the outdoors ..."
306 Second Avenue West, Seattle WA 98119

Published simultaneously in Canada by Douglas & McIntyre
1615 Venables St., Vancouver B.C. V5L 2H1

All rights reserved. No part of this publication may be reproduced or transmitted in any form or by
any means, electronic or mechanical, including photocopy, recording, or any information storage
and retrieval system, without permission in writing from the publishers.

ISBN 0-89886-291-4 (North America)

Acknowledgements
Writing this guide proved to be a much bigger task than I had anticipated. Many of my friends came
up with extra information that I simply could not leave out, and in consequence the book grew
considerably. I must thank Malcolm MacPherson for supplying me with a portable AT computer and
Shakespeare program, without which I would never have dared to even start such a gigantic task.
Many people have helped me in collecting information, and I thank them all. In particular a mention
must go to Joe Healey, Guy McLelland, Paul Innes, Bruno Cormier, Christine Coquio, Bernard Thun,
Felicity Butler, Stephan Gschwendtner, Matt Saunders, Fred Simpson, Miranda Ruffell, Geoff Odds,
Mike Ratcliffe, Bradley Jackson, Simon Nadin, John Hartley, Chris Addey, Steve Earnshaw, Tony
Ryan, Dave Turner, Chris Harding, Nigel Slater, Mark Pretty, Chris Plant, Sean Myles, Simon Carr,
Barry Knight, Brian Parr, Sue Bloggs, Uli Hofsteder and Ben Moon. I am also particularly indebted to
Jean-Pierre Bouvier whose 1982 guide came out at a time when we were struggling to find areas other
than Verdon and Fontainebleau, and also thank *Vertical* magazine for giving me so much
photographic inspiration to climb in Europe.

Picture Credits
Front cover photograph: Ben Moon on CHOUCAS 8a + , Buoux, France, by Takashi Nakagawa.
Back cover photograph: Steve Morley on CHARLES DE GAUL 7a + , Volx, France, by Dave Turner.

Manufactured in Great Britain

Contents

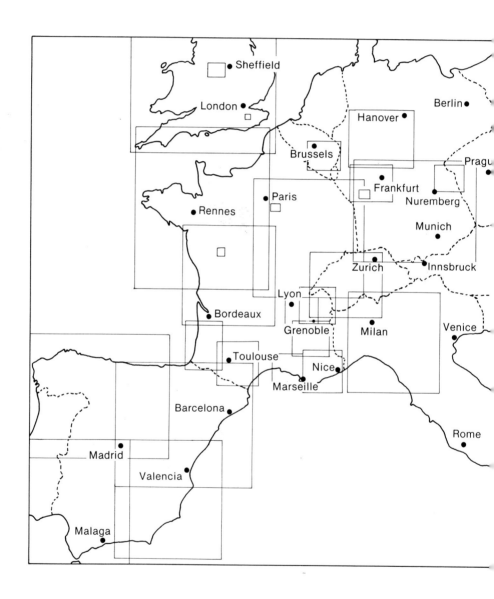

List of Maps

Preface

Welcome, and thank you for purchasing the first edition of this crag climbing guide to Europe. You now have at your fingertips 640 crags and 58 topo diagrams from right across Europe. I have not included every crag there is for obvious reasons, most importantly because the book must go to print now to be ready in time for the 1991 season. Still, there is enough climbing here for about 100 people over about 100 years. I have tried to cover as wide an area as possible and in consequence the depth of information varies considerably. France is very well represented since I have spent over two years there in total. My visits to Spain, Italy and Germany have been a bit more sporadic, so the amount of info on them is not so great.

I have brought the whole of Europe into line by using the French grading system throughout; no doubt this will become the norm over the next 5 years. I have included topo diagrams for British crags since they are often unavailable and the ones that do exist have the British Stone Age grading system.

If I have missed out any crag, or you feel that any of my comments seem unjust then I would be very pleased to receive details, however minor. Send to David Jones, c/o The Crowood Press, Gipsy Lane, Swindon, SN2 6DQ.

The Guide

HOW TO USE IT

Each crag has certain information presented in a quick, easy-to-use formula. After a few minutes' use the figures will give clear and exceptionally useful vital information. The top line gives the **general overall picture** of the crag, including:

The name of the crag.

Sun hours − the hours (preceded by the symbol ✳) when the sun shines on the crag. This is very important in hot climates. Most European crags suffer temperatures of over 100°F (37°C) in the hot summer sun, while in spring and autumn you will appreciate some sunshine.

The **number of routes** − in each grade, from 4 to 8. If they are not spread evenly (for example, if all the grade 6 are in fact 6a and there are hardly any 6b and 6c), this will be said in the crag description. Most crags do seem to offer a fair average in each grade.

The **total number of routes**, which may include grade 1−3 climbs and unbolted routes or overgrown ones.

The **province**. For those familiar with a country this will help to identify the crag's location quickly without having to refer to maps.

The **number of the crag** in this guide.

The information is set out as follows:

Name of main crag: ✳ hours routes in grades (4.5.6.7.8) total (00) area of country, province crag number

For example:

ORPIERRE: ✳ 06.00→22.00 (24.20.37.5.1)(78)   HAUTES ALPES [286]

Information is then given about the **climbing** on the cliff, the size and style of routes. In many cases this is quite brief (a combination of lack of space and precise information available), but it will always be adequate. **Information** is also given about the *in situ* **protection**. This does *not* guarantee any safety or imply that the bolts will hold in the event of a fall. The information given is to describe the type of bolts used, and for simplicity they have been divided into six categories, as follows:

[1]   15mm ring bolts with resin glue fixments
[2]   13mm ring bolts with resin glue fixments
[3]   10mm expansion bolts with hangers
[4]   Pegs in concrete and expansion bolts
[5]   8mm expansion bolts with hangers
[6]   Various bolts and pegs with loose placements

Class 1 are obviously stronger than class 6, however, you should remember that even a loose peg in a horizontal crack could hold better than a 15mm bolt in a roof where, 5mm under the hard rock skin, the rock might be like putty.

The following is an example of the climbing information.

One of the great French crags with just about everything going for it. Limestone from 30→150m. The rock is superb with plenty of water pockets on the large walls and overhangs. Bolts [3] and a lovely situation. The crag faces many different ways and offers climbing all year round.

After the climbing information, **directions to find the crag** are given. Because of the size of Europe, this has been a nightmare to collect, but it should be very accurate. The directions are intended to get you to the crag even if you lose your road map, and in using reference material to locate crags I have pulled out almost all of my hair. Many books quote only 'East' or 'West' and a typing slip will send you 50km in the opposite direction. As all guides are equally open to such mistakes, I would advise you to use the town names wherever possible; if they do not match up with the E or W indicated, go by the towns.

First of all, the distance from the nearest major town on almost any map of the whole country concerned is given, with a geographic direction. If in doubt, refer to the main map. Next there are details of how to drive to the nearest parking spot for the crag, and then there are approach details. The wording has been carefully planned to avoid confusion but one good tip is that there is a distinct difference between 'to' a town and 'towards' a town. If it says 'to', go right to the town. 'Towards' means you should follow the direction, but there will be another instruction before you reach the town. There are a few crags for which exact descriptions were unavailable but, rather than exclude them, the lack of info has been mentioned.

Finally, each crag description has a reference in brackets. This is the page number and cross reference of the crag on the most popular and available road atlas of each country. Those listed below offer the best value for money in navigating around Europe. There is also the Michelin road atlas to Europe which is very good and was used when describing directions for every single crag. Directions might read as follows:

Dir: 24km NW of Sisteron, 10km W of Laragne-Montéglin. From that town take the N75 northwards to Eyguians, turn L on to the D30 which leads to Orpierre after 10km. Park in the village. The crags overlook the village and can be reached in about 15 mins. Please use the footpaths which prevent erosion and damage to local property. (145:F2)

The following road atlases were used to locate crags, and references to locations will match.

Great Britain: *Ordnance Survey Superscale Atlas* (1:144, 132)
Belgium: No road atlas but where possible references are to French *Michelin*
Luxembourg: French *Michelin*
Germany: *Auto-Atlas*, Reise und Verkehrsverlag, Deutschland (1:200,000)
Switzerland: *Automobile Club de Suisse* loose map, Kümmerly + Frey (1:250,000)
France: *Michelin Motoring Atlas* (1:200,000)
Spain: *Gran Atlas de Carreteras*, Plaza & James (1:300,000)
Italy: *Atlant Stradale d'Italia*, Touring Club Italiano (1:200,000)

The atlases are readily available from bookshops or motoring organisations. If you have any difficulty, contact Stanfords, Long Acre, London WC2E 9LP (071-836 1321), or McCarta Ltd, 122 Kings Cross Road, London WC1X 9DS (071-278 8276).

If camping is a particular problem in the area a local site will be suggested but otherwise the climber will be left to enquire. Normally campsites are easy to locate and very good value for money. Information on where to buy local topo guides is given but this is very much a seasonal thing — supplies run out, shops close and so on — all out of my control. In general, local info from other climbers is usually more than helpful. 'Mid-season' means spring or autumn.

NOTES FOR NON-EUROPEAN CLIMBERS

Those climbers visiting Europe for the first time will be impressed at the amount of climbing on offer. One major difficulty, though, is transport; if you don't have wheels you have problems. Many crags *can* be reached by public transport or hitch-hiking but on weekdays getting to them is very awkward — there are fewer climbers around to pick people up. Think about flying to Barcelona in Spain. Of the European countries Spain is the cheapest for car hire and from Barcelona you can reach the southern French crags in 4–5 hours. In Britain car hire is expensive but hitching is a good idea with the good road network. In Spain and Italy you must have a car. In Germany and Switzerland car hire (and just about everything else) is expensive, so stock up on what you can in France. Drinking out in Europe (with the exception of Britain) is also expensive, so always quench your thirst *before* entering a bar!

The equipment needed is very simple — boots or slippers, a single 10mm rope and 7 quick draws per person, belay brake and 1 screwgate. Two ropes for 55m abseils are definitely a luxury and are not necessary if you are restricted on baggage allowance.

GRADES

GRADE COMPARISON CHART

English	French	German	USA	Australian
Diff	2	I	5.2	10
V Diff	3	II	5.4	12
Severe	4	III	5.5	14
Hard Severe	5a	IV	5.6	15
Very Severe	5b	V	5.8	17
HVS	5c	VI	5.9	18
E1,5b	6a	VII −	5.10b	19
E2,5c	6a	VII	5.10c	21
E3,5c	6b	VII +	5.10d	22
E3,6a	6b	VIII −	5.11b	23
E4,6a	6c	VIII	5.11c	24
E4,6b	7a	VIII	5.11d	25
E5,6a	7a	VIII +	5.12a	26
E5,6b	7b	IX −	5.12b	27
E6,6b	7c	IX +	5.12c	29
E6,6c	7c +	X	5.13a	32
E7,7a	8a	X +	5.13c	40
E8,7a	8b +	XI −	5.14a	
E9,7b	8c			

Accidents

In most cases accidents will be minimal and it is unlikely that rescue services will be needed. Most of the crags in the book are near a road and even with a broken leg, getting to hospital should not provide a problem. Medical attention in Europe is excellent but expensive, and I suggest that you are fully insured both for medical and personal belongings. In the case of more serious injury, for example a back or spinal fracture, do not move the patient unless absolutely necessary. If you are in doubt as to what to do, contact the police first, as they will know who will be most helpful.

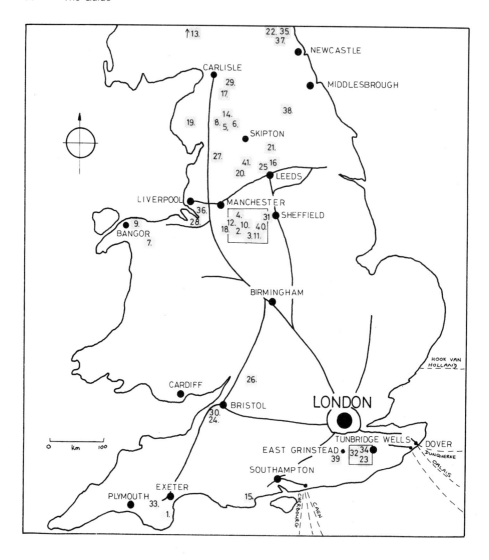

1. ANSTEY'S COVE
2. THE CORNICE — Cheedale
3. THE CORNICE — Water Cum Jolly
4. THE EMBANKMENT
5. GORDALE SCAR
6. KILNSEY CRAG
7. LLANBERIS SLATE QUARRIES
8. MALHAM COVE
9. PEN TRWYN
10. RAVEN TOR
11. RUBICON WALL
12. TWO TIER BUTTRESS — Cheedale
13. UPPER CAVE CRAG
14. YEW COGAR

15. THE AGGLESTONE
16. ALMSCLIFF
17. ARMATHWAITE
18. BALDSTONES
19. BOWDERSTONE
20. BRIDE STONES
21. BRIMHAM ROCKS
22. BOWDEN DOORS
23. BOWLES ROCKS
24. BURRINGTON COOMBE
25. CALEY
26. CASTLE ROCK
27. CRAIG Y LONGRIDGE
28. FRODSHAM

29. THE GELT BOULDER
30. GOBLIN COMBE
31. GRITSTONE EDGES
32. HARRISON'S ROCKS
33. HAYTOR
34. HIGH ROCKS
35. KYLOE CRAGS
36. PEX HILL
37. SANDY CRAG
38. SLIPSTONE CRAG
39. STONE FARM ROCKS
40. STONEY MIDDLETON
41. WIDDOP

Great Britain

England and Wales are included in this guide so that climbers from America and Europe can easily identify how many crags have *in situ* gear. There are about 2,000 crags in Britain of which only a small number have been bolted. The reason for this is tradition — not such a bad thing — but, still, more and more British climbers are seeing the benefit of bolt-protected routes.

The crags described here are climbing places that necessitate only the use of a rope, karabiners and quick draws. For a comprehensive guide to the naturally-protected crags in Britain, *see Crag Guide to England and Wales*, also published by The Crowood Press.

Placing protection in Britain is worse than in Europe or North America since the weather is often cool and windy. Routes are awkward to find, it is awkward to place protection, and they are graded poorly, so a leader will often take over an hour to lead one pitch. The second begins to feel the cold, feet stuck solid in mud at the bottom of the crag, and eventually has to climb, shivering and fed up. There are no bolts at the top of the crags either, so an abseil to clean a route of gear is a long and arduous business.

Many British climbers have grown up with this type of climbing and never travelled to the Continent. However, trends are slowly changing. Limestone routes are getting bolted up, and top-roping routes are also increasing. These changes are looked on with disgust by the old traditionalists, but modern climbing is here to stay. One day perhaps whole families will be able to visit the British crags and enjoy climbing in safety together, as they do in Europe.

BOLTED CRAGS

Anstey's Cove:
✳ 12.00→19.00 (0.0.4.12.2)(18)
DEVON [1]

An old limestone crag which has been developed to give some good hard steep routes. *In situ* gear [4−6]. 10−25m. Tides not a problem.

Dir: At Babbacombe 2km NE of Torquay. From Torquay take the B3199 to Babbacombe, after 1.5km park in car park on the right. A path just further on the right is signposted to Anstey's Cove. (7:F3)

The Cornice − Cheedale:
✳ Never (0.0.0.22.5)(27) PEAK [2]

The Cornice is a strange crag which, due to two good summers in a row, has become very popular with the hard climbers and new bolted routes have become very popular. Limestone. None of the routes are easy and all are steep and overhanging. The problem with the area is that it seeps for a long time after winter and never gets the sun. However, in a hot summer this is a blessing as it remains very cool. All are single pitch to 25m with bolts [3−6]. Worth a visit.

Dir: 7km E of Buxton. From Buxton take the A6 towards Bakewell. After 3km there is a car park on the L opposite a quarry. Park here and walk downstream beside the river. A long 20-min walk leads you beside the river with Two Tier Buttress on the R low down; stepping stones. Go round the corner, cross by bridge then cross back again over the river. Here are some stepping stones and the crag is on the L with lots of bolts with hangers. (79:F3)

The Cornice − Water Cum Jolly:
✳ Never (0.0.0.4.4)(8) PEAK [3]

A good steep crag with some fine limestone climbing. There are a few routes in the lower grades but these are not bolt protected. Definitely worth a visit for the 7c climber. Also stays in the shade in the hot summer afternoons.

Dir: 80 km NW of Bakewell, 25km SW of Sheffield. From Sheffield take the A621 towards Bakewell. About 4km before turn R on to the A623 towards Stoney Middleton and Manchester. Carry on for 10km then turn L on to the B6465. Pass through Wardlow and carry on to the pub at Monsal Head. Turn R and go

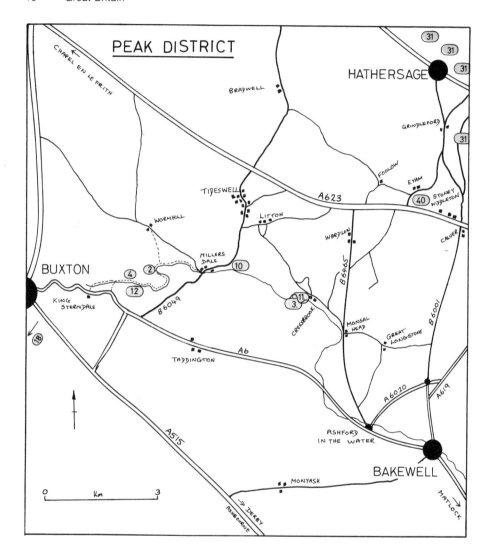

PEAK DISTRICT

2. THE CORNICE – Cheedale
3. THE CORNICE – Water Cum Jolly
4. THE EMBANKMENT
10. RAVEN TOR
11. RUBICON WALL
12. TWO TIER BUTTRES – Cheedale
18. BALDSTONES
31. GRITSTONE EDGES
40. STONEY MIDDLETON

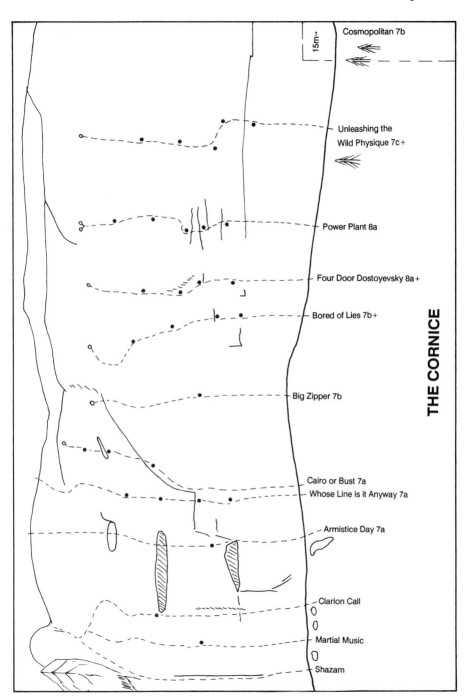

Cosmopolitan 7b

15m→

Unleashing the Wild Physique 7c+

Power Plant 8a

Four Door Dostoyevsky 8a+

Bored of Lies 7b+

Big Zipper 7b

Cairo or Bust 7a

Whose Line is it Anyway 7a

Armistice Day 7a

Clarion Call

Martial Music

Shazam

THE CORNICE

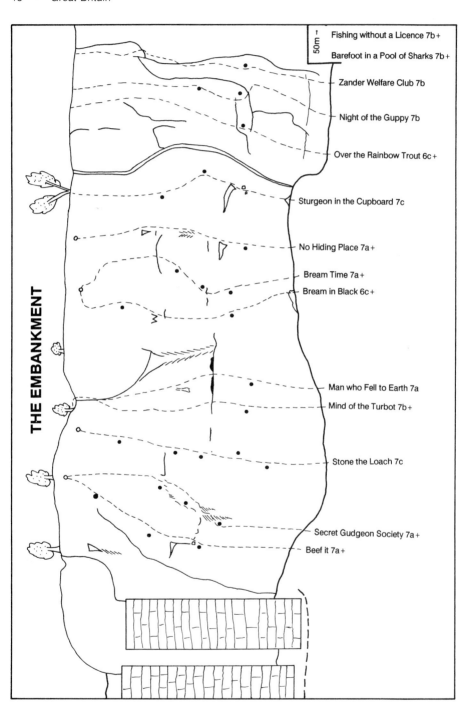

THE EMBANKMENT

50m

Fishing without a Licence 7b+

Barefoot in a Pool of Sharks 7b+

Zander Welfare Club 7b

Night of the Guppy 7b

Over the Rainbow Trout 6c+

Sturgeon in the Cupboard 7c

No Hiding Place 7a+

Bream Time 7a+

Bream in Black 6c+

Man who Fell to Earth 7a

Mind of the Turbot 7b+

Stone the Loach 7c

Secret Gudgeon Society 7a+

Beef it 7a+

down the steep hill and along the valley to Cressbrook. Park just before the road starts to go uphill and by a disused mill house. Take a footpath on the L which goes upriver to a small lake and a crag on the R. Pass this and walk upstream for 10 mins. The crag can be seen on the other side at the large bend in the river. Cross (wet feet) to the crag. It can be reached by footpath from above but for the first time this is very awkward. (79:F3)

The Embankment:
✳ 10.00→16.00
(0.0.1.18.0)(20) PEAK [4]

This cliff is quite small and very popular. 10−20m high with all routes having *in situ* protection [5−6]. There are 20 routes, 7a→7c, with most being around 7b. All are steep and slightly overhanging, the limestone being smooth and quite technical, no pockets. The cliff faces S and is well protected from the wind; trees offer shade in summer. Climbing possible all year round. There are campsites at Buxton and to the north at Castleton.

Dir: 25km SW of Sheffield, 7km E of Buxton. Take the A6 going E out of Buxton. After 4km the road goes uphill; carry on to a layby on the L, often with a tea van. Park here. Go down the steep N slope to the old railway track in the valley, turn R and go W along the disused track for 1km. Before going into the tunnel take a small footpath on the R, the cliff is here directly on the L. (79:F3)

Gordale Scar:
✳ 18.00→20.00
(0.0.0.0.6.1)(7) YORKSHIRE [5]

A very large sombre limestone crag offering some of the hardest routes in Yorkshire. 30−40m routes, grade 8a − and above. The crag is very wet in winter and only dries out in a good summer spell. Steep and very overhanging with some of the spaces in between the bolts being rather large. Bolts [3−6]. Some are not bolt protected but this is very obvious. Plenty of tourists.

Dir: See Malham Cove. (93:H5)

Kilnsey Crag:
✳ 06.00−12.00
(0.0.0.12.4)(18) YORKSHIRE [6]

A good large limestone crag up to 30m high. A cold crag generally but perfect on hot summer afternoons. Bolts [4−6]. The routes are very good, sustained and overhanging. The main roof is around 8b.

Dir: 16km ENE of Settle. From Skipton take the B6265 N to Threshfield, then turn L on to the B6160 which passes through Kilnsey village. The crag is obvious from the pub in the village. Drive to the N end of the crag and then park about 200 yds further on at a parking spot. (94:A5)

Llanberis Slate Quarries:
✳ 10.00−18.00 (0.0.0.21.6)(30) N WALES [7]

Across the road from Llanberis are a collection of old slate quarries at Dinorwic. Most of the routes are naturally protected and others are bolted. A lot of routes only have an occasional bolt but there are a handful of fully bolted-up routes. Info can be found in Llanberis. The crags do dry very quickly after rain.

Dir: 12km SE of Caernarfon. Take the A4086 to Llanberis and enquire locally. (74:E4)

Malham Cove:
✳ 10.00→18.00
(0.0.7.43.18)(68) YORKSHIRE [8]

The best crag in England with very good routes varying from steep walls at about 6c to very steep overhanging walls at 8c. About 60 routes, mostly 7a to 8b. Pockets, overlaps and a lot of powerful climbing. Limestone with bolts [3−6]. There are several areas in the cove to climb but as yet only the L side is well bolted up. There are two tiers, the lower one staying very dry even in heavy rain. Climbing possible here all year round but it can get cold in winter and very hot in the summer. S-facing and very sheltered from N winds.

Dir: 50km NW of Leeds, 15km NW of Skipton. Take the A65 NW out of Skipton for 10km, then take a small road running N to Airton and then Malham. Park in the village and then a path leads due N to the Cove. A small road leads off to the E over the bridge in the village centre. After 1km this bends and you can park

NEW DAWN, 7c, Malham Cove. (Climber Jean-Baptiste Tribout, Photo David Jones)

there for Gordale Scar. Gordale Scar is then directly up the valley from here. There is a campsite very near to the village, just to the NW. (93:G5)

Pen Trwyn:
✳ 05.00→12.00 (0.0.0.26.7)(300)
15.00→22.00 NORTH WALES [9]

There are several parts of Pen Trwyn on which to climb. Most of the crags are naturally protected but there are about 30 bolt-protected routes, limestone. Recently there has been a landslide and access to the crags is proving difficult. The main bolted [4−6] area is LOWER PEN TRWYN which is just above the sea and can be seen straight ahead from the Pier at Llandudno above the rocky beach at low tide. Above it is the large crag of Pen Trwyn with only a couple of fully bolted routes. There is some good wet weather bouldering in the caves, though. Ask climbers locally for Pidgeon's Cave. There are no trees at the top for top-roping unfortunately.

Dir: 1km NNE of Llandudno. From the town do a R at the Empire Hotel then a L at the Grand Hotel to The Great Orme, through the toll gate and after 200m round a bend the crag is seen. (75:G2)

Lower Pen Trwyn is 1km N of Llandudno. Go past the toll on the Ormes road and, at the first big caves on the L, park. Go over the wall and down the gully to the boulder beach below; quite a walk. Not possible to climb at high tide but in the shade all day.

Raven Tor:
✳ 13.00→21.00
(0.0.0.18.8)(26) PEAK [10]

A large limestone crag with many hard routes, indeed, some are classic test pieces. About 30 routes, 7b to 8c. 5−70m and W facing. The crag overhangs everywhere and especially at the base, most of the starts being very hard indeed. The small routes on the R require very strong fingers whilst the routes up the centre are long and relentless. For spring and autumn afternoon climbing and, in summer, morning only. The crag seeps a lot after the winter and the big routes only come into condition mid-summer through to late autumn. Bolts [5−6].

Dir: 24km SW of Sheffield, 8km E of Buxton. Take the A6 E from Buxton, after 10km turn L on to the B6049 and go down to Millers Dale. Turn R down the small road past the Happy Angler pub. The crag is by the road on the L after 1km. (79:F3)

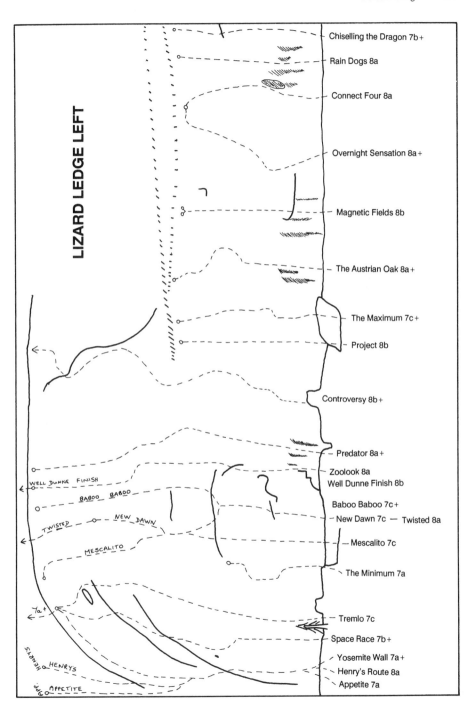

LIZARD LEDGE LEFT

Chiselling the Dragon 7b+

Rain Dogs 8a

Connect Four 8a

Overnight Sensation 8a+

Magnetic Fields 8b

The Austrian Oak 8a+

The Maximum 7c+

Project 8b

Controversy 8b+

Predator 8a+

Zoolook 8a
Well Dunne Finish 8b

Baboo Baboo 7c+

New Dawn 7c — Twisted 8a

Mescalito 7c

The Minimum 7a

Tremlo 7c

Space Race 7b+

Yosemite Wall 7a+

Henry's Route 8a

Appetite 7a

WELL DUNNE FINISH

BABOO BABOO

TWISTED   NEW DAWN

MESCALITO

7a+

S. HENRY'S   HENRYS

APP.   APPETITE

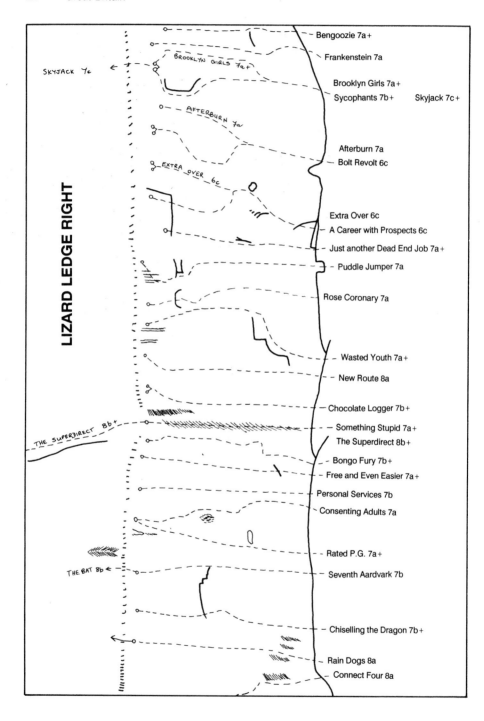

LIZARD LEDGE RIGHT

Skyjack 7c

Brooklyn Girls 7a+

Afterburn 7a

Extra Over 6c

The Superdirect 8b+

The Bat 8b

Bengoozie 7a+

Frankenstein 7a

Brooklyn Girls 7a+

Sycophants 7b+   Skyjack 7c+

Afterburn 7a

Bolt Revolt 6c

Extra Over 6c

A Career with Prospects 6c

Just another Dead End Job 7a+

Puddle Jumper 7a

Rose Coronary 7a

Wasted Youth 7a+

New Route 8a

Chocolate Logger 7b+

Something Stupid 7a+

The Superdirect 8b+

Bongo Fury 7b+

Free and Even Easier 7a+

Personal Services 7b

Consenting Adults 7a

Rated P.G. 7a+

Seventh Aardvark 7b

Chiselling the Dragon 7b+

Rain Dogs 8a

Connect Four 8a

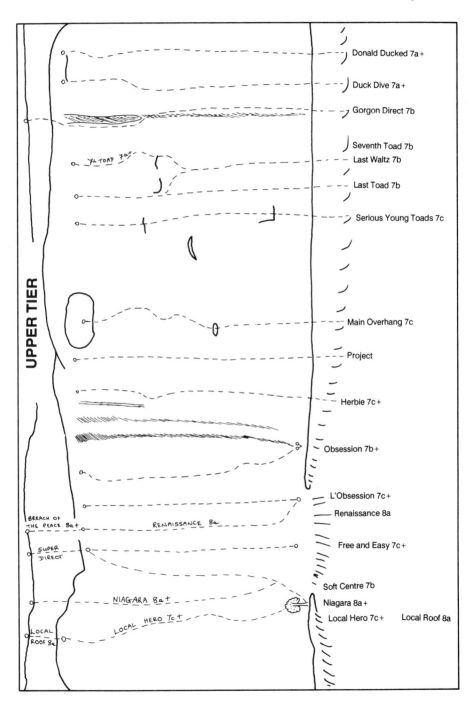

UPPER TIER

Donald Ducked 7a+
Duck Dive 7a+
Gorgon Direct 7b
Seventh Toad 7b
Last Waltz 7b
Last Toad 7b
Serious Young Toads 7c
Main Overhang 7c
Project
Herbie 7c+
Obsession 7b+
L'Obsession 7c+
Renaissance 8a
Free and Easy 7c+
Soft Centre 7b
Niagara 8a+
Local Hero 7c+   Local Roof 8a

7L TOAD 7a+
BREACH OF THE PEACE 8a+
RENAISSANCE 8a
SUPER DIRECT
NIAGARA 8a+
LOCAL HERO 7c+
LOCAL ROOF 8a

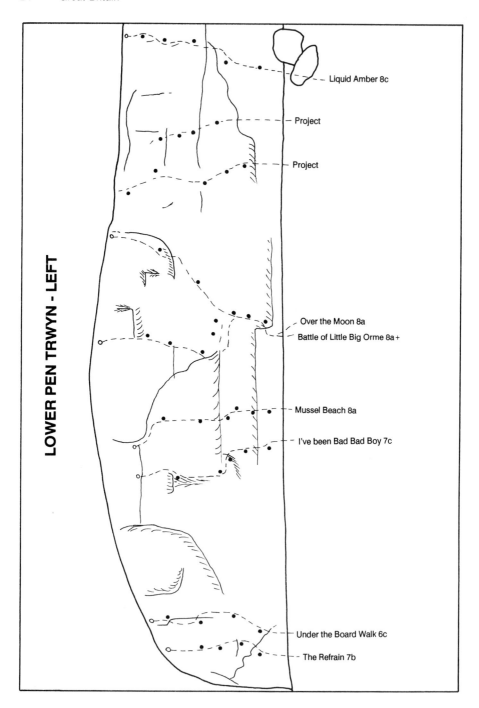

LOWER PEN TRWYN - LEFT

Liquid Amber 8c

Project

Project

Over the Moon 8a
Battle of Little Big Orme 8a+

Mussel Beach 8a

I've been Bad Bad Boy 7c

Under the Board Walk 6c

The Refrain 7b

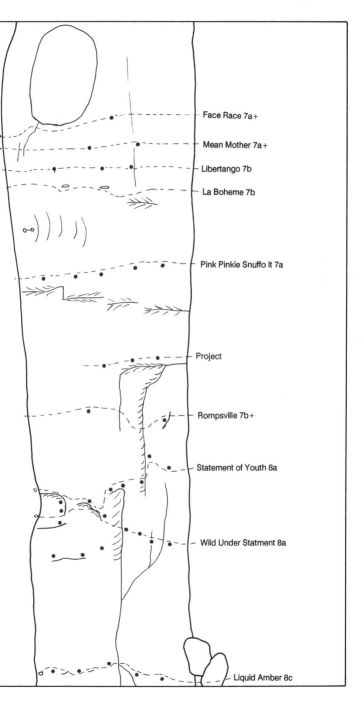

LOWER PEN TRWYN - RIGHT

Face Race 7a+

Mean Mother 7a+

Libertango 7b

La Boheme 7b

Pink Pinkie Snuffo it 7a

Project

Rompsville 7b+

Statement of Youth 8a

Wild Under Statment 8a

Liquid Amber 8c

HUBBLE, 8c +, Raven Tor. (Climber Ben Moon, Photo David Jones)

Rubicon Wall:
✳ 12.00→18.00
(0.0.4.22.5)(35)   PEAK [11]

A 10m natural limestone crag in a very pleasant setting by the river. A large white wall offering some very fingery routes, with an overhanging section with very powerful routes. Bolted [3] routes are in the 8b grade, all the others need nuts also but can be very easily top-roped from the trees above. These can be reached from either end. Most of it stays dry in the rain but it can seep a lot after heavy rain. A popular spot with limestone anorexic stick insects. There is also an access problem with local fishermen, so good behaviour is of vital importance.

Dir: 8km NW of Bakewell, 25km SW of Sheffield. From Sheffield take the A621 towards Bakewell. About 4km before turn R on to the A623 towards Stoney Middleton and Manchester. Carry on for 10km then turn L on to the B6465, pass through Wardlow and carry on to the pub at Monsal Head. Turn R and go down the steep hill and along the valley to Cressbrook. Park just before the road starts to go uphill and by a disused mill house. Take a footpath on the L which goes upriver and the crag is shortly on the R by a lake. (79:F3)

Two Tier Buttress – Cheedale:
✳ 14.00→20.00
(0.0.0.15.2)(17)   PEAK [12]

An excellent-looking crag. On close inspection the size of the holds becomes depressing, unless you are a superstar. Only the hardest routes so far have been bolted [3–6]. Many should follow but this will always be a crag for 7b upwards. The cliff is limestone and in two parts. The climbs are on the lower tier and are 20m high.

Dir: 7km E of Buxton. *See* Cornice directions (page 15). (79:F3)

Upper Cave Crag:
✳ 12.00→17.00
(0.0.0.5.4)(9)   SCOTLAND [13]

A beautifully-situated crag in the lowland valleys of Scotland just N of Perth. A volcanic schist crag of unrelenting steepness 20m high,

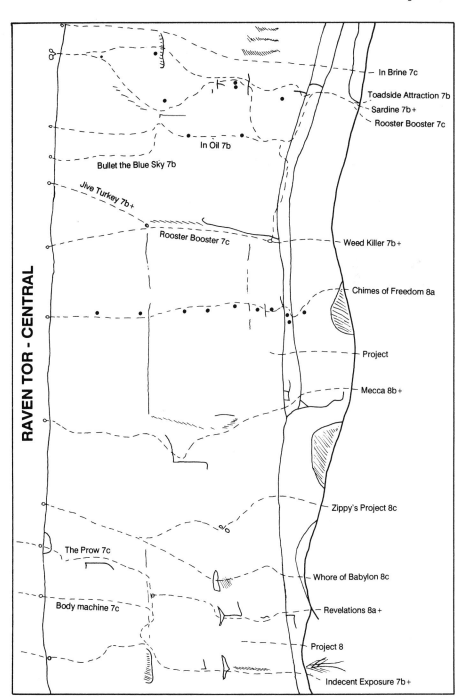

RAVEN TOR - CENTRAL

In Brine 7c
Toadside Attraction 7b
Sardine 7b+
Rooster Booster 7c
In Oil 7b
Bullet the Blue Sky 7b
Jive Turkey 7b+
Rooster Booster 7c
Weed Killer 7b+
Chimes of Freedom 8a
Project
Mecca 8b+
Zippy's Project 8c
The Prow 7c
Whore of Babylon 8c
Body machine 7c
Revelations 8a+
Project 8
Indecent Exposure 7b+

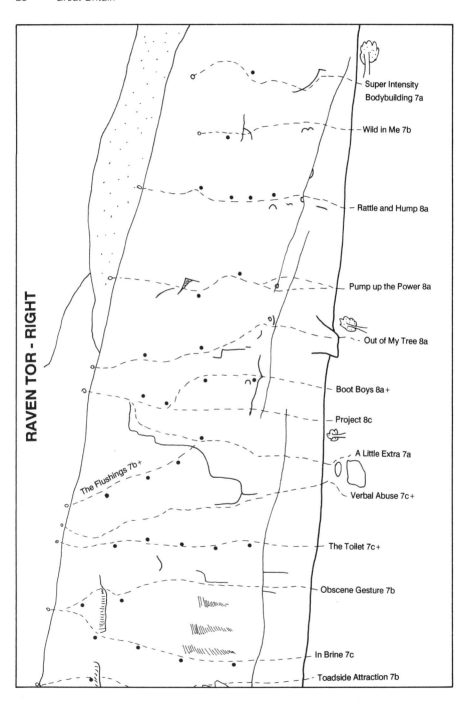

RAVEN TOR - RIGHT

Super Intensity
Bodybuilding 7a

Wild in Me 7b

Rattle and Hump 8a

Pump up the Power 8a

Out of My Tree 8a

Boot Boys 8a+

Project 8c

A Little Extra 7a

Verbal Abuse 7c+

The Flushings 7b+

The Toilet 7c+

Obscene Gesture 7b

In Brine 7c

Toadside Attraction 7b

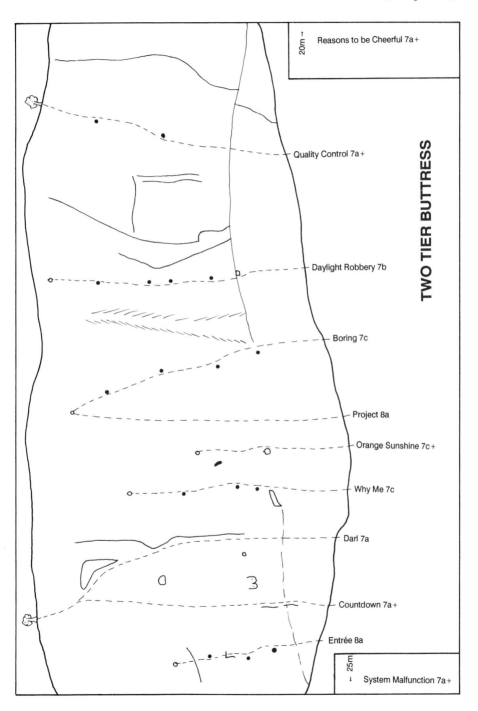

Reasons to be Cheerful 7a+

20m ↑

Quality Control 7a+

Daylight Robbery 7b

Boring 7c

Project 8a

Orange Sunshine 7c+

Why Me 7c

Darl 7a

Countdown 7a+

Entrée 8a

25m ↓

System Malfunction 7a+

TWO TIER BUTTRESS

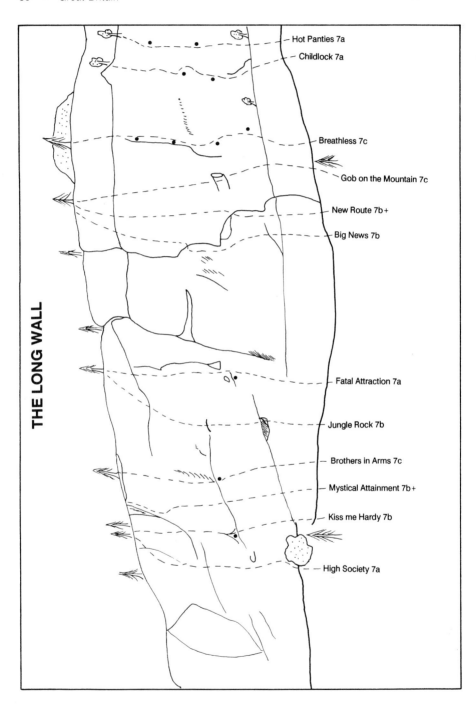

THE LONG WALL

Hot Panties 7a
Childlock 7a
Breathless 7c
Gob on the Mountain 7c
New Route 7b+
Big News 7b
Fatal Attraction 7a
Jungle Rock 7b
Brothers in Arms 7c
Mystical Attainment 7b+
Kiss me Hardy 7b
High Society 7a

offering some excellent routes in the higher grades. Bolts [3−6]. Very cold in winter. Sometimes referred to as CRAIG-A-BARNS.

Dir: 21km NNW of Perth. Take the A9 N towards Pitlochry. Turn off to the R at Dunkeld. The crag is directly ahead to the N overlooking the village. Park in a car park and walk to the crag in 10 mins. (137:G4)

Yew Cogar:
✳ 17.00→19.00
(0.0.0.10.1)(11) YORKSHIRE [14]

A fair limestone crag up to 25m with a range of recently developed and equipped routes. Bolts [4−6].

Dir: 13km NE of Settle. From Settle go N for about 1km then turn R on to a small road towards Malham Tarn, then L to the village of Arncliffe. The crag is about 1m on the S side of the impressive valley running SW from Arncliffe. The best approach is from the village itself. Park here by the pub (handy for the disillusioned retreat), then walk up the valley for 2km to the crag. (93:H4)

TOP-ROPING AND BOULDERING

The Agglestone:
✳ 9.00→17.00
(Bouldering) DORSET [15]

This is a small bouldering area with quite hard problems going up to 7m. Hard sandstone but not a lot of it; worth a visit if passing.

Dir: 7km N of Swanage, 1km NW of Studland. Leave studland going N and after 300m, park and take the track that forks left. Follow on to a path leading to Godlingstone Heath, and the rock. 15 mins. (10:B4)

Almscliff:
✳ 9.00→21.00
(Bouldering) YORKSHIRE [16]

One of the best gritstone outcrops in the world with fantastic bouldering. Not over-large but offering upwards of 200 problems. The actual outcrop is reserved for natural protection, but the bouldering is where the real action is. Dries very quickly indeed after rain. Always worth a visit.

Dir: 8.5km ENE of Otley. Take the A659 to Pool, then turn L on to the A658 going NE. At Huby turn L and go through the village on the small road to Stainburn. After 1.5km the road bends to the L and the crag is on the R. 1 min. (86:D2)

Armathwaite:
✳ 10.00→18.00
(Bouldering) CUMBRIA [17]

A very good bouldering area with pleasant landings. Sandstone but nothing like Fontainebleau. Walls and occasional boulders with friction problems. A very beautiful setting and busy on good evenings in summer, but never that busy really. There are some routes that can be top-roped, but you must use a long sling to protect the rock from rope grooves. 5−15m high and situated at just above sea level, all year round for the hardy.

Dir: 15km N of Penrith. Take the A6 N to High Hesket then turn off R to Armathwaite. At the village turn R and go over the bridge and park. A footpath leads down under the bridge and along the S bank. Follow this into the trees keeping R on a well-worn path and to the crag in about 10 mins. (102:B2)

Baldstones:
✳ 07.00→14.00
(Bouldering) PEAK [18]

This outcrop is neighboured by NEWSTONES and RAMSHAW ROCKS, all of which are excellent gritstone crags and areas for bouldering. To the S are THE ROACHES but these are more orientated towards routes with natural protection. They are from 3−15m high with about 200 problems. Situated at 1,400ft and more of a summer crag. Worth a visit.

Dir: 9km NNE of Leek. Take the A53 for 8.5km, 2km past Upper Hulme. Here a road leads off L to Newstone Farm on the L in 1km. From here the rocks can be seen on the ridge to the N. 5 mins. (78:E4)

Bowderstone:
✳ 9.00→21.00
(Bouldering)   LAKE DISTRICT [19]

An area whose true potential has been realised by Pete Kirton and Jerry Moffatt. Good bouldering in a beautiful setting perhaps unrivalled in the whole universe. Not a large area but good problems to work on and also the driest spot in the Lake District (but unfortunately the wettest recorded spot in England). There are many small faces around the area to give fun soloing or wild top-roping. The rock is basically volcanic of no certain description except very hard on the joints in cracks. Worth a boulder.

Dir: 7.5km S of Keswick. Take the B5289 S for 8.5km to a car park on the L just past the turn-off to Grange. Here a footpath leads off S through the woods past Woden's Face to The Bowderstone, then a path can be taken on the L up to the Bowderstone Crag. Alternatively, go L from the car park, and up above in the trees is Quayfoot Buttress. (101:G5)

Bride Stones:
✳ 09.00→22.00
(Bouldering)   YORKSHIRE [20]

One of the best gritstone bouldering areas to be found, with problems at all grades in a very peaceful setting. Best on a good summer's evening. Quite exposed and quick drying. 15ft.

Dir: 7.5km NE of Bacup. From the roundabout at Todmorden take the A646 towards Burnley. After 4.5km at Cornholme turn R on to a small road which leads up to Shore and then take the road going across the moor after 2km. Here turn R and go for 1km to the Sportsman's Inn. The rocks are over on the R, reached by a track. (85:H4)

Brimham Rocks:
✳ 09.00→21.00
(Bouldering)   YORKSHIRE [21]

The best gritstone outcrop in the world. The climbing here is very good, but the geological make-up of the area is superb. Lots of buttresses with paths running between them, and problems at every turn. Absolutely varied climbing throughout. Over 200 listed climbs on natural protection with thousands of boulder problems. The rocks can get green in winter but nearly always offer some good rock to climb on. Good running on the moors nearby and around the outcrops. A must for climbers and the family. 10–15m.

Dir: 15km NW of Harrogate. Take the B6165 to Summerbridge. Here a small road on the R leads up the steep hill to the rocks in about 2.5km. The area is owned by the National Trust; please use the car park. (94:D5)

Bowden Doors:
✳ 9.00→17.00 (Bouldering)
NORTHUMBERLAND [22]

The largest sandstone outcrop in the area, 10m high and with over 300 problems. The climbing is very good but also very exposed. Always worth a visit except in the rain; no real roofs. BACK BOWDEN is another outcrop nearby which is very similar but also has good roofs.

Dir: 6.5km ENE of Wooler. Turn off the B6348 on to the B6349 and continue for 6.5km. The crag can be seen on the L. Please be careful of fences and walls. To reach Back Bowden Doors carry on the road for another 200m then turn L; after 1.5km a path leads down the edge of a forest to the crag. 5 mins. (123:E4)

Bowles Rocks:
✳ 10.00→18.00
(45.36.62.54.9)(200)   SUSSEX [23]

An excellent sandstone crag 5–10m high offering superb climbing in a very sheltered spot. Too high for really good bouldering but some excellent wall and roof climbs. Strenuous climbing on very rounded holds. Terrifically varied climbing in all grades.

Dir: 5km SSW of Tunbridge Wells. Follow A26 (Crowborough) SW, past Eridge station for 1km. Turn left (Bowles outdoor centre). A road leads to the centre, enter and park. The rocks are 100m on the R. (22:B1)

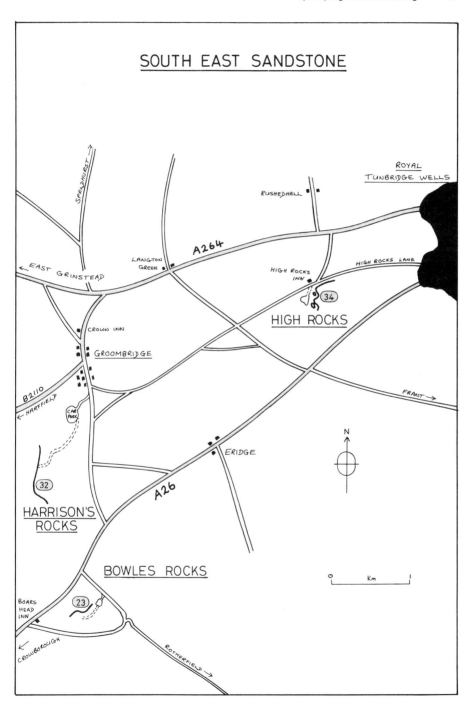

SOUTH EAST SANDSTONE

SPEDHURST →

ROYAL
TUNBRIDGE WELLS

RUSHEDHALL

A264

← EAST GRINSTEAD

LANGTON
GREEN

HIGH ROCKS LANE

HIGH ROCKS
INN

(34)

HIGH ROCKS

CROWN INN

GROOMBRIDGE

B2110

← HARTFIELD

FRANT →

CAR
PARK

N

(32)

ERIDGE

HARRISON'S
ROCKS

A26

BOWLES ROCKS

Km

BOARS
HEAD
INN

(23)

← CROWBOROUGH

ROTHERFIELD →

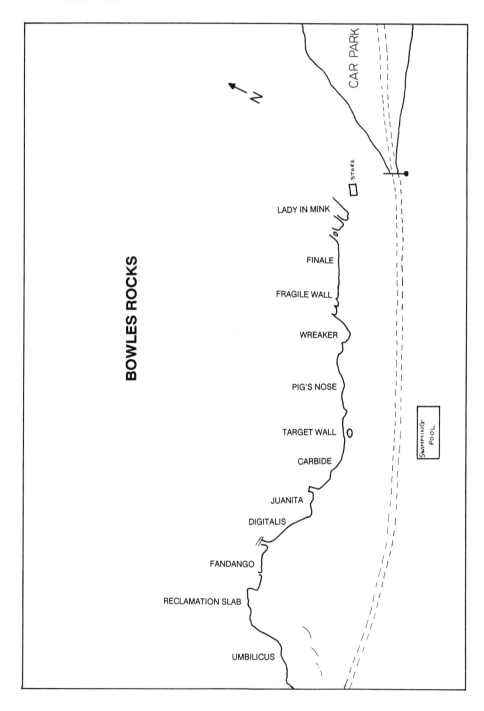

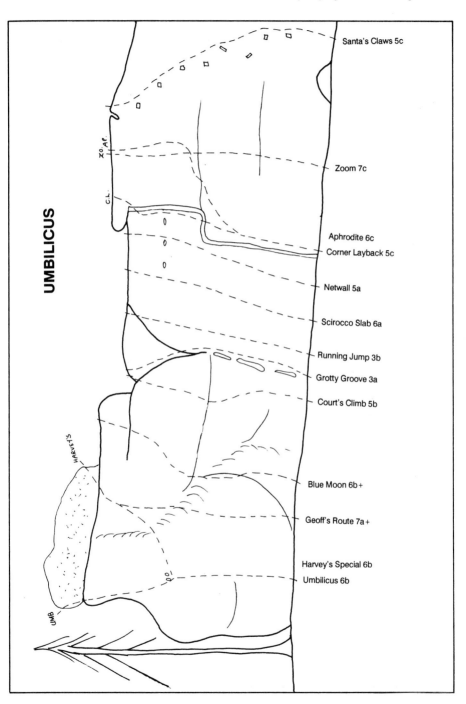

UMBILICUS

Santa's Claws 5c

Zoom 7c

Aphrodite 6c
Corner Layback 5c

Netwall 5a

Scirocco Slab 6a

Running Jump 3b

Grotty Groove 3a

Court's Climb 5b

Blue Moon 6b+

Geoff's Route 7a+

Harvey's Special 6b
Umbilicus 6b

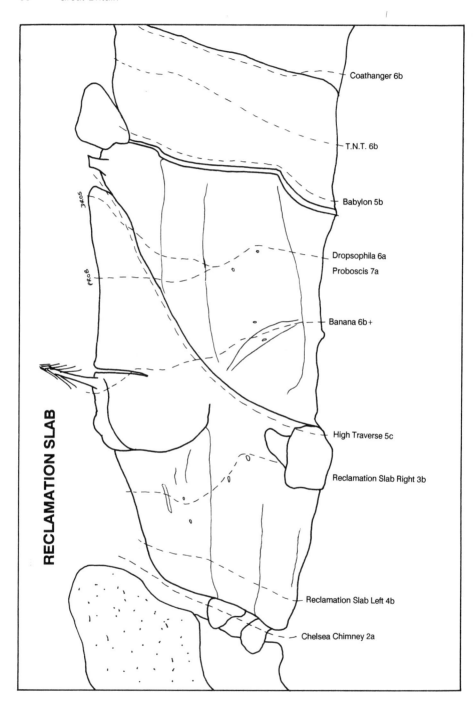

Coathanger 6b

T.N.T. 6b

Babylon 5b

Dropsophila 6a
Proboscis 7a

Banana 6b+

High Traverse 5c

Reclamation Slab Right 3b

Reclamation Slab Left 4b

Chelsea Chimney 2a

RECLAMATION SLAB

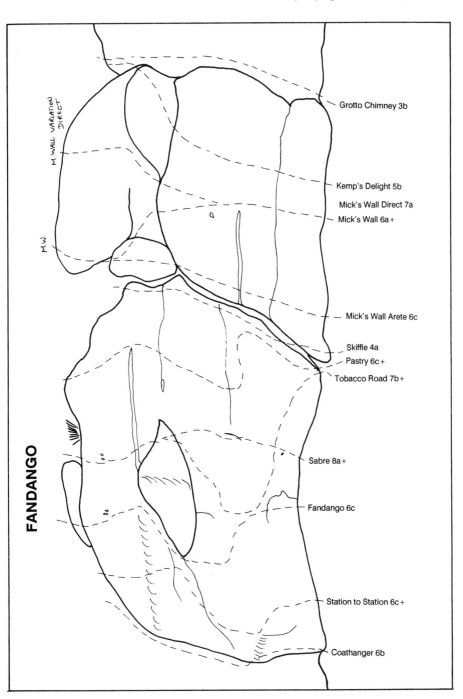

FANDANGO

M. WALL VARIATION DIRECT

M.W.

Grotto Chimney 3b

Kemp's Delight 5b

Mick's Wall Direct 7a

Mick's Wall 6a +

Mick's Wall Arete 6c

Skiffle 4a

Pastry 6c +

Tobacco Road 7b +

Sabre 8a +

Fandango 6c

Station to Station 6c +

Coathanger 6b

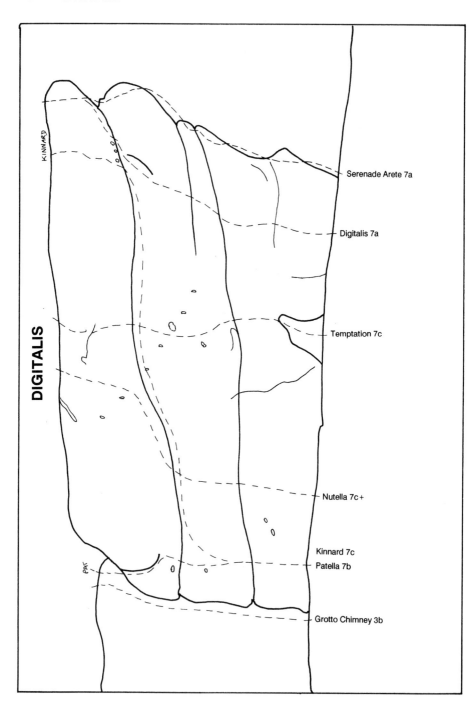

KINNARD

PAT

DIGITALIS

Serenade Arete 7a

Digitalis 7a

Temptation 7c

Nutella 7c+

Kinnard 7c
Patella 7b

Grotto Chimney 3b

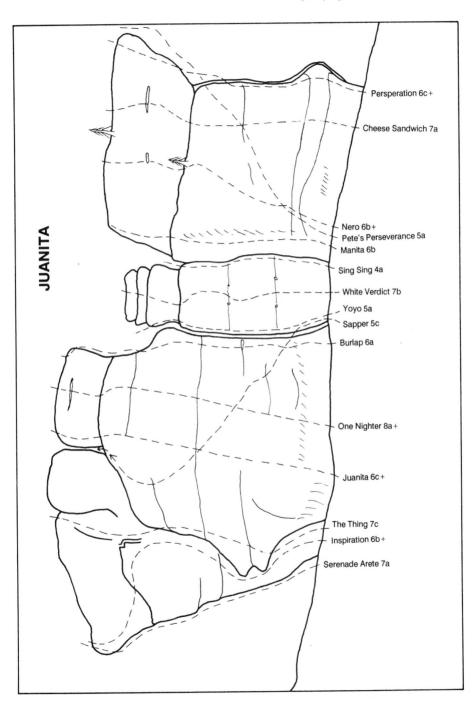

JUANITA

Persperation 6c+

Cheese Sandwich 7a

Nero 6b+
Pete's Perseverance 5a
Manita 6b

Sing Sing 4a

White Verdict 7b

Yoyo 5a
Sapper 5c

Burlap 6a

One Nighter 8a+

Juanita 6c+

The Thing 7c
Inspiration 6b+
Serenade Arete 7a

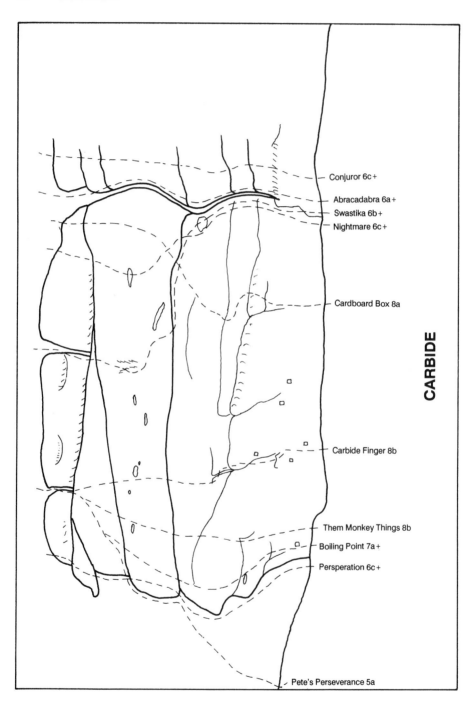

Conjuror 6c+
Abracadabra 6a+
Swastika 6b+
Nightmare 6c+
Cardboard Box 8a

CARBIDE

Carbide Finger 8b
Them Monkey Things 8b
Boiling Point 7a+
Persperation 6c+
Pete's Perseverance 5a

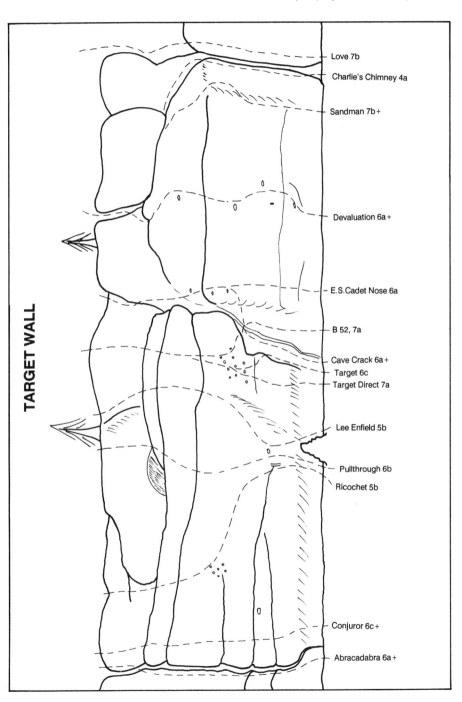

TARGET WALL

Love 7b
Charlie's Chimney 4a
Sandman 7b+
Devaluation 6a+
E.S.Cadet Nose 6a
B 52, 7a
Cave Crack 6a+
Target 6c
Target Direct 7a
Lee Enfield 5b
Pullthrough 6b
Ricochet 5b
Conjuror 6c+
Abracadabra 6a+

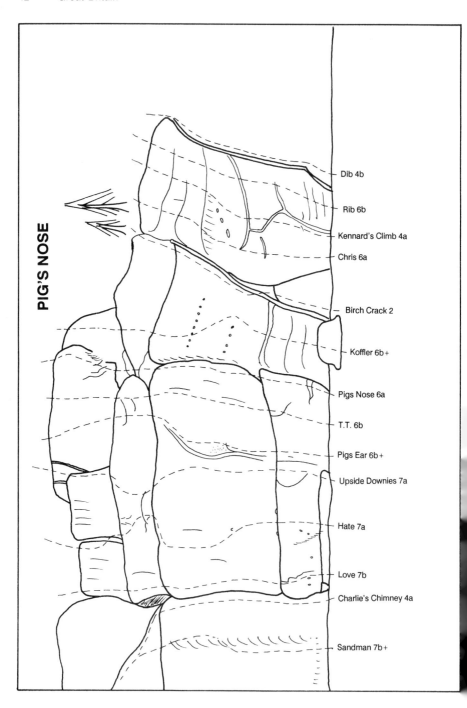

PIG'S NOSE

Dib 4b

Rib 6b

Kennard's Climb 4a

Chris 6a

Birch Crack 2

Koffler 6b+

Pigs Nose 6a

T.T. 6b

Pigs Ear 6b+

Upside Downies 7a

Hate 7a

Love 7b

Charlie's Chimney 4a

Sandman 7b+

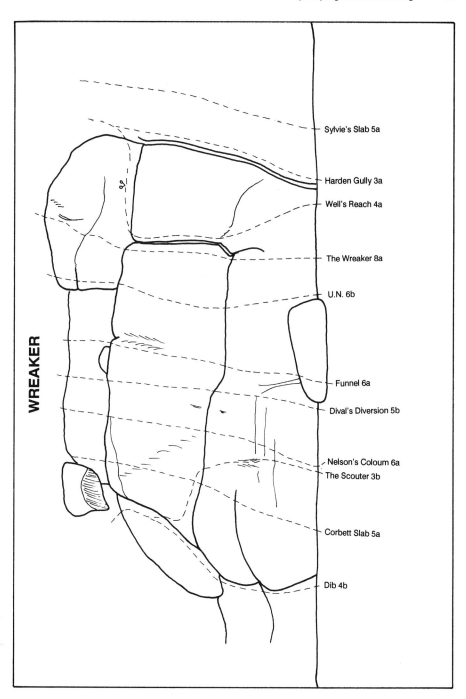

WREAKER

Sylvie's Slab 5a

Harden Gully 3a

Well's Reach 4a

The Wreaker 8a

U.N. 6b

Funnel 6a

Dival's Diversion 5b

Nelson's Coloum 6a
The Scouter 3b

Corbett Slab 5a

Dib 4b

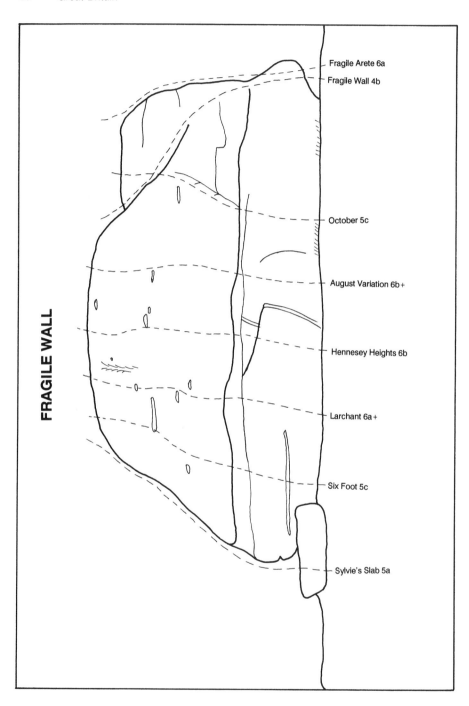

FRAGILE WALL

Fragile Arete 6a
Fragile Wall 4b
October 5c
August Variation 6b+
Hennesey Heights 6b
Larchant 6a+
Six Foot 5c
Sylvie's Slab 5a

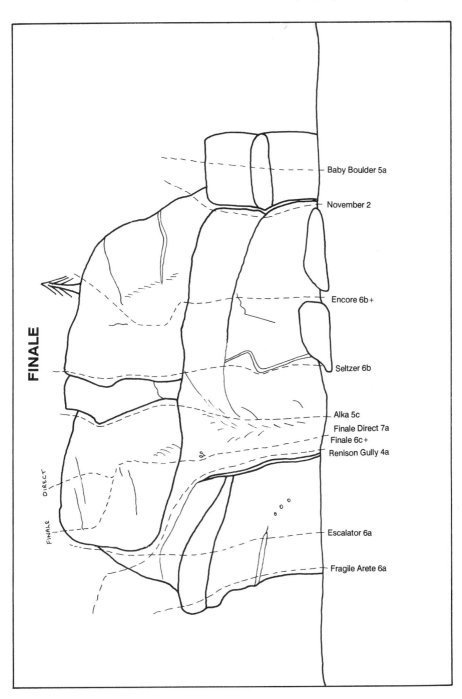

FINALE

Baby Boulder 5a

November 2

Encore 6b+

Seltzer 6b

Alka 5c
Finale Direct 7a
Finale 6c+
Renison Gully 4a

DIRECT

FINALE

Escalator 6a

Fragile Arete 6a

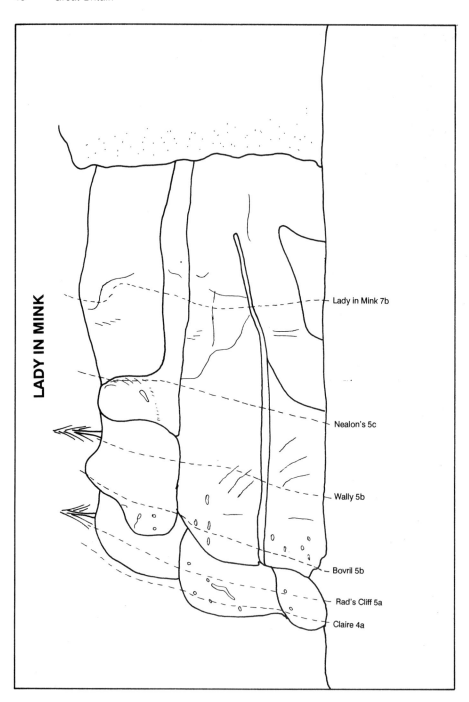

LADY IN MINK

Lady in Mink 7b

Nealon's 5c

Wally 5b

Bovril 5b

Rad's Cliff 5a

Claire 4a

Burrington Coombe:
(Bouldering) Somerset [24]

Some small cliffs in this area give good bouldering and some short climbs of varying difficulty. Limestone.

Dir: 20km E of Weston-super-Mare. From Bristol take the A38 S to Churchill, then the A368 E towards West Harptree. After 3.5km turn R on to the B3134. Arrive at the Coombe after 1.6km. (26:D4)

Caley
✶ 06.00→12.00 (18.00)
(Bouldering) YORKSHIRE [25]

A very good gritstone bouldering area with about 150 problems. Most of the problems get the morning sun but there are exceptions. There are problems of all sizes here up to 15m high. Worth a few hours if passing.

Dir: 3km ESE of Otley. The crags are just to the S of the A660 between Leeds and Otley, 1km before the roundabout when entering Otley. Park at the side of the road and walk to the crag in 3 seconds. (86:D2)

Castle Rock:
(Bouldering) GLOUCESTERSHIRE [26]

This small 30ft limestone outcrop offers a good 20 routes to entertain climbers of almost any standard, and is very good for bouldering.

Dir: 8km NE of Cheltenham. Take the A46 N from Cheltenham to Cleeve Hill and The Rising Sun pub. The rocks are 5 mins' walk along and up the hill. (42:A2)

Craig Y Longridge:
✶ 10.00→17.00
(Bouldering) LANCASHIRE [27]

An excellent crag offering superb bouldering on good to poor gritstone. The rock deteriorates towards the top and it is usual not to complete the routes. The crag is quite steep and offers nothing below 6b. Good grade 7 bouldering.

Dir: 11.5km NE of Preston. Drive to Longridge. From the town centre take the road leading NE towards the golf course on Jeffrey Hill, after 1km fork R, after 0.5km there is an iron gate and a track which leads to the quarry. (84:E3)

Frodsham:
✶ 14.00→19.00
(12.15.32.25.2)(70) LIVERPOOL [28]

Some very small sandstone overhangs 3−5m giving superb roof problems in the middle grades. Can stay damp in winter with holds seeping under the overhangs. Gets a bit too crowded with midges in the late summer months, good climbing though. Worth a visit.

Dir: 3km SSW of Frodsham which is 25km SE of Liverpool. Going W on the A56 leaving Frodsham, turn L on to the B5393. After 2.3km the road turns R, carry straight on for 700m. Here a path leads off L into the woods and the rocks. (77:G3)

The Gelt Boulder:
(Bouldering) CUMBRIA [29]

A very good limestone boulder offering steep and excellent problems. Worth a boulder. 20ft.

Dir: 26.5km NNE of Penrith, 16km E of Carlisle. Drive to Castle Carrock on the B6413. From the village take the road going E to the river Gelt. After 2km the road turns R, park here and walk straight on down to the river to a bridge, cross over and turn R to go upstream for about 400m to the boulder. (102:B1)

Goblin Combe:
✶ 13.00→18.00
(4.7.25.12.0)(43) SOMERSET [30]

A good limestone crag up to 25m high with trees at the top for top-roping. The crag is steep and gives very good routes.

Dir: 13km WSW of Bristol. Take A370 SW to Cleeve. Take the lane on the L before The Rising Sun pub, towards Wrington. Park after 300m. A track and then a footpath leads to the crag E direction in about 15 mins.

Gritstone Edges:
✶ 10.00→21.00 (4000) PEAK [31]

These have been grouped as one since they are all very similar and offer the same type of climbing. All are 3−15m high and W facing. They run down the complete E side of the Peak

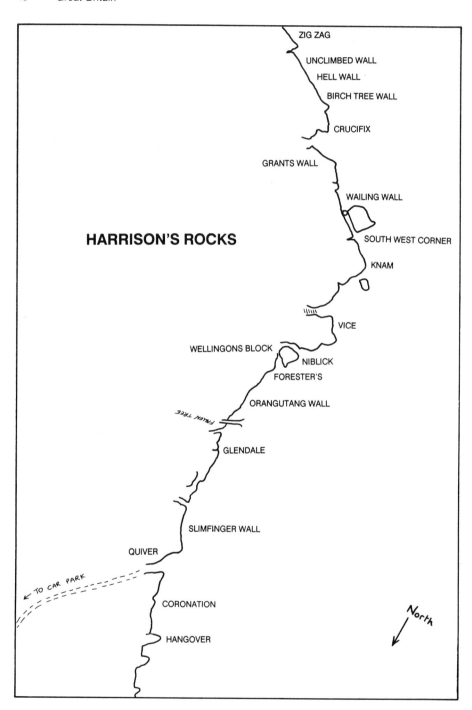

ZIG ZAG

UNCLIMBED WALL

HELL WALL

BIRCH TREE WALL

CRUCIFIX

GRANTS WALL

WAILING WALL

HARRISON'S ROCKS

SOUTH WEST CORNER

KNAM

VICE

WELLINGONS BLOCK

NIBLICK

FORESTER'S

ORANGUTANG WALL

FALLEN TREE

GLENDALE

SLIMFINGER WALL

QUIVER

← TO CAR PARK

CORONATION

HANGOVER

North

District National Park. The most popular are known as Stanage, Millstone, Burbage, Froggatt and Curbar. All offer thousands of bouldering possibilities in all grades and give hours of entertainment.

Dir: 10km SW of Sheffield. From Sheffield take the A625 out towards Hathersage and the Gritstone Edges are obvious on the western tops of the moors. (79:G2−3)

Harrison's Rocks:
✶ 10.00→22.00
(65.68.54.52. − 5)(290) SUSSEX [32]

A very popular crag, especially at weekends. Sandstone 5−10m with all types of climbing in all the grades. Steep and bulging routes often make on-sight flashes quite difficult. At weekends it gets very popular. Always worth a visit. Please always leave a small donation to help with the upkeep of the crag, and take litter home with you.

Dir: 3.5km W of Tunbridge Wells. Take the A264 (East Grinstead) from Tunbridge Wells. Continue on the B2188 to Groombridge, fork left at the Victoria Pub, and go over railway. After 400m fork R (Eridge), then after 70m turn R into a lane signposted Harrison's Rocks and Birchden Wood. Park in car park and walk 10 mins (or sprint 2 mins) to the crag. It is hoped that the Forestry Commission will open a small lightweight campsite here in the future. (22:B1)

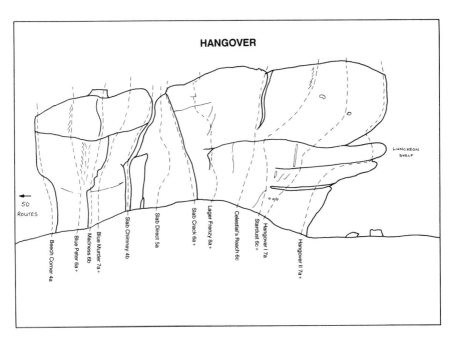

HANGOVER

LUNCHEON SHELF

← 50 ROUTES

Beech Corner 4a
Blue Peter 6a +
Madness 6b
Blue Murder 7a +
Slab Chimney 4b
Slab Direct 5a
Slab Crack 6a +
Lager Frenzy 8a +
Celestial's Reach 6c
Stardust 6c +
Hangover I 7a
Hangover II 7a +

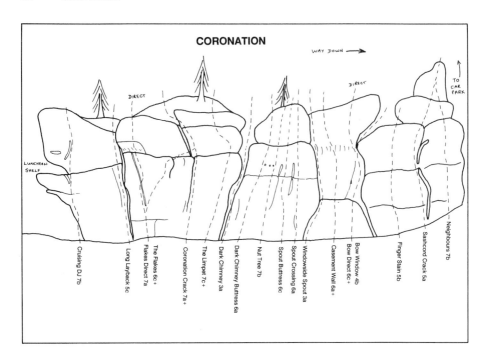

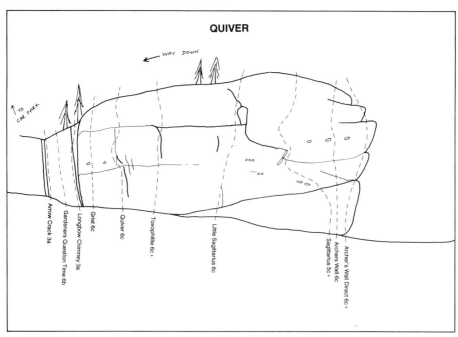

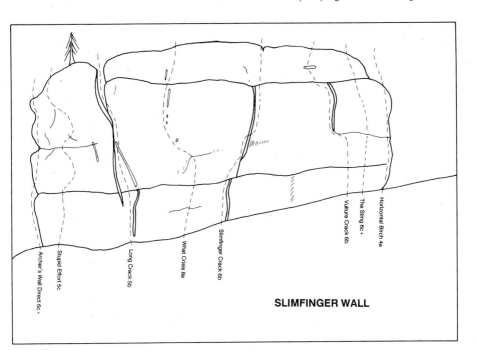

Archer's Wall Direct 6c+
Stupid Effort 5c
Long Crack 5b
What Crisis 8a
Slimfinger Crack 6b
Vulture Crack 6b
The Sting 6c+
Horizontal Birch 4a

SLIMFINGER WALL

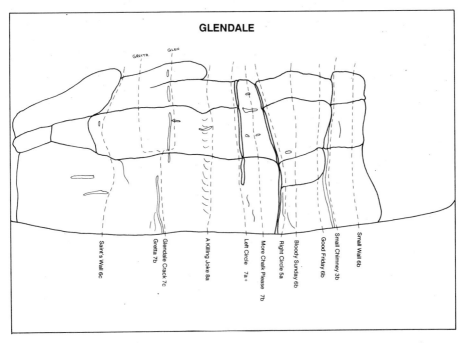

GLENDALE

GRETTA   GLEN

Saint's Wall 6c
Gretta 7b
Glendale Crack 7c
A Killing Joke 8a
Left Circle 7a+
More Chalk Please 7b
Right Circle 5a
Bloody Sunday 6b
Good Friday 6b
Small Chimney 3b
Small Wall 6b

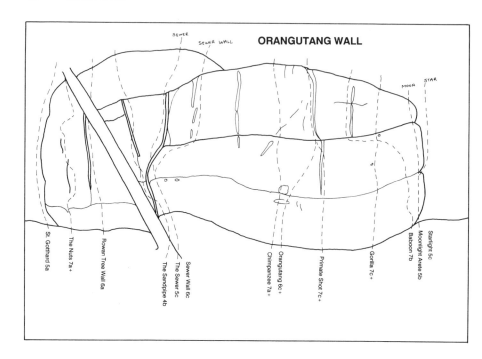

SEWER

SEWER WALL

ORANGUTANG WALL

MOON STAR

- St. Gothard 5a
- The Nuts 7a+
- Rowan Tree Wall 6a
- The Sandpipe 4b
- The Sewer 5c
- Sewer Wall 6c
- Chimpanzee 7a+
- Orangutang 6c+
- Primate Shot 7c+
- Gorilla 7c+
- Baboon 7b
- Moonlight Arete 5b
- Starlight 5c

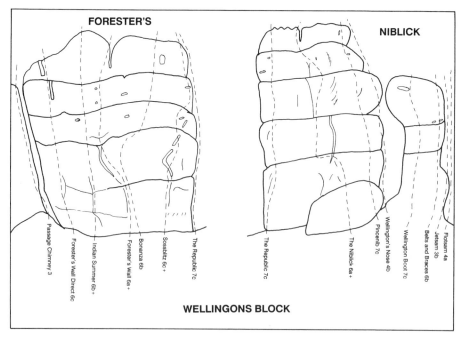

FORESTER'S

NIBLICK

- Passage Chimney 3
- Forester's Wall Direct 6c
- Indian Summer 6b+
- Forester's Wall 6a+
- Bonanza 6b
- Sossblitz 6c+
- The Republic 7c

- The Republic 7c
- The Niblick 6a+
- Princenib 7c
- Wellington's Nose 4b
- Wellington Boot 7c
- Belts and Braces 6b
- Jetsam 3b
- Flotsam 4a

WELLINGONS BLOCK

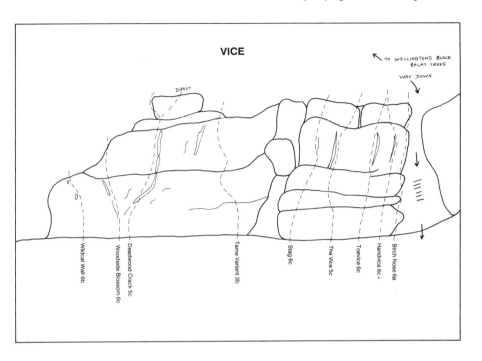

VICE

DIRECT

TO WELLINGTON'S BLOCK
BELAY TREES

WAY DOWN

Wildcat Wall 6b
Woodside Blossom 6c
Deadwood Crack 5c
Tame Variant 3b
Stag 6c
The Vice 5c
Toevice 6c
Handvice 6c+
Birch Nose 6a

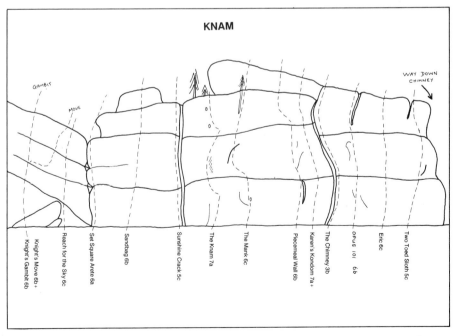

KNAM

GAMBIT

MOVE

WAY DOWN
CHIMNEY

Knight's Move 6b+
Knight's Gambit 6b
Reach for the Sky 6c
Set Square Arete 6a
Sandbag 6b
Sunshine Crack 5c
The Knam 7a
The Mank 6c
Piecemeal Wall 6b
Karen's Kondom 7a+
The Chimney 3b
Opus 101 6b
Eric 6c
Two Toed Sloth 5c

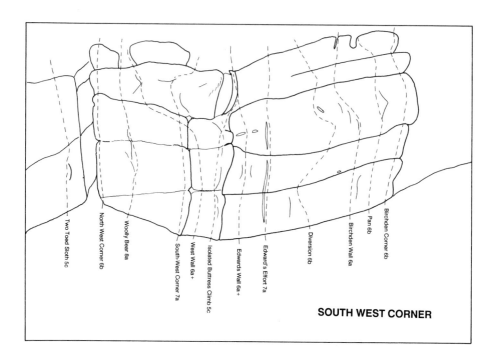

Two Toed Sloth 5c
North West Corner 6b
Woolly Bear 8a
South-West Corner 7a
West Wall 6a+
Isolated Buttress Climb 5c
Edwards Wall 6a+
Edward's Effort 7a
Diversion 6b
Birchden Wall 6a
Pan 6b
Birchden Corner 6b

SOUTH WEST CORNER

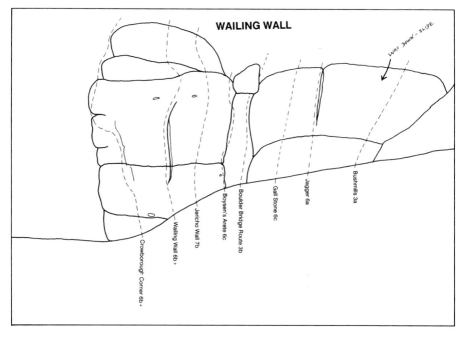

WAILING WALL

WAY DOWN - SLIDE

Crowborough Corner 6b+
Wailing Wall 6b+
Jericho Wall 7b
Boysen's Arete 6c
Boulder Bridge Route 3b
Gall Stone 6c
Jagger 6a
Bushmills 3a

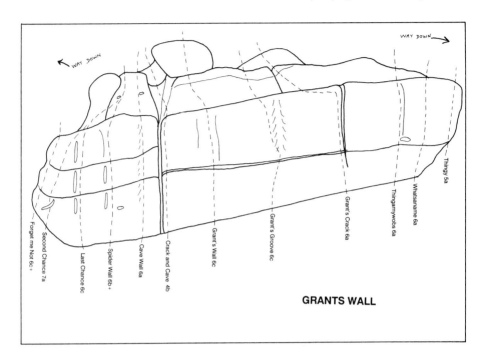

WAY DOWN

WAY DOWN

Thingy 5a

Whatsaname 6a

Thingamywobs 6a

Grant's Crack 6a

Grant's Groove 6c

Grant's Wall 6c

Crack and Cave 4b

Cave Wall 6a

Spider Wall 6b+

Last Chance 6c

Second Chance 7a

Forget me Not 6c+

GRANTS WALL

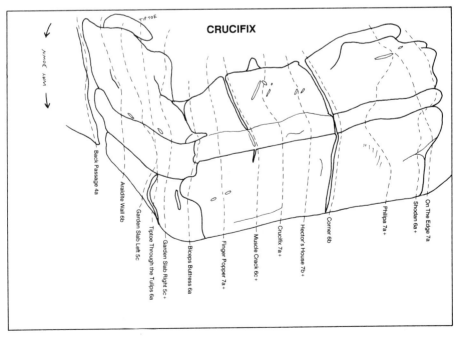

TIP TOE

CRUCIFIX

WAY DOWN

Back Passage 4a

Araldite Wall 6b

Garden Slab Left 5c

Tiptoe Through the Tulips 6a

Garden Slab Right 5c+

Biceps Buttress 6a

Finger Popper 7a+

Muscle Crack 6c+

Crucifix 7a+

Hector's House 7b+

Corner 6b

Philipa 7a+

Shodan 6a+

On The Edge 7a

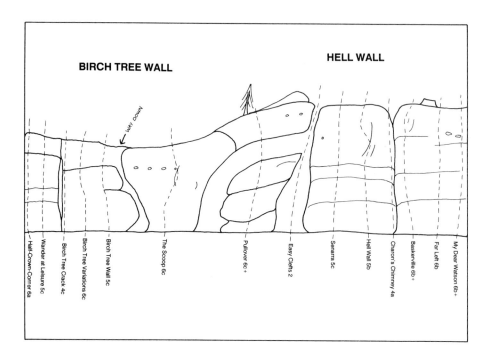

BIRCH TREE WALL

HELL WALL

WAY DOWN

- Half-Crown-Corner 6a
- Wander at Leisure 5c
- Birch Tree Crack 4c
- Birch Tree Variations 6c
- Birch Tree Wall 5c
- The Scoop 6c
- Pullover 6c+
- Easy Clefts 2
- Senarra 5c
- Hell Wall 5b
- Charon's Chimney 4a
- Baskerville 6b+
- Far Left 6b
- My Dear Watson 6b+

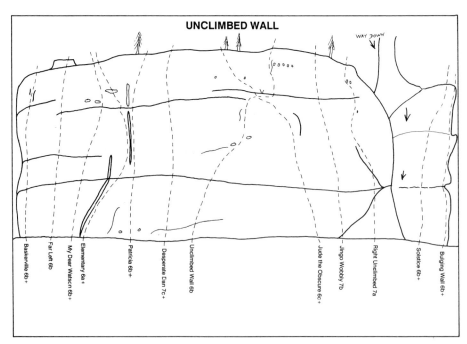

UNCLIMBED WALL

WAY DOWN

- Baskerville 6b+
- Far Left 6b
- My Dear Watson 6b+
- Elementary 6a+
- Patricia 6b+
- Desperate Dan 7c+
- Unclimbed Wall 6b
- Jude the Obscure 6c+
- Jingo Wobbly 7b
- Right Unclimbed 7a
- Solstice 6b+
- Bulging Wall 6b+

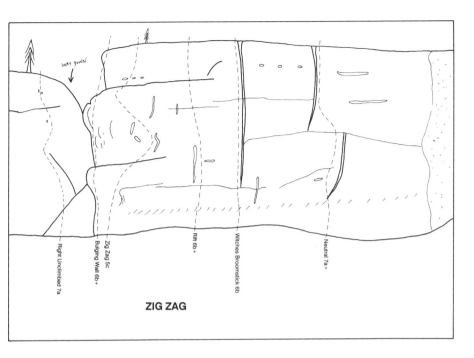

Right Unclimbed 7a · Bulging Wall 6b+ · Zig Zag 5c · Rift 6b+ · Witches Broomstick 6b · Neutral 7a+

ZIG ZAG

Haytor:
✴ 07.00→21.00
(Bouldering)   DEVON [33]

The National Park of Dartmoor offers about 30 areas of granite crags with endless bouldering possibilities, the largest of which is Haytor. This is split into High Man and Low Man, both giving superb climbing. There are unbolted routes up to 30m high and plenty of areas on which to boulder. In winter the area is very cold and often with snow, so it is best in the summer months. Situated at 500m. For other areas *see Crag Guide to England and Wales* (Crowood).

Dir: 7km WSW of Bovey Tracey. From BT take the B3344 towards Manaton, after 1km fork left up a smaller lane to Haytor, which is reached after 5.5km, car park. Walk to the Tor. 10 mins. (6:D2)

High Rocks:
✴ 10.00→16.00
(35.54.76.87. – 17)(250)   KENT [34]

A very good sandstone crag 5–10m but very different from the other crags in the area. The harder routes are of great quality and demand

SALAD DAYS, 7c, High Rocks. (Climber Guy McLelland, Photo David Jones)

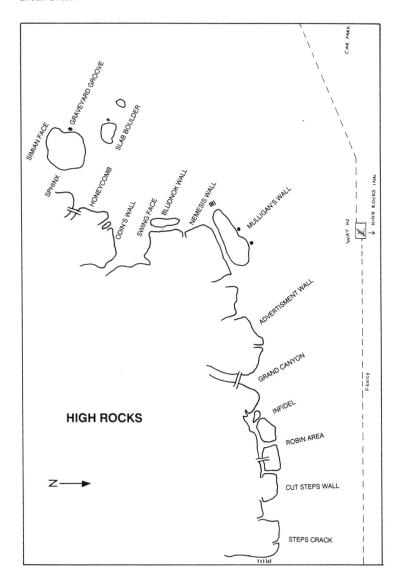

HIGH ROCKS

Z ⟶

very good technique and strength in both arms and fingers. The crag is often damp but is the best place to be on a very hot day. There are more routes to the L end of the crag which are not on the topo diagrams. They are smaller but still good fun. Worth a trip.

Dir: 3km W of Tunbridge Wells. From TW take A264 (East Grinstead), after 2km at Rusthall Common take a road left signposted High Rocks. High Rocks Inn and yuppie complex is reached. The rocks opposite are fenced in and an admission fee is charged (unfortunately). It is common to protest before paying to enjoy the countryside and the owners should be made to feel uneasy about adopting this outrageous practice. (22:B1)

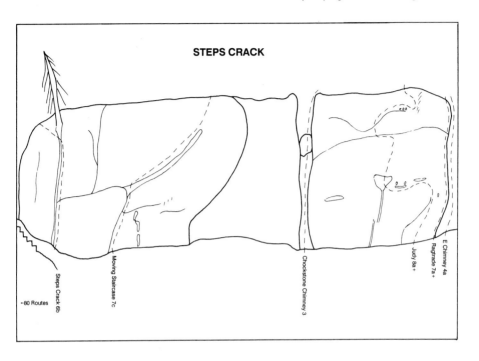

STEPS CRACK

Steps Crack 6b

~80 Routes

Moving Staircase 7c

Chockstone Chimney 3

Judy 8a+

Ragtrade 7a+

E Chimney 4a

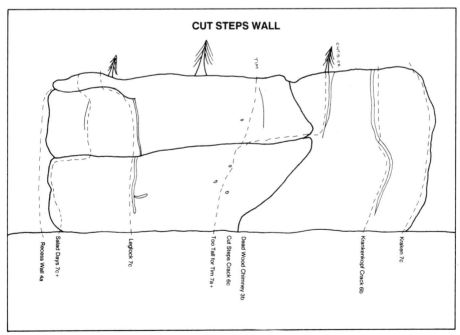

CUT STEPS WALL

TIM

CUTS CK

Salad Days 7c+

Recess Wall 4a

Legjock 7c

Too Tall for Tim 7a+

Cut Steps Crack 6c

Dead Wood Chimney 3b

Krankenkopf Crack 6b

Kraken 7c

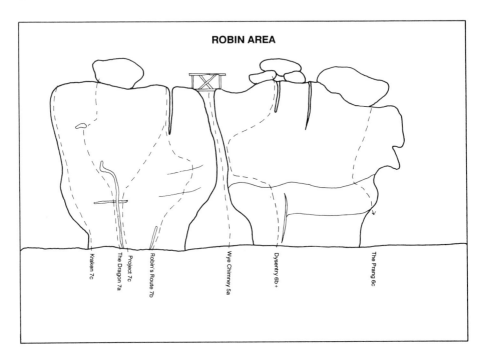

ROBIN AREA

Kraken 7c
The Dragon 7a
Project 7c
Robin's Route 7b
Wye Chimney 5a
Dysentry 6b+
The Prang 6c

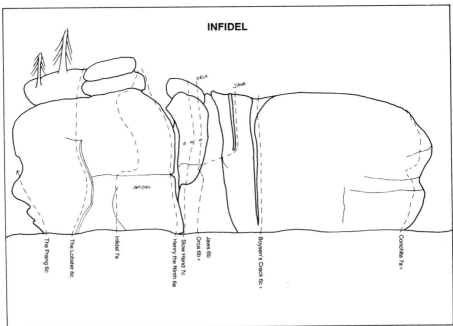

INFIDEL

ORCA
JAWS
INFIDEL

The Prang 6c
The Lobster 6c
Infidel 7a
Slow Hand 7c
Henry the Ninth 6a
Orca 6b+
Jaws 6b
Boysen's Crack 6c+
Conchita 7a+

GRAND CANYON

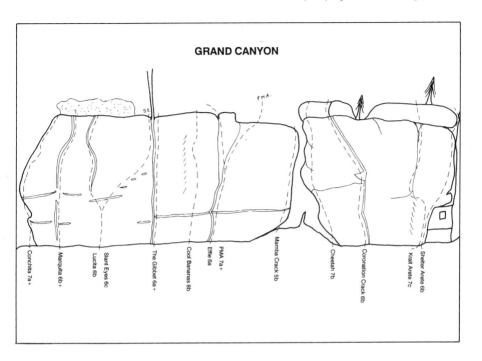

Conchita 7a+
Marquita 6b+
Lucita 6b
Slant Eyes 6c
The Gibbet 6a+
Cool Bananas 8b
Effie 6a
PMA 7a+
Mamba Crack 5b
Cheetah 7b
Coronation Crack 6b
Krait Arete 7c
Shelter Arete 6b

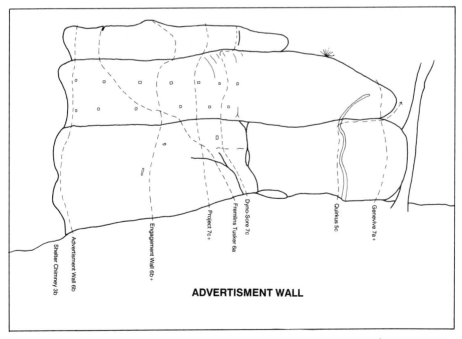

Shelter Chimney 3b
Advertisment Wall 6b
Engagement Wall 6b+
Project 7c+
Fremlins Tusker 6a
Dyno-Sore 7c
Quirkus 5c
Genevive 7a+

ADVERTISMENT WALL

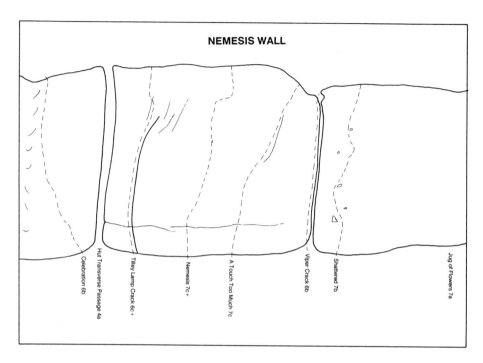

NEMESIS WALL

Celebration 6b

Hut Transverse Passage 4a

Tilley Lamp Crack 6c +

Nemesis 7c +

A Touch Too Much 7c

Viper Crack 6b

Shattered 7b

Jug of Flowers 7a

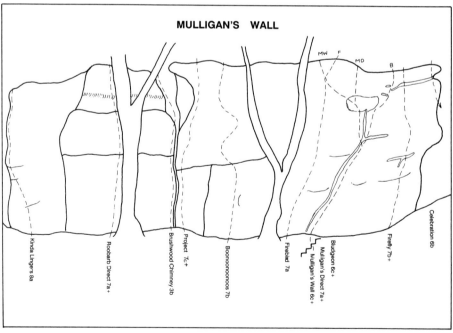

MULLIGAN'S WALL

Kinda Linger's 8a

Roobarb Direct 7a +

Brushwood Chimney 3b

Project 7c +

Boonoonoonoos 7b

Firebird 7a

Bludgeon 6c +
Mulligan's Direct 7a +
Mulligan's Wall 6c +

Firefly 7b +

Celebration 6b

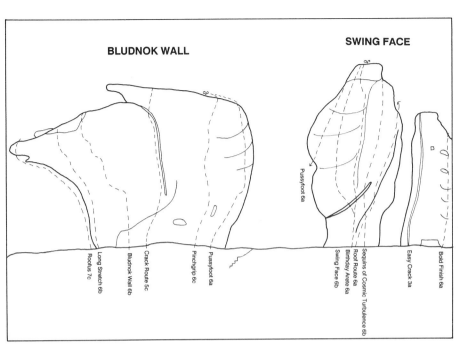

BLUDNOK WALL

SWING FACE

Pussyfoot 6a

Long Stretch 6b
Roofus 7c
Bludnok Wall 6b
Crack Route 5c
Pinchgrip 6c
Pussyfoot 6a

Swing Face 6b
Birthday Arete 6a
Roof Route 6a
Sequins of Cosmic Turbulence 6b
Easy Crack 3a
Bold Finish 6a

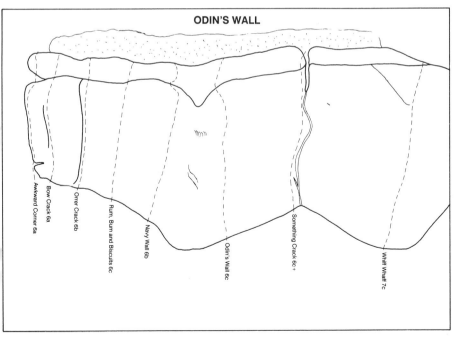

ODIN'S WALL

Awkward Corner 6a
Bow Crack 6b
Orter Crack 6b
Rum, Bum and Biscuits 6c
Navy Wall 6b
Odin's Wall 6c
Something Crack 6c+
Whiff Whaff 7c

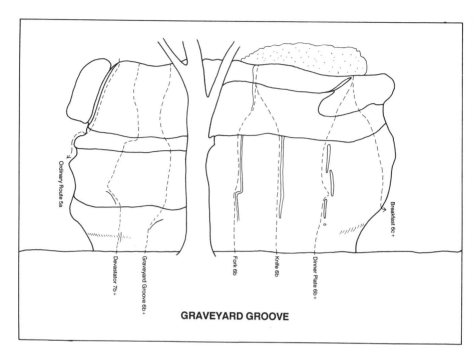

GRAVEYARD GROOVE

Ordinary Route 5a

Devastator 7b+

Graveyard Groove 6b+

Fork 6b

Knife 6b

Dinner Plate 6b+

Breakfast 6c+

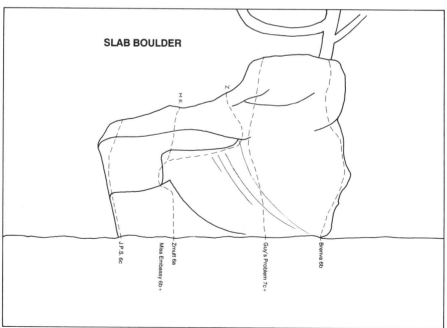

SLAB BOULDER

M.E.

Z

J.P.S. 6c

Miss Embassy 6b+

Zmutt 6a

Guy's Problem 7c+

Brenva 6b

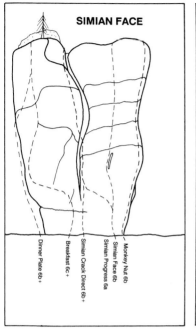

SIMIAN FACE

Dinner Plate 6b+
Breakfast 6c+
Simian Crack Direct 6b+
Simian Progress 6a
Simian Face 6b
Monkey Nut 6b

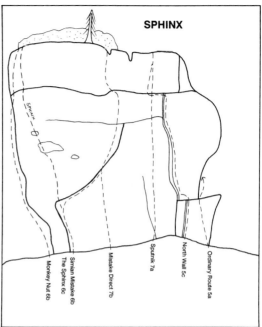

SPHINX

Monkey Nut 6b
The Sphinx 6c
Simian Mistake 6b
Mistake Direct 7b
Sputnik 7a
North Wall 5c
Ordinary Route 5a

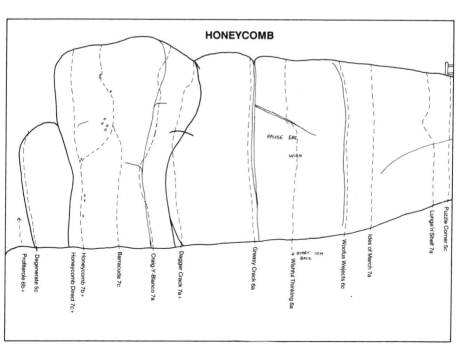

HONEYCOMB

PAUSE ERE
WISH

Profiterole 6b+
Degenerate 5c
Honeycomb 7b+
Honeycomb Direct 7c+
Barracuda 7c
Craig-Y-Blanco 7a
Dagger Crack 7a+
Greasy Crack 6a
Wishful Thinking 6a
START 10M BACK
Woolus Wejects 6c
Ides of March 7a
Lunge'n'Shell 7a
Puzzle Corner 5c

Kyloe Crags:
✳ 10.00→19.00 (Bouldering)
NORTHUMBERLAND [35]

There are two sandstone crags here — KYLOE CRAG and KYLOE IN THE WOOD. Kyloe is 10–15m high and offers some very good climbing in all grades, very sheltered and facing SW. The latter crags are in the woods, stay dry in rain and are a must for the 7b upward climber. The problems are only 3m high but are very good indeed. Both worth a visit.

Dir: 15km SSE of Berwick-upon-Tweed. From Lowick on the B6353 go E for 2.1km, turn R and after 500m a track leads off to the L. This leads to the crags in about 5 mins. Kyloe Crag is obvious. The crags in the wood are reached by taking the small road for 1.5km to a gate on the L with some fire beaters. A track leads into the forest, after 5 mins bear R on a track marked WS7; the crag is reached in 5 mins. (123:E4)

Pex Hill:
✳ 9.00→22.00 (30.45.56.65.4)(180)
LIVERPOOL [36]

NEMESIS, 7c+, High Rocks. (Climber Paul Widdowson, Photo David Jones)

A quarry of very hard sandstone offering very hard wall routes of 3m–15m. Most of the routes are soloed, but the longer hard ones are best top-roped. Very hard on the fingertips and requires good balance on the tiptoes. This is a dubious area and cars left unattended should not have valuables in them.

Dir: 10km from the outskirts of Liverpool. Leave the M62 at junction 7 going S on the A569. After 1.2km at a junction turn R on to the A5080. After 400m there is a turning on the R with some green posts. This leads to the quarry in about 200m. (77:G2)

Sandy Crag:
(Bouldering)
NORTHUMBERLAND [37]

A reasonable sandstone crag up to 20m high with some very good bouldering. Worth a visit if passing.

Dir: 26km NW of Morpeth. Take the B6341 SW from Rothbury about 10km to the village of Hepple. After 2.5km there is a track which leads straight on where the road goes over a

THE ICEMAN, 8a, Kyloe in the Wood. (Climber Joe Healey, Photo David Jones)

bridge. This leads to Midgy House after 1.2km. The crag is on the hill up to the L. (112:C3)

Slipstone Crag
✲ 10.00→18.00
(Bouldering)   YORKSHIRE [38]

A good small gritstone crag with about 200 boulder problems. All grades. Situated at 450m and very cool in winter but still climbable if the snow keeps off. Worth a detour.

Dir: 23km NW of Ripon, 1.5km NE of Colsterdale. From Masham on the A6108 take a small road leading W through the village of Healey to the fork leading to Colsterdale. Take this going R for 2.8km to a parking spot on the R. Walk along the road for 300m where a footpath leads off up to the R and the rocks in about 5 mins. (94:C3)

Stone Farm Rocks:
✲ 9.00→19.00
(32.32.5.2.0)(70)   SUSSEX [39]

An outcrop of sandstone boulders reaching up to 20ft offering about 60 routes in the lower and middle grades. A very enjoyable spot, south facing and quick drying. Worth a visit.

Dir: 5km SSW of East Grinstead. Find East Grinstead old town centre. By Clarendon House and the Ship pub, take the B2110 (Turners Hill). After 2.2km turn L to St Hill Green. After 1km at a T-junction turn R to West Hoathly, after 1.3km cars can be parked on the L. A track 50 yds back on the left leads to the crag in 100 yds. (21:H1)

Stoney Middleton:
✲ 10.00→18.00
(10.25.64.55.8)(150)   PEAK [40]

A 30m limestone crag which over the years has become very polished and is similar to Saffres and La Dube in France. Most of it was once quarried but some is natural. There are two parts — the Main Crag, which has some excellent routes in all grades, and The Quarry, which has mostly grade 7 climbs. Leading with nuts does occur here but considering all the factors — polished rock with poor nut placements in flared cracks — you are far better off with top-roping. Worth a detour.

Dir: 6km NNE of Bakewell, 25km SW of Sheffield. From Sheffield take the A621 towards Bakewell. About 4km before turn R on to the A623 towards Stoney Middleton and Manchester. The crag is just past the town on the R. Also carry on up the road to a B road on the R towards Eyam. Turn R here and after 100m there is a quarry on the R by an electric sub-station with 20 very good routes. (79:G3)

Widdop:
✲ 9.00→19.00
(Bouldering)   YORKSHIRE [41]

A good gritstone outcrop on the moor overlooking Widdop Reservoir at 367m. Not the place for a bleak winter's day. Some very good rock offers about 30 climbs when in condition, N facing. All standards of problems and grades. On the other side of the road to the N is an outcrop known as SCOUT CRAG — WIDDOP, and JACKSON'S RIDGE. These both offer plenty of bouldering and being S facing are often a good alternative to the larger and colder Widdop. Worth a visit.

Dir: 10km E of Burnley. Go to the N part of town and a village called Harle Syke. From here take the small road over the moor towards Hebden Bridge. Halfway, at Widdop Reservoir, the crag is easily visible. Cross over the dam and follow the track to the crag. By carrying on along the track, up the valley on the L and taking the path around the hill in a E direction, you can reach Gorple outcrop in 15 mins, visible to the L. (85:H3)

NAMUR

Aiguilles de Chaleux:
✶ 10.00→18.00 (50)   NAMUR [1]

Some very fine pinnacles with routes in most grades up to 70m long, in a very fine setting overlooking the Lesse river. *In situ* gear is unknown but presumed adequate. Definitely worth looking in for a couple of days.

Dir: 28km SSE of Namur, 6km SSE of Dinant. From Dinant cross to the E side of the river and take the N94 in the direction of Beauraing. After 3km go under the dual carriageway then turn L to Dréhance, then R to Furfooz. From here the Aiguilles are only 1km away and signposted to the R. (11:E2)

WALKING THE WHITE STICK, 7a, Freyr. (Climber Barry Knight, Photo Brian Parr)

Freyr:
✶ 10.00→18.00
(77.76.189.112.4)(460)   NAMUR [2]

This is the best-known crag in Belgium and deservedly so. Limestone up to 120m high. There are both very good and very bad areas in which to climb. Mostly the climbing is steep walls with *in situ* gear [2–6]. It is a very popular crag so don't expect to be alone at weekends. There is a topo guide which can be bought locally in the café and is superb, with perfectly adequate info on the routes. Definitely worth a visit. The crag is situated low down by the river and can be climbed on all year round but is best in the cooler summer days. A good alternative to the British limestone for those living in England. There are good camping facilities nearby to the E of the crags; enquire at the cafés. Café Chamonix has been recommended.

Dir: 30km S of Namur, 5km SSW of Dinant. From the town of Dinant go to the E side of the river and take the N95 which fol,ows the river Meuse towards Beauraing. (Do not go to Freyr château which is on the other side of the river.) Just as the road leaves the river after 10km the crags are on the R. (11:E2)

La Longariesse:
(14)   NAMUR [3]

A limestone crag up to 60m high. Good routes which are a lot less popular than those at nearby Freyr. This is a chance to get away from the crowds.

Dir: 31km S of Namur, 6km SSW of Dinant. From the town of Dinant go to the E side of the river and take the N95 which follows the river Meuse towards Beauraing. (Do not go to Freyr château which is on the other side of the river.) Just as the road leaves the river after 10km there is the area of Freyr on the R. From here a footpath leads upstream to the crags of ROCHERS DE WAULSORT, and then La Longariesse. (11:E2)

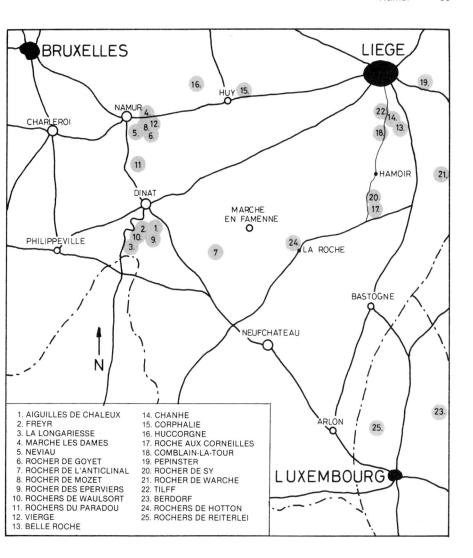

1. AIGUILLES DE CHALEUX
2. FREYR
3. LA LONGARIESSE
4. MARCHE LES DAMES
5. NEVIAU
6. ROCHER DE GOYET
7. ROCHER DE L'ANTICLINAL
8. ROCHER DE MOZET
9. ROCHER DES EPERVIERS
10. ROCHERS DE WAULSORT
11. ROCHERS DU PARADOU
12. VIERGE
13. BELLE ROCHE
14. CHANHE
15. CORPHALIE
16. HUCCORGNE
17. ROCHE AUX CORNEILLES
18. COMBLAIN-LA-TOUR
19. PEPINSTER
20. ROCHER DE SY
21. ROCHER DE WARCHE
22. TILFF
23. BERDORF
24. ROCHERS DE HOTTON
25. ROCHERS DE REITERLEI

Marche Les Dames:
✷ 10.00→16.00

(4−7c)(250)   NAMUR [4]

This is one of the most popular crags in Belgium and has plenty of routes in all grades. The bolts [2−4] are not that old and are plentiful. Up to 80m high. Definitely worth a visit.

Dir: 7km ENE of Namur. From Namur take the small road on the N side of the river going downstream towards Liège, and opposite the N90 on the other bank. After 6km the crag is obvious on the L side of the road. (11:E1)

Climber on a route on Freyr. (Photo Barry Knight)

Neviau:
✳ 11.00→19.00
(4−8a)(130)   NAMUR [5]

A very good crag of good solid limestone with occasional pockets offering superb climbing. There was some very poor *in situ* gear here for a while and hopefully much of it has been renewed. The crag reaches up to 75m high and is in several large sections. There are routes here for all standards but many tend to be quite polished as it is the closest crag to Namur. Worth a visit though.

Dir: From Namur cross over the river Meuse to the S and immediately turn R on to the N947 which leads to Dave and Yvoir. After 4km the crag is obvious on the L side of the road (before Dave). (11:E1)

Rocher de Goyet:
(4c−8a)(50)   NAMUR [6]

A very good crag with not that many routes on, however. All routes are single pitch with lowering off points. Bolts [2−3]. Very good for the lower-grade climber.

Dir: 11km ESE of Namur. From the town on the S side take the N90 towards Liège. After 10km opposite Namêche turn R to Samson and Goyet. On arriving at Goyet the crag can be seen on the L side of the road. (11:E1)

Rocher de l'Anticlinal:
(30)   NAMUR [7]

This crag is sometimes known as LES GRIGNAUX. A small crag but well equipped with bolts [2−3] and all are single pitch routes.

Dir: 26km SE of Dinant. Take the N94 going S which runs almost parallel with the *autoroute*. After about 30km turn L on to the N86 towards Rochefort. After 5km enter Han-sur-Lesse. At the town take the road upstream on the R which leads to the crag after 1.5km and the crag is seen on the R. (11:F3)

Rocher de Mozet:
(70)   NAMUR [8]

A good crag with some fine slab routes up to 30m high as well as a few desperates. *In situ* gear [2−4]. Worth a visit.

Dir: 9km E of Namur. From the town on the S side take the N90 towards Liège, after 10km opposite Namêche turn R to Samson, carry on to the café Le Samsonnet where a path leads off to the R and to the crag. A topo should be on sale at the café. (11:E1)

Rochner des Eperviers:
(4−7c)(45)   NAMUR [9]

A very good crag with routes up to 50m and very good rock. In a natural park area, very scenic and attractive in summer.

Dir: 28km SSE of Namur, 6km SSE of Dinant. From Dinant take the N95 in a S direction towards Beauraing. After 8km arrive in Falmange, turn L on a small road to Hulsonniaux, then turn L on to the N910 towards Celles. After 2km the road drops down into the Lesse valley and towards the

AIGUILLES DE CHALEUX. The crag is on the L. (11:E2)

Rochers de Waulsort:
✻ Not a lot (4 – 7b)(25)   NAMUR [10]

Previously an under-developed crag, but the routes are slowly becoming equipped and eventually it should provide good complementary climbing to Freyr.

Dir: *See* La Longariesse. (11:E2)

Rochers du Paradou:
(30)   NAMUR [11]

Some very good slab climbing to be found here on good rock, so worth a visit. The crag has a lot of potential and should develop into one of Belgium's premier crags.

Dir: 15km S of Namur, 1km N of Yvoir. From Namur you can take the N92 S to Yvoir. From the village go on the N947 back towards Namur and the crag is shortly on the R (marked on the map as Rocher du Fitevoye). (11:E1)

Vierge
(100)   NAMUR [12]

This crag is becoming more popular in recent years. The scope for routes is not very good but reports have said that not all of the routes have been equipped yet. Bring some nuts along too. The crag is up to 45m and of volcanic rock.

Dir: 9km E of Namur. From the town cross to the S side of the river Meuse and then take the N90 towards Liège. The crag is reached after about 10m and is on the R before the bridge which leads N across the river to Namêche. (11:E1)

LIÈGE

Belle Roche
(Unknown)   LIÈGE [13]

Not much info on this crag I'm afraid. It was once quarried and to the best of my knowledge still is. Access is at weekends only but climbing here has been popular in the past so have a look at it if in the area. The rock is limestone and routes of up to 100m have been reported.

Dir: 20km S of Liège. The quarry lies to the N of the N633 between Comblain-au-Pont (2km) and Aywaille (7km).

Chanhe
(3 – 7a)(100)   LIÈGE [14]

A limestone crag up to 100m high. The *in situ* bolts [1 – 4] are quite recent and much of the crag's development has been over the last 10 years. The rock is limestone but the climbing is more akin to granite slabs. The area is still quarried and it is not possible to climb here on working days. Have a reserve crag in mind in case they have decided to quarry here.

Dir: 15km SSE of Liège. Take the N30 towards Bastogne, and after 12km just before Sprimont turn R towards Chanhe. After 3.5km there are some quarries on the R.

Corphalie:
✻ 09.30 → 16.00
(3 – 7b)(38)   LIÈGE [15]

A very good limestone crag with long routes up to 50m high. The *in situ* gear situation is not known, so bring some nuts along too. There is also a smaller crag up to 20m high which is excellent for beginners or very part-time climbers. The climbing is very enjoyable even though some of the routes are quite polished.

Dir: 24km WSW of Liège. Go to the town of Huy on the river Meuse. Cross to the N side of the river and take the small road by the riverside which leads downstream towards Liège. After 4km the crag is on the L and obvious (opposite Tilhange).

Huccorgne:
(40)   LIÈGE [16]

Little is known of current development here but there should be *in situ* gear with routes grade 4 to possibly in the high grade 7s. The crag is in two parts, one up to 20m with easy routes on, the other a large 30m pillar with very steep possibilities.

Dir: 24km ENE of Namur. Take the N90 to Huy, then go N on the N64 towards Hannut. After 6km turn L to Moha then follow the road to Huccorgne. The crags are before the village near the bridge (*autoroute*).

Roche aux Corneilles:
(50)   LIÈGE [17]

A very good crag for hard climbers. The crag is up to 40m high and very steep limestone. *In situ* gear situation is not known at present, but should have improved over the last few years.

Dir: 24km S of Liège, 4.5km S of Hamoir. From Liège take the N30 S towards Bastogne, after 15km pass through the town of Aywaille then turn R on to the N86 towards Barvaux. After 14km arrive at Vieuxville and the crags are on the R nearby.

Comblain-la-Tour:
(100)   LIÈGE [18]

A very good crag with routes up to 40m high in all grades. The cliff has been popular for many years now and has been undergoing recent development. *In situ* bolts [1−4]. Visit if passing.

Dir: 20km S of Liège. Take the N654 which runs S from Liège up the valley of the Ourthe river towards Hamoir. After 30km reach the village of Comblain-au-Pont. Carry on for 2km then turn L over the river to the village of Comblain-la-Tour. The crag is very close to the railway and the river.

Pepinster:
✳ 9.00−21.00
(4−7c)(200)   LIÈGE [19]

There are some very good routes here and the area is popular with local climbers. There is also plenty of bouldering as well. The largest climbs are 40m with many different styles of climbing. Worth a visit. There are *in situ* bolts [1−2].

Dir: 18km ESE of Liège. Take the N61 towards Verviers and after 20km reach the town of Pepinster and the crags.

Rocher de Sy:
(300)   LIÈGE [20]

One of the most popular and largest crags in Belgium. There are climbs in all grades here, from easy to ridiculous. *In situ* bolts [1−4]. There are 12 different buttresses which give very varied climbing. Worth a visit.

Dir: 28km S of Liège, 4km S of Hamoir. From Liège take the N30 S towards Bastogne, after 15km pass through the town of Aywaille then turn R on to the N86 towards Barvaux. After 14km arrive at Vieuxville but turn off to the R just before to the village of Sy. The crags are very near by on the banks of the river.

Rocher de Warche:
(40)   LIÈGE [21]

A small 20m quartzite crag with routes mainly in the lower grades. All the bolts [1−4] are recent. A nice spot near the river and very close to the motor-racing circuit of Francorchamps.

Dir: 42km SE of Liège. Take the A27 to the Malmédy turn-off. Go towards the town and after passing under the railway bridge turn R and take the road to Bellevaux. Turn R and follow the road to the village of Warche; the crag is very near.

Tilff:
(3−7c)(65)   LIÈGE [22]

A very good crag with three different parts, each having a character of its own. All the climbs are single pitch and bolted [1−3]. They vary in length from 20−50m high. There are plenty of routes to suit all standards of climber. Worth visiting. There is also a campsite very near by as well as many along the length of the river Ourthe.

Dir: 8km S of Liège. Leave the S of Liège on the A26 towards Bastogne, and take the first turn-off to Tilff. Take the road towards Esneux and the cliff is shortly on the L. The crag of ESNEUX is smaller and just further on up the valley.

Luxembourg

Berdorf:
(50.70.140.40.0)(300)
LUXEMBOURG [23]

A sandstone crag which is 50m high in parts and well worth bringing a full 50m rope to. There is *in situ* gear [1 − 3]. There are all types of climbs here from slabs to overhangs but in the main it is quite steep walls. In addition to the climbs there are a few sandstone bouldering circuits. There is a topo to the crag which can be bought locally.

Dir: 29km NNE of Luxembourg, 6km WNW of Echternach. From Echternach take the N10 going W towards Diekirch, after about 2km turn L on to the CR364 which leads to Berdorf in 7km. In the village follow signs to the camping and swimming pool (*piscine*). Park here and take a signposted footpath to the crag. 15 mins. (23:F1 − *Michelin*, France)

Rochers de Hotton:
(4c − 7c)(130)   LUXEMBOURG [24]

A good large crag up to 40m high and sometimes referred to as Rénissart. *In situ* gear [2 − 5]. One of the more important crags in Benelux.

Dir: 41km S of Liège, 9km ENE of Marche-en-Famenne. From Marche take the N86 to the village of Hotton, 9km. About 0.5km before the village there is a track on the R which leads to the crag in about 150m.

Rochers de Reiterlei:
✳ 10.00→16.00
(4c − 7b)(40)   LUXEMBOURG [25]

Some sandstone crags up to 30m high situated in a very picturesque spot. *In situ* bolts [1 − 4].

Dir: 13km NNW of Luxembourg. From the city take the N12 towards Saeul, pass through Kopstal, Quatre Vents. Pass through Dondelange then after 300m turn R on to a road which leads down to the river Eisch and the town of Hollenfels after 5km. The crag is near the old monastery. (23:E2 − *Michelin*, France)

Germany

Climbing in Germany is very popular and quite mixed. Some of the limestone areas, although famous, offer little for the climber who struggles desperately on grade 6 climbs. There has been much development and *in situ* gear is plentiful, however, the bolts are generally farther apart than those in France. This should change as the European directive on bolt placing comes into force, stipulating safe distances between bolts on certain types of rock with certain types of bolt.

There is good climbing to be found in most parts of Germany with the exception of the area north of Hanover. The weather in the winter is quite awful and, even though people do climb, I would recommend skiing instead. In the summer it does get hot but it is nothing like the searing heat of France, Spain and Italy. Many of the crags are in areas where shaded parts can be found — the Frankenjura is particularly good for this, for example — and in all my trips to Germany I have never found it too hot to climb.

A single 55m rope is the norm here and 10–14 quick draws represent ample equipment. The Germans tend to be rather over-sized, especially in height, so practise clipping bolts at full reach, or even by dyno!

The countryside in general is very beautiful, the beer is very good and Germany is altogether a great place to climb and have a holiday. Access is also very good, on *autobahns* that do not have speed limits and main roads or *Bundesstraße* (BS in the directions).

Maps in Germany are very awkward to recommend. The German language is very cumbersome, with very long names, and RV maps are almost completely filled with typeset. However, they do have a lot of info, and if you can decipher them they are the best. Shell also do a good series, which are slightly easier to use — the number 17 to the Frankenjura is particularly useful.

NORTH GERMANY

Bodensteiner Klippen:
✳ 10.00→20.00
(Bouldering)   WESER [1]

Some very good limestone bouldering and climbing to be found here. The rock is up to 15m high in places so it is worth bringing a top rope, but it is equally good just for bouldering.

Dir: 18km NW of Goslar. Take the BS82 to Langelsheim, for 5km then turn R to Lutter. In the town take a L turn to Bodenstein where a small road leads up towards the crags. (64:Ib,36)

Dörenther Klippen:
(4–7a)(250)   EMS [2]

A very good sandstone area with many climbs in the mid-grades up to 25m high. Worth a visit.

Dir: 21km WSW of Osnabrück, 6km S of Ibbenbüren. From that town take the BS219 to the *autobahn*, carry on for 1km, then the crags are on the hill to the L. (47:He,35)

Göttinger Wald:
✳ 10.00→20.00
(4–8a)(100)   LEINE [3]

This is a large area to the E of Göttingen which has recently been developed. Bolts [1–4].

Dir: 6km NE of Göttinger. Local topo guides can be bought in the town at climbing shops. The crags are in the forest to the E of the town. (72:Ia,39)

Hallelujasteinbruch:
(6–8a)(33)   LUTTER [4]

There is an old disused sandstone quarry here which has been developed to give some single pitch routes across the grades. Not a lot but the only crag in the close area.

Dir: 8km SW of Bielefeld. Go S to Brackwede and ask locally for exact details of the quarry. (60:Ic,37)

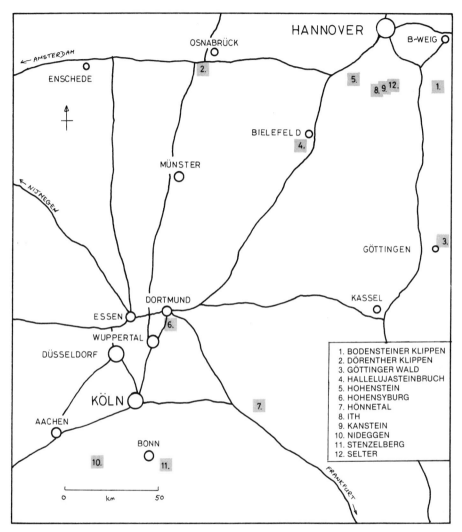

Hohenstein:
(4 – 6b)(50)   WESER [5]

A limestone crag not of the highest quality but with some good climbing nevertheless. All the routes are two pitch and have *in situ* gear [1 – 4].

Dir: 34km SW of Hannover, 11km NNE of Hameln. From Hameln take the BS83 road towards Minden, and after 10km at the village of Krückeberg turn R and go to Wickbolsen.

Follow the road N to a hill and the crag. (50:Kb,37)

Hohensyburg:
☆ 12.00→19.00
(4 – 7b)(100)   RUHR [6]

Some good climbing to be found here as well as bouldering. Routes up to 25m high.

Dir: 11km S of Dortmund centre, 6km N of Hagen. Take the *autobahn* going S out of

Dortmund, carry on for 2km after it ends and turn L towards the river and the crags on the N bank of the river.

Hönnetal:
(5 – 8a)(300)   RUHR [7]

This area is one of the most important in the northern part of Germany. The crags are good-quality compact limestone, all with bolts [1 – 4]. The crags are in various buttresses and some of the climbs are 70m long, however, most are only single pitch.

Dir: 30km N of Siegen. Take the road leading N through Kreuztal and carry on to Lennestadt. From here go to Meggen and seek local advice for the exact location of the crags. (78:Ia,42)

Ith:
(4 – 8a)(1000)   WESER [8]

A very good area to visit. Limestone crags, not very large but up to 30m high in parts and very good climbs. *In situ* gear [1 – 4]. There are many hard routes here, so arrive fit.

Dir: 24km NNE of Holzminden. Take BS64 to Eschershausen, turn L in the town then second R on to a minor road towards Salzhemmendorf. Pass through the town of Sa Wallensen (the campsite here is popular with climbers) and the crags are up on the L. (62:Kd,36)

Kanstein
✳ 11.00→20.00
(4 – 7a)(300)   WESER [9]

A good limestone area with nearly 40 limestone towers up to 25m high. A good aspect and worth visiting. *In situ* gear [1 – 4]. It takes about half an hour to walk to the crag, which remains quiet. The compact rock and quality make it definitely worth a visit.

Dir: 28km NNE of Holzminden. Take BS64 Eschershausen, turn L in the town then second R on to a minor road towards Salzehemmendorf. Pass through the town of Sa. Wallensen and past Ith on the L. Arrive at the town of Salzhemmendorf and take a R turn up to the peak and car park at Kanstein, 4km. The crags are to the S. (62:Kd,36).

Nideggen:
(4 – 8a)(1000)   RHEIN [10]

The area is sometimes referred to as NORDEIFEL. Some very good sandstone-puddingstone crags here up to 40m high with *in situ* gear [1 – 4]. It is very extensive and offers climbing at all grades, especially in the middle to lower. The chalk situation here has been mixed in the past, from a complete to coloured chalk only; the situation will be obvious upon arrival.

Dir: 44km SW of Koln, 13km S of Düren. From Düren go S through Kreuzau and on to Nideggen. The crags are on the riverbank and reach as far as Hausen to the S and Üdingen to the N. The main outcrop though is beneath the château at Nideggen. (75:Gc,44)

Stenzelberg:
(4 – 8b)(200)   RHEIN [11]

Good crags with routes up to 45m and bolts [1 – 2]. Worth a visit.

Dir: 16km SE of Bonn. From Bonn take the dual carriageway up the E side of the Rhein to Königswinter. Here turn L and go to the Naturpark called Siebengebirge at its N end and the crags. (76:Hb,44)

Selter:
(4 – 8b)(300)   WESER [12]

A good limestone area with *in situ* gear [1 – 4] and up to 25m high. The harder routes are some of the best in the area and are worth a trip. Don't miss this one. There are a lot of large roofs here which stay dry in the rain.

Dir: 50km S of Hannover. From Hannover take the BS3 south to Elze (to the W of Hildesheim). Carry on to Alfeld where the limestone edge is obvious. The best cliffs perhaps are the southernmost but the overhangs are towards the N. (63:Kf,37)

CENTRAL GERMANY

There is a lot of climbing around here and it is by far the most popular part of Germany for climbers. There are two principal areas – the sandstone of the Pfalz to the west and the limestone of the Frankenjura to the East. Both are very good and exciting places to climb.

Alter Konrad:
(5 – 7a)(24)   LAHN [13]

A limestone crag up to 35m high with *in situ* gear [1 – 2]. Not a bad crag and worth visiting if passing.

Dir: 45km E of Koblenz, 7km E of Limburg. From Limburg go E on a road to the town of Runkel then, staying on the S side of the river, take the road to Villmar in the E. The crag will be seen on the S side of the river. (87:lb,46)

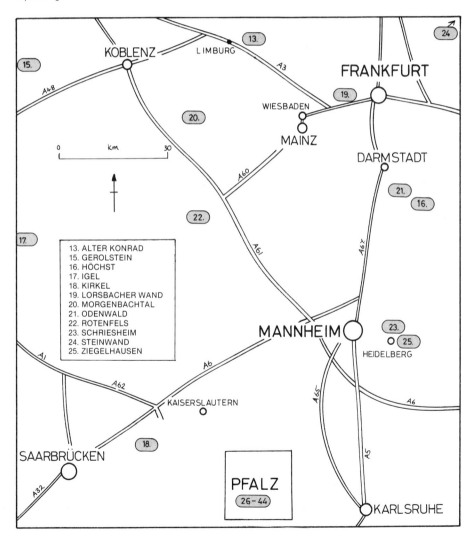

Fichtelgebirge:
(5 – 8a)(230) WUNSIEDEL [14]

This crag and STEINWALD are the largest in the area around Weissenstadt. The crags are granite and up to 40m high. A lovely area and often quite quiet. *In situ* gear situation is unknown. There is a topo guide to the area which can be purchased locally; it is by Bernhard Thun, so it should be very good and easy to use.

Dir: 28km NE of Bayreuth. Take the *autobahn* N for 20km to the turn-off to Gefrees. Carry on going E to the town of Weissenstadt. The crags are quite near locally to the town. (106:Mf,48)

Gerolstein:
(4 – 7c)(100) KYLL [15]

One of the less popular areas in which to climb but still not bad. Limestone crags up to 30m high. Bolts [2 – 6].

Dir: 66km W of Koblenz. Use a map to find or go from Mayen to the W of Koblenz. Carry on the BS258 for 8km then turn L on to the BS410 which after 20km reaches Gerolstein. The crags are to be found locally. (84:Gd,47)

Höchst:
(5 – 7b)(30) DARMSTADT [16]

An old sandstone quarry which has been well developed and has *in situ* gear [1 – 4]. All are reasonably long at 20 – 25m.

Dir: 26km ESE of Darmstadt. Take the BS449 to Reinheim then after winding through the town take the BS426 to Höchst. Seek locally for the quarry. (100:If,50)

Igel:
(4 – 7c)(60) TRIER [17]

Some good sandstone crags with *in situ* gear [1 – 4] and offering single pitch routes in the middle grades. Not a bad spot.

Dir: 8km SW of Trier. From Trier take the BS49 up the W side of the Mosel river towards Wasserbilling. This leaves the river after a short while and after about 8km Igel is reached where the crag should be obvious. (96:Gd,50)

Kirkel:
✱ 09.00 → 18.00
(Bouldering) SAARBRÜCKEN [18]

One of the best bouldering areas in Europe. Hard sandstone which is very good to climb on and in places quite high. The largest are up to 40m high with bolts [1 – 2] so it is worth bringing a rope along. Good for all standards of climber and a great spot for a heatwave in the summer months.

Dir: 16km ENE of Saarbrücken, 6km SW of Homburg. From Homburg take the BS40 towards St Ingbret, after 5km reaching the town of Kirkel. The crags are in the forest to the S only a few km from here. (110:Hb,53)

Lorsbacher Wand:
(6a – 8a)(61) FRANKFURT [19]

A good climbing area for the harder climber with *in situ* gear [1 – 4].

Dir: 20km W of Frankfurt, 11km NE of Wiesbaden. Leave the *autobahn* in between the two cities at the Hofheim turn-off to the N. Carry on N towards Eppstein, just before the village turn L to Hofheim and the crag. (99:Ic,48)

Morgenbachtal:
(3 – 7b)(118) BINGEN [20]

Some very nice quartzite crags for the middle grade climber. *In situ* gear [1 – 4]. Worth a visit.

Dir: 30km W of Wiesbaden, 7km NW of Bingen. From Bingen take the BS9 down the L side of the Rhein towards Bacharach. After about 7km reach the village of Trechtingshausen, turn L and up into the Morgenbachtal valley and the crags, which are reached in a couple of km. (98:Hf, 48 → 49)

Odenwald:
(4 – 7c)(100) DARMSTADT [21]

A sandstone area with an assortment of small outcrops and quarries. Climbs of all grades.

Dir: To the SE of Darmstadt, about 10 – 15km away.

Rotenfels:
(3 – 6a)(30)   BAD KREUZNACH [22]

There is a bird restriction at this crag – no climbing from 15 Feb to 15 May. The crag is volcanic porphyry and up to 160m high. There is *in situ* gear [1 – 6], but the rock itself demands more caution than usual. A bit of a veggie crag.

Dir: 32km SW of Mainz, 4km SW of Bad Kreuznach. From that town take the BS48 up the river Nahe to Bad Münster am Stein. The crags are on the N side of the river nearby. (98:Hf,50)

Schriesheim:
(5 – 8a)(100)   HEIDELBERG [23]

A now disused porphyry quarry with some very good hard routes. *In situ* gear [1 – 4] and routes up to 30m high.

Dir: 8km of Heidelberg. Take the BS3 N to the town of Schriesheim and locate the quarry which is near to the town. (113:Ld,52)

Steinwand:
(3 – 7c)(120)   FULDA [24]

Some very good volcanic rock with a lot of climbing in the lower grades. The crag is up to 20m high with *in situ* gear [1 – 4]. A guide can be bought locally.

Dir: 14km E of Fulda. Leave Fulda on the BS458 which after 7km passes through Dipperz. Carry on for 7km to a crossroads, Poppenhausen is to the R and Steinwand is to the L.

Ziegelhausen:
(4 – 7c)(45)   HEIDELBERG [25]

A good sandstone quarry with some fine routes up to 30m high and worth a visit. *In situ* gear [1 – 4].

Dir: 5km E of Heidelberg. Take the BS37 going E from the city along the river Neckar. After 7km turn L over the river into the town of Ziegelhausen to locate the quarry. (113:Le,52)

Pfalz

This area is (after the Frankenjura) one of the best places to climb in Germany. The rock is a hard sandstone which often has plentiful bolts and pegs. Natural protection is uncommon and a waste of time anyway, since nearly all the best routes are face routes. The area can get a bit greasy in winter but even so year-round climbing is possible. In the summer the trees often shade the rock and belayer. It is worth spending a while in the region in order to get the most from it. The rock is very nice to the skin and, when the fingers are sore from the sharp-edged limestone, it offers a great relief.

There are many crags in the area and the major ones are listed in this section. For good local info and topos I suggest a trip to the climbing store in Busenberg. Peter Lischer, who runs it, is a climber and is in touch with all the local goings-on. Topos for the area can also be purchased at Barrenbrunnerhof or Dahn.

Asselstein:
(5 – 7c)(25)   PFALZ [26]

Quite a good crag which gives single pitch routes up to 50m. There are a few easier routes here and it is not a bad crag for the VS climber to sample.

Dir: 13km E of Landau, 36km WNW of Karlsruhe. From Landau take the BS10 all the way to Annweiler. From the town follow signs to Trifels and soon the crag will be seen towering up above the forest. (124:Hf,53)

Bruchweiler Geierstein:
(5 – 8a)(68)   PFALZ [27]

A very popular crag and one of the best in the Pfalz. A few very hard climbs but generaly middle grade routes. It is always worth a visit. If you like cracks (ugh!) then there are a few good samples here. Bolts [1 – 2].

Dir: 44km WNW of Karlsruhe. Drive NW to Bad Bergzabern, then take the BS427 towards Dahn. Pass through Busenberg then after 2km turn L towards Wieslautern, and after 2km the crag is up on the L. (124:He,54)

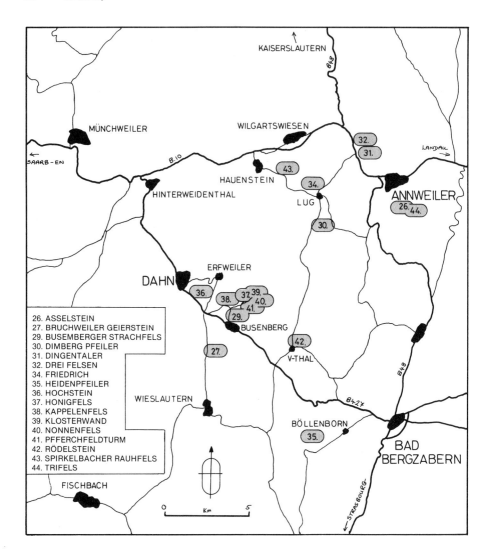

Burghaldefels:
(5 – 8a)(26)   PFALZ [28]

A well recommended crag with some good middle grade and easy routes. There are a couple of desperates as well, so it is good for a mixed group.

Dir: Unknown.

Busemberger Strachfels:
(Bouldering)   PFALZ [29]

A good spot for bouldering if the summer heat gets too strong. There are a few routes here, so bring a rope. There have been reports in the past of the *in situ* gear being poor, so be careful.

Dir: 12km ENE of Bad Bergzabern. From there take the BS427 towards Dahn. After

14km pass through Busenberg, and soon after turn R to Schindhard. About 300m further on you can park and the crag is on the R not very far away. (124:He,54)

Dimberg Pfeiler:
(6 – 7c)(22)   PFALZ [30]

A well recommended crag. The cliff has long climbs at not too steep an angle.

Dir: 39km WNW of Karlsruhe. Go NW to Landau, take the BS10 to Annweiler. Pass the turn-off to Bad Bergzaberg but 1km later turn L over the river and under the railway on the road which leads to Lug. From here take a small road to the S which leads to Dimbach. The crag is just to the E of the village. (124:Hf,53)

Dingentaler:
(6b – 8a)(60)   PFALZ [31]

A very good crag of nice solid sandstone. Bolts [1 – 4], but most of the routes tend to be in the mid to harder grades. Worth a visit.

Dir: 38km NW of Karlsruhe, 3km NW of Annweiler. From Landau to the NW of Karlsruhe take the BS10 to Annweiler. Carry on and bear R to Rinnthal. Turn R up a road which after 1km the crags can be seen to the R. (124:Hf,53)

Drei Felsen:
(6b – 7c)(35)   PFALZ [32]

A very good crag with good 40m climbs. *In situ* bolts [1 – 4].

Dir: 19km W of Landau. Take the BS10 through Annweiler and on to Rinnthal. After 1km the BS48 goes off to the R, the crags are on the R to thè other side of the river. (124:Hf,53)

Fladestine:
(4 – 6c)(26)   PFALZ [33]

A good crag worthy of a visit, I am told.

Dir: Unknown.

Friedrich:
✳ 10.00→17.00
(5 – 7c)(24)   PFALZ [34]

A large crag offering some fine routes.

Dir: 40km WNW of Karlsruhe. Go NW to Landau, take the BS10 to Annweiler. Pass the turn-off to Bad Bergzabern but 1km later turn L over the river and under the railway on the road which leads to Lug. The crag is just to the N of the village. (124:Hf,53)

Heidenpfeiler:
(4 – 7b)(28)   PFALZ [35]

There are a few good slab routes here as well as plenty of others. Quite a well-known crag.

Dir: Not quite sure but try. From Bad Bergzabern take the BS427 towards Dahn but turn off L after 1km. This should be signposted to Böllenborn. Carry on for another 3km to a hut where the road turns to the S. To the N here 1km is the peak of Heidenberg. I presume the crag is near. (124:Hf,54)

Hochstein:
✳ 10.00→17.00
(3 – 7b)(65)   PFALZ [36]

This is one of the most important crags in the Pfalz area. The crag reaches up to 50m high in parts but most of the routes are 25 – 35m long. The rock is very good, bolts [1 – 2]. There are a lot of routes here in the 5 – 6 grade and it is a popular crag because of it. Definitely worth a visit. On the opposite side of the valley near Dahn are the cliffs of LAMMERFELSEN which are also worth looking at.

Dir: 16km ENE of Bad Bergzabern, 1km SE of Dahn. From Bad Bergzabern take the BS427 towards Dahn. Pass through Busenberg, after 2km pass the turn-off to Erfweiler, after almost 1km the crag will be seen up to the R. (124:He,54)

Honigfels:
✳ 08.00→14.00
(5 – 8a)(115)   PFALZ [37]

A good limestone crag with some excellent new hard routes on. Popular with grade 7 – 8 climbers.

Dir: *See* Klosterwand.

Kappelenfels:
(5 – 7a)(24) PFALZ [38]

A reasonable crag but not so many good routes as other crags in the area.

Dir: 13km ENE of Bad Bergzabern. From that town take the BS427 towards Dahn. After 14km pass through Busenberg, and soon after turn R to Schindhard. The crag is above the village and a track leads to it from the sports ground. (124:He,54)

Klosterwand:
☀ 08.00→15.00

(5 – 7b)(22) PFALZ [39]

A crag situated in the area of Barrenbrunnerhof.

Dir: 12km ENE of Bad Bergzabern. From that town take the BS427 towards Dahn. After 14km pass through Busenberg, and soon after turn R to Schindhard. As the road bears round L coming into the main part of the village, turn R and follow this road for 2km to the parking at Barrenbrunnerhof. Across to the L are some fields and two crags, Klosterwand on the L and Nonne to the R. The crag of Honigfels is to the W of the other two, but check this locally. (124:Hf,54)

Nonnenfels:
☀ 12.00→19.00
(5 – 8a)(35) PFALZ [40]

A good crag which is very close to the road and pleasant to climb on. All the routes are single pitch. Worth a visit.

Dir: 12km ENE of Bad Bergzabern. *See* Klosterwand. (124:Hf,54)

Pfferchfeldturm:
☀ 10.00→16.00
(5 – 8a)(65) PFALZ [41]

A good crag with plenty of different types of climbing. There is also a bird restriction, 15 Feb to 15 June. All routes are single pitch and have bolts [1 – 2].

Dir: 12km ENE of Bad Bergzabern. From that town take the BS427 towards Dahn. After 14km pass through Busenberg, and soon after turn R

to Schindhard. As the road bears round L coming into the main part of the village turn R and follow this road for 1.5km and just before Barrenbrunnerhof the back of the crag can be seen up to the R. A track winds its way up to the crag from here, follow it around to the base of the crag. (124:Hf,54)

Rödelstein:
☀ 10.00→16.00
(5 – 7c)(50) PFALZ [42]

This is perhaps the most important crag in the whole of the Pfalz. Most of the routes are 20m high but there are a few higher. *In situ* gear [1 – 4]. There is a good equal spread across the grades with some very fine hard routes as well. Worth a good few days.

Dir: 9km ENE of Bad Bergzabern. Take the BS427 towards Dahn but after about 10km turn R to Vorderweidenthal which is reached in 2km. From here the crag can be seen easily. A track (parking) and a path lead to the crag. (124:Hf,54)

Spirkelbacher Rauhfels:
☀ 12.00→19.00
(4 – 7b)(35) PFALZ [43]

A good crag with some fine routes.

Dir: 42km WNW of Karlsruhe, 8km W of Annweiler. From Landau to the NW of Karlsruhe take the BS10 to Annweiler. Carry on and after 10km turn off L to Hauenstein. The crag is here to the E overlooking the town. (123:Hf,53)

Trifels:
(6a – 8a)(30) PFALZ [44]

A nice crag which has both short climbs of around 20m and longer pitches up to 45m high. Bolts [1 – 2].

Dir: 11km W of Landau, 34km NNW of Karlsruhe. From landau take the BS10 towards Annweiler. About 1km before the town turn L and take the small road to Trifels which is reached in 3km. The crag is beneath the castle. (124:Hf,53)

North Frankenjura

This is by far the best part of Germany to go climbing, well on its way to a thorough development and bolting-up programme. Nearly all the routes are single pitch and around 30m high. It is a great summer area, and you will find it quiet in relation to Verdon, for example. The valleys are really beautiful and there are plenty of good campsites. The main centre is Pottenstein, from where all the crags can be reached quite quickly. There are a few really large crags so you do have to travel around quite a lot, but this just adds to the fun and enjoyment. There is a highly recommended topo guide to the whole area by Bernhard Thun which can be purchased locally, but carry this guide in case it sells out.

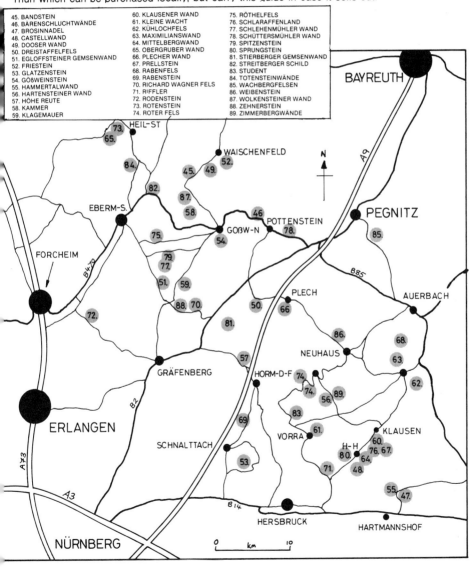

45. BANDSTEIN
46. BÄRENSCHLUCHTWÄNDE
47. BROSINNADEL
48. CASTELLWAND
49. DOOSER WAND
50. DREISTAFFELFELS
51. EGLOFFSTEINER GEMSENWAND
52. FRIESTEIN
53. GLATZENSTEIN
54. GÖBWEINSTEIN
55. HAMMERTALWAND
56. HARTENSTEINER WAND
57. HÖHE REUTE
58. KAMMER
59. KLAGEMAUER

60. KLAUSENER WAND
61. KLEINE WACHT
62. KÜHLOCHFELS
63. MAXIMILIANSWAND
64. MITTELBERGWAND
65. OBERGRUBER WAND
66. PLECHER WAND
67. PRELLSTEIN
68. RABENFELS
69. RABENSTEIN
70. RICHARD WAGNER FELS
71. RIFFLER
72. RODENSTEIN
73. ROTENSTEIN
74. ROTER FELS

75. RÖTHELFELS
76. SCHLARAFFENLAND
77. SCHLEHENMÜHLER WAND
78. SCHÜTTERSMÜHLER WAND
79. SPITZENSTEIN
80. SPRUNGSTEIN
81. STIERBERGER GEMSENWAND
82. STREITBERGER SCHILD
83. STUDENT
84. TOTENSTEINWÄNDE
85. WACHBERGFELSEN
86. WEIBENSTEIN
87. WOLKENSTEINER WAND
88. ZEHNERSTEIN
89. ZIMMERBERGWÄNDE

Bandstein:
✴ 06.00→14.30
(5−7c)(25)   FRANKENJURA [45]

A good roadside crag with some quite large routes. There is also room for the development of harder routes. *In situ* gear [1−6]. Just to the S is the smaller crag of SCHWARZE WAND, with a handful of middle grade routes.

Dir: 30km SE of Bamberg. From Forchheim take the BS470 to Ebermannstadt. Carry on towards Pottenstein but after 9km enter Muggendorf. Turn L to Doos, carry on towards Waischenfeld. After about 2km and before Rabeneck the crags are on the L. (105:Mb,50)

Bärenschluchtwände:
✴ 11.00→19.00
(4−8b)(10)   FRANKENJURA [46]

A very good crag indeed, but all the routes are hard with about 4 exceptions. There is a lot of scope here for grade 8 routes. Great spot, single pitch climbs, *in situ* gear [1−4], but hot in summer. Opposite, on the other side of the road in the shade, is the small, very steep crag of ERINNERUNGSWAND. There are a couple of easy routes and a couple of 7c+ routes which require above average middle finger strength.

Dir: 24km SW of Bayreuth. Take the A9 S towards Nürnberg and turn off to Pottenstein. From the town take the BS470 towards Tüchersfeld. After 2km there is a campsite on the R and the crag is obvious above. (105:Mc,50)

Brosinnadel:
✴ 12.00→19.00
(1.3.1.1.0)(6)   FRANKENJURA [47]

A limestone crag with a few routes and some harder possibilities. The right-hand buttress is known as BROSINNADEL and the L buttress is OEDER WAND. *In situ* protection [1−2].

Dir: 37km ENE of Nürnberg. Take the BS14 from Nürnberg going E, pass Hersbruck and carry on for 10km. Just past Hartsmanshof turn ott to the L at Weigendorf to Oef, go under the railway and as the road turns round to the L the crags are on the R (118:Md,51)

Castellwand
(3.1.6.2.0)(12)
FRANKENJURA [48]

A longish rambling crag which is very steep in parts offering a few desperates. *In situ* gear [1−4].

Dir: 37km ENE of Nürnberg. *See* Mittelbergwand.

Dooser Wand:
✴ 15.00→21.00
(5−7a)(7)   FRANKENJURA [49]

A small crag to the side of the road with a handful of good routes on clean rock. There is scope for harder routes so watch press for details, but only a few. All are single pitch and have *in situ* gear [1−6].

Dir: 32km ESE of Bamberg. From Forchheim take the BS470 to Ebermannstadt. Carry on towards Pottenstein but after 9km enter Muggendorf. Turn L to Doos, carry on towards Waischenfeld. Pass through Rabeneck then after about 1km the crag is seen on the R. (105:Mc,49)

Dreistaffelfels:
(3−6b)(40)
FRANKENJURA [50]

A rambling group of cliffs giving plenty of scope for the lower grade climber. None of the routes are over 20m but all are bolted [1−4]. Very easy to get to and good as an introductory crag for the beginner or climber new to the area.

Dir: 31km SSW of Bayreuth. Take the A9 S towards Nürnberg. Turn off at the Plech− Ottenhof exit. Take the road to Betzenstein, go into the village then turn L on the road to Ittling and Hetzendorf. Very shortly turn L on to a track which soon leads to the crags. (118:Mc,51)

Egloffsteiner Gemsenwand:
✴ 12.00→21.00
(3−6a)(12)   FRANKENJURA [51]

Quite a large rambling crag with some slightly vegetated routes on, bolts [1−4]. A nice crag in the afternoon, especially after a good heavy lunch and perhaps too many beers for anything over-energetic.

Dir: 34km SW of Bayreuth. Take the A9 towards Nürnberg and then leave at the Pegnitz exit. Continue S on the BS2 towards Grafenberg, pass through Wiedensees, Leupoldstein, then 2km later turn R to Obertrubach. From here turn L and take the road to Wolfsberg, then Hammerbühl, and to Egloffstein. Instead of turning L into the village go straight on towards Mostviel and shortly a track and a path lead off to the R and the crag. (105:Mb,50)

Friestein:
(6b − 7c)(5)   FRANKENJURA [52]

A small crag but a good one. Steep and uncompromising. There is scope for harder routes and lots of variations. *In situ* gear [1 − 4] but hopefully more will be placed. Single pitch routes. Worth a day for the middle grade climber.

Dir: 32km E of Bamberg. From Forchheim take the BS470 to Ebermannstadt. Carry on towards Pottenstein but after 9km enter Muggendorf. Turn L to Doos, carry on to Waischenfeld. Go over the river and turn R, follow the river for a while then a track leads off to the L and the crag. (105:Mc,49)

Glatzenstein:
✳ 9.00→12.00
(1.2.8.5.2)(18)   FRANKENJURA [53]

A limestone crag made up of two buttresses beside each other. A small one on the L has a few routes on, one 7b + . The larger crag on the right has some good routes around 6b/c. Height unknown.

Dir: 24km ENE of Nürnberg. Take the A9 N from Nürnberg, turn off on the BS14 to Hersbruck. After 2.2km turn L on to a road to Schnaittach. After 3km turn R to Kersbach (2km), take a small road on the R to Weibenbach. Go through the village and carry on for a few hundred metres where a valley leads to the north at a bend in the road. A path runs up the valley and to the crag in 10 mins. (118:Mc,51)

Gössweinstein:
✳ 16.00→21.00
(5 − 7c)(110)   FRANKENJURA [54]

The main crag near the village offers plenty of grade 7 climbing with one magnificent wall, 8 grade 7 climbs in a row and not easy ones at that. For the other parts there are easier routes. The other crags include NAPOLEON, EMPORWAND, EIBENWÄNDE and FEHENSTEINE. All are worth visiting and are nice and cool on hot summer days.

Dir: 33km SE of Bamberg. Take the BS470 from Forchheim towards Pegnitz. Pass through Ebermannstadt and follow the valley all the way to Gössweinstein. Turn up the road which leads to the village. Just arriving, look for a track on the L which leads through the woods to the crags. (105:Mc,50)

Hammertalwand:
✳ 07.00→13.00
(1.2.4.2.0)(9)   FRANKENJURA [55]

Quite a steep and large limestone crag, good for those hot summer afternoons out of the sunshine. Many new harder possibilities here.

Dir: 37km ENE of Nürnberg. Take the BS14 towards Amberg from the A9 near Lauf, bypass Hersbruck and carry on for 10km. Just past Hartmanshof turn off on the L to Oed. Follow the road around past the crags of Brosinnadel and after 200m a small road on the L is seen. The crag is above this. (118:Md,51)

Hartensteiner Wand:
(4 − 6b)(20)   FRANKENJURA [56]

Not a very high crag but easy-angled and quite long, offering nice middle to easy grade routes. *In situ* gear is varied [1 − 6].

Dir: 38km ENE of Nürnberg, 12km ENE of Hersbrock. From Nürnberg take the A9 to the Lauf North turn-off, then the BS14 towards Sulzbach. After 16km turn L to Hohenstadt and carry on towards Neuhaus. After nearly 20km arrive at Velden, turn R to Hartenstein. In the village turn R just before the cemetery and take a track which leads quickly to the crag. (118:Md,51)

Höhe Reute:
(3 – 6a)(20)   FRANKENJURA [57]

A small easy-angled limestone crag. None of the routes exceed 15m high but offer worthwhile climbing for the lower grade climber. *In situ* gear [1 – 4].

Dir: 32km NE of Nürnberg. Take the A9 N towards Bayreuth. Pass Schnaittach then turn off at the Hormersdorf exit and go to the village of Schermshöhe very close by. Just to the N of the village a road leads up to a TV – radio tower. Take this and the crag is on the L. (118:Mc,51)

Kammer:
✳ 06.00→21.00
(3 – 6a)(25)   FRANKENJURA [58]

A good little crag, but only suitable for beginners. Easy-angled with *in situ* gear [1 – 4].

Dir: 31km SE of Bamberg. From Forchheim take the BS470 to Ebermannstadt. Carry on towards Pottenstein but after 9km enter Muggendorf. Turn L towards Doos but after 1km turn R to Engelhardsberg. From the village a track leads off to the S and the craggy hollow. (105:Mb,50)

Klagemauer:
✳ 10.00→16.00
(6a – 8b)(22)   FRANKENJURA [59]

A very good crag for the hard climber. There is an overhanging base with good bouldering, and the top half is not exactly a slab either. Not a lot below grade 7 here. Bolts [1 – 4]. There is also the small outcrop of SIGNALSTEIN close by which offers a couple of routes in the lower grades.

Dir: 33km SW of Bayreuth. Take the A9 towards Nürnberg and then leave at the Pegnitz exit. Continue S on the BS2 towards Grafenberg, pass through Wiedensees, Leupoldstein, then 2km later turn R to Obertrubach. From here carry on through Wolfsberg then turn R up to Dörfles, and then on to Sorg. A track leads off to the R and the crag shortly after you leave the village heading N. The crag is seen on the R above a parking spot. (105:Mb,50)

Klausener Wand:
✳ 17.00→21.00
(5 – 7a)(8)   FRANKENJURA [60]

A good large limestone crag which should see more development. At present there are several grade 6 climbs bolted [1 – 4]. All are single pitch.

Dir: 34km ENE of Nürnberg, 8km ENE of Hersbrock. From Nürnberg take the A9 to the Lauf North turn-off, then the BS14 towards Sulzbach. After 16km turn L to Hohenstadt, then Eschenbach, then Fischbrunn, then Hirschbach. From here carry on to Unterklausen to a parking spot just before the town on the R. From here a path leads off and up to the R to the crag. (118:Md,51)

Kleine Wacht:
(3 – 6b)(22)   FRANKENJURA [61]

A large cliff with lots of easy routes on, great for the family and beginners. *In situ* gear [1 – 4]. Some parts are vegetated but this can only be expected as the angle is kind enough to support plant life.

Dir: 32km ENE of Nürnberg, 5km NE of Hersbrock. From Nürnberg take the A9 to the Lauf North turn-off, then the BS14 towards Sulzbach. After 16km turn L to Hohenstadt, then take the road towards Neuhaus. After 8km reach Vorra. The crag is up and to the R of the village. Best reached by turning down the road on the R and after a few hundred metres a path leads off to the L and the crag. (119:Md,51)

Kühlochfels:
✳ 11.00→17.00
(5 – 8a)(20)   FRANKENJURA [62]

Some good crags which are all quite small and offer good sporting fun. Routes of all grades and *in situ* gear [1 – 4]. It is a bit of a walk to the crag, though.

Dir: 36km S of Bayreuth. Turn off the A9 (30km to the S of Bayreuth) and take the BS85 to Auerbach. Carry straight on towards Sulzbach. After 10km look for the village of Gaibach, here turn R and go to Loch (midway to Königstein). Turn L and follow a track forking L then R, carry on for a while until a footpath on the L leads to the crag. (118:Md,51)

Maximilianswand:
✴ 08.00→19.00
(5 – 8b)(100)   FRANKENJURA [63]

One of the main areas in the Frankenjura and very popular. A lot of good routes which are set down out of the wind in, an excellent sun trap. There are several crags in the area which include STEINERNE STADT and KROTTENSEER TURM. All offer single pitch limestone routes with bolts 75 per cent [1 – 2], 25 per cent [3 – 6]. Definitely worth a trip.

Dir: 44km NE of Nürnberg. Take the A9 for 30km towards Bayreuth and turn off to Neuhaus. In town go under the railway and towards Krottensee. Instead of turning L to the village go straight on to the crag which should be signposted, 1km from here. (118:Md,51)

Mittelbergwand:
✴ 11.00→19.00
(2.5.9.3.1)(20)   FRANKENJURA [64]

One of the larger limestone crags in the area, and very close to the Schlaraffenland group of crags. Worth a visit. Some of the routes have aid on but by now this may have been eliminated. Good for the 6b/c climber.

Dir: 37km ENE of Nürnberg. From Hersbruck take the road going N towards Velden. After 2km take the road on the R towards Hirschbach. After 5km (having passed through Fischbrunn) the small hamlet of Unter is reached. The crags are here on the R. Mittelbergwand is on the L of the river and Castellwand is on the R. (118:Md,51)

Obergruber Wand:
(6a – 7c)(6)   FRANKENJURA [65]

A small crag worthy of inclusion for the good quality of its short routes and possibilities. *In situ* gear [1 – 4].

Dir: 17km ESE of Bamburg. From Forchheim take the BS470 to Ebermannstadt, carry on just past then turn off L and go to Heiligenstadt. Carry straight on to Burggrub then turn L to Obergrub. After 1.5km the crag is seen on the L near the road. (105:Ma,50)

Plecher Wand
(3 – 6a)(12)   FRANKENJURA [66]

Not a crag for the super climber, but an excellent crag for the beginner or perhaps the 'comfortable climber'. Small routes with *in situ* pro [1 – 4].

Dir: 34km SSW of Bayreuth. Take the A9 S towards Nürnberg for 35km to the Plech turn-off. From Plech turn R before the end of town on the road towards Hormersdwarf. After a few hundred metres turn L on to a track which leads up and round to the crag. (118:Mc,51)

Prellstein:
✴ 12.00→20.00
(4 – 7c)(15)   FRANKENJURA [67]

Quite a large crag with two distinct faces, N and W facing. All *in situ* gear [1 – 4]. A lot of grade 6 routes.

Dir: 34km ENE of Nürnberg, 8km ENE of Hersbrock. From Nürnberg take the A9 to the Lauf North turn-off, then the BS14 towards Sulzbach. After 16km turn L to Hohenstadt, then Eschenbach, then Fischbrunn, then to Hirschbach. From here a path leads up the crag which is almost due S. (118:Md,51)

Rabenfels:
✴ 07.00→21.00
(6 – 8b)(12)&(25)   FRANKENJURA [68]

This is the more famous of the crags called Rabenfels even though there are not many routes on it. The classic test piece of its time is here – Gettoblaster, 8b. All the routes are single pitch, *in situ* gear [1 – 4], on good clean rock. There are some very good other crags in the area which should not be missed since they all have grade 7 and 8 routes on. These are MOSQUITO ROCK, FOLTERKAMMER and KANZELSTEIN.

Dir: 43km NE of Nürnberg. Take the A9 for 30km towards Bayreuth and turn off to Neuhaus. In town go under the railway and towards Auerbach. After 2km there is a R turn to Krottensee. Ignore this, then take a track off to the R 300m further on and before a church. Follow it for 1.7km, ignoring the turning off to the L after 800m, then fork L and the crags are soon reached and are to the L and R. (118:Md,51)

Rabenstein:
✳ 11.00→17.00
(0.4.3.6.0)(13)   FRANKENJURA [69]

Two limestone crags TALSEITE and BERG-
SEITE, with a good handful of routes to occupy
an afternoon. Sheltered and close to the motorway.

Dir: 27km NE of Nürnberg. Take the A9 N
from Lauf for 6km to the Schnaittach turn-off,
and almost immediately turn L on to a road to
Osternohe. At that village turn L to Haidling.
Here a small road on the L leads to a fork after
a few hundred metres; go L and the crag is
found shortly on the R. (118:Mc,51)

Richard Wagner Fels:
✳ 06.00→21.00
(4−8b)(130)   FRANKENJURA [70]

One of the best areas in the Frankenjura. There
are many different crags here under various
names, only of significance if you are following
a guidebook. They are HARTELSTEIN,
WOLFSBERGER WAND, DACHLWAND,
BLEISTEINNE and ELDORADO, home of the
route No More Babysitting for Neurotic Girls
Today, 7c and a must for any visiting climber.
The crag of Richard Wagner Fels has one of
the first 8as in Europe, *Amadeus
Schwarzenegger*. There has been much
activity here over the years and most of the
routes are bolted [1−3]. There is still scope for
even harder routes and a visit to this area is
compulsory for any extreme climber. All the
routes are single pitch.
  The crag of Hartelstein offers more to the
lower grade climber, as does Wolfsberger to
the middle grade climber. All are near each
other and a route can always be found in or out
of the sun.

Dir: 33km SW of Bayreuth. Take the A9
towards Nürnberg and then leave at the
Pegnitz exit. Continue S on the BS2 towards
Grafenberg, pass through Wiedensees,
Leupoldstein, then 2km later turn R to
Obertrubach. From here turn L and take the
road towards Wolfsberg. The crags are on
either side of the road between the two towns.
If you carry straight on through the town of
Wolfsberg on the way to Untertrubach a few
hundred metres later the crag of ZEHNERSTEIN
is seen on the R above a parking spot.
(118:Mb,50)

Riffler:
✳ 12.00→19.00
(4−7a)(38)   FRANKENJURA [71]

Some very fine limestone pinnacles on the side
of the hill offering plenty of climbing across the
grades. The climbs are quite long, 65m, and
can be split in half. *In situ* gear [1−6]. Some of
the gear is old and may well have been
replaced.

Dir: 30km ENE of Nürnberg, 4km NE of
Hersbrock. From Nürnberg take the A9 to the
Lauf North turn-off, then the BS14 towards
Sulzbach. After 16km turn L to Hohenstadt,
then instead of turning R to Eschenbach carry
straight on towards Vorra. After 2km arrive at
the village of Alfalter. From here a path leads
up to the R and the crag. (118:Md,51)

Rodenstein:
✳ 09.00→20.00
(3−6a)(67)   FRANKENJURA [72]

An excellent area for the lower grade climber
and novice. Plenty of bolted [1−4] routes and
a pleasant angle to the crag. There are several
sections and two other separate climbing
areas to the N, ZWILLINGE and
GEIERSWAND. The latter is larger. Worth a
visit.

Dir: 27km SE of Bamberg, 7km E of
Forchheim. From Forchheim take the BS470
towards Ebermannstadt, but after 4km turn R
to Wiesenthau. From here carry on to
Schlaifhausen then turn L up to a parking spot
on the Walberla. The crags are here.
(105:Ma,50)

Rotenstein
✳ Not a lot
(5−8a)(45)   FRANKENJURA [73]

A very good area when the sun really gets
going in the summer. There are some superb
climbs here on good clean steep faces, and no
shortage of *in situ* gear [1−4]. There is a group
of crags which include BURGGRUBER and
LUISENWAND. All offer similar climbing
and are essentially the same outcrop. Worth a
detour.

Dir: 17km ESE of Bamberg. From Forchheim
take the BS470 to Ebermannstadt, carry on just
past then turn off L and go to Heiligenstadt.
Carry straight on to Burggrub then very shortly

on the road to Oberngrub a track leads off to the L and the crags. (105:Ma,50)

Roter Fels:
✳ 07.00→20.00
(5 – 8b)(150)   FRANKENJURA [74]

This area is one of the very good spots in the Frankenjura. There are about 5 crags very close together – ANKATAWAND, BRÜCKEN-WAND, ROTER FELS, EMPORWAND and ZSIGMONDY. All are very good and offer many routes across the grades. All have their own character and plenty of *in situ* gear [1 – 6]. Not too many easy routes but certainly enough for a couple of days. The harder routes individually often take several days. Worth including in a trip to the Frankenjura.

Dir: 33km ENE of Nürnberg, 11km NNE of Hersbrock. From Nürnberg take the A9 to the Lauf North turn off, then the BS14 towards Sulzbach. After 16km turn L to Hohenstadt, then take the road towards Neuhaus. After 8km reach Vorra. Carry on to Rupprechstegen (before Velden). After passing through the village the road winds its way down by the river and the crags are to the L and the R. (119:Mc,51)

Röthelfels:
✳ 10.00→17.00
(4 – 7b)(85)   FRANKENJURA [75]

A very good area for the lower grade climber. There are a couple of harder routes but on the whole the crag is easy-angled and perfect for novices or beginners. Certainly not to be missed. All the routes are single pitch and have bolts [1 – 4]. There are about 6 sections, all with pleasant routes.

Dir: 34km NNE of Nürnberg, 13km E of Forchheim. From Forchheim take the BS470 towards Ebermannstadt, but 2km before turn R and go to Pretzfeld. From here take the road which, after a short while, forks to Utspring. Here turn L and take the Morschreuth road, pass through Eberhardstein then very soon after the crags are on the L, with a parking spot on the R side of the road. (105:Mb,50)

Schlaraffenland:
✳ Not often
(5 – 7c)(52)   FRANKENJURA [76]

This is a group of about 7 limestone crags giving some very good summer routes. All types of climb and *in situ* gear [1 – 2]. Worth a visit.

Dir: 34km ENE of Nürnberg, 10km ENE of Hersbrock. From Nürnberg take the A9 to the Lauf North turn-off, then the BS14 towards Sulzbach. After 16km turn L to Hohenstadt, then Eschenbach, then Fischbrunn, then to Unterhirschbach. From here going up the valley to Hirschbach the crags are on the R side of the valley. (118:Md,51)

Schlehenmühler Wand:
✳ 10.00→16.00
(3 – 7a)(12)   FRANKENJURA [77]

A nice crag for the middle grade climber, bolted routes [1 – 4]. Not all the routes go to the top of the crag but abseil points are usually in place if needed. A couple of very easy routes but most in grade 6. Usually quiet.

Dir: 32km SW of Bayreuth. Take the A9 towards Nürnberg and then leave at the Pegnitz exit. Continue S on the BS2 towards Grafenberg, pass through Wiedensees, then turn R to Weidenhüll, then to Kleingesee, and to Bieberbach. Go through this village and take the road to Schlehenmüle, signposted Äpfelbach, and just after the village the crag is on the R. (105:Mb,50)

Schüttersmühler Wand:
✳ 11.00→17.00
(6a – 8b)(5)   FRANKENJURA [78]

A very impressive crag with an increasing number of routes of which few will be below 7c. There is only one easy route and the rest are very good indeed. Watch for development.

Dir: 24km SSW of Bayreuth. Take the A9 S towards Nürnberg and turn off towards Pottenstein. Pass through the village of Wannberg then after about 1km the crag is on the R. (105:Mc,50)

Spitzenstein:
✳ 09.00→19.00
(5−7b)(6)   FRANKENJURA [79]

A small crag worthy of a single visit. Most routes are worth doing and have *in situ* gear [1−4]. There is an E and W side to suit sun-seekers, all single pitch routes.

Dir: 32km SW of Bayreuth. Take the A9 towards Nürnberg and then leave at the Pegnitz exit. Continue S on the BS2 towards Grafenberg, pass through Wiedensees, then turn R to Wiedenhüll, then to Kleingesee, and to Bieberbach. Go into the centre of the village then turn R and follow the road all the way to the town of Wichsenstein. From here a footpath leads directly to the S and the crag, 10 mins. (105:Mb,50)

Sprungstein:
✳ 09.00→16.00
(0.0.1.1.1)(3)   FRANKENJURA [80]

Quite a large buttress with a handful of hard routes, worth a visit for the hard climber for Direttissima 8a.

Dir: 36km ENE of Nürnberg. From Hersbruck take the road going N towards Velden. After 2km take the road on the R towards Hirschbach. After 4km having passed through Fischbrunn and not reached Hirschbach the crag can be seen on the L. (118:Md,51)

Stierberger Gemsenwand:
✳ 09.00→15.30
(3−6b)(12)   FRANKENJURA [81]

A crag for the low grade climber with little scope for harder climbing. *In situ* gear [1−6]. A nice aspect and a worthwhile crag.

Dir: 34km SSW of Bayreuth. Take the A9 S towards Nürnberg. Leave at the Betzenstein exit midway to Nürnberg. Go to the town centre then take the road towards Weidenhüll. After 0.5km turn L and go to the village of Stierberger. From here the road carries on towards Münchs and after a short while the crag is seen on the L. (118:Mc,50)

Streitberger Schild:
✳ 08.00→17.00
(4−7b)(41)   FRANKENJURA [82]

Three very good crags, quite large and dominant, in close proximity to one another. Streitberger is the largest and offers two pitch climbs, SCHAUERTALER, a smaller pinnacle, and HUNNENSTEIN, which has easier climbs than the other two crags. Worth a trip, but on a very hot day the availability of a beer very close by can be too much of a distraction!

Dir: 25km ESE of Bamberg. From Forchheim take the BS470 to Ebermannstadt. Carry on towards Pottenstein but after 4km enter the village of Strietberg. The crags are obvious above the village to the North. (105:Mb,50)

Student:
✳ 12.00→19.00
(4−8a)(12)   FRANKENJURA [83]

A large crag with a few easy routes but rapidly becoming one of the good hard crags. Several really hard desperates here. The climbs are mostly two pitch of which both are very hard indeed. *In situ* gear [1−4].

Dir: 33km ENE of Nürnberg, 9km NNE of Hersbruck. From Nürnberg take the A9 to the Lauf North turn-off, then the BS14 towards Sulzbach. After 16km turn L to Hohenstadt, then take the road towards Neuhaus. After 8km reach Vorra. Carry on to Artelshofen then after 1km and before you reach Enzendorf there is a parking spot on the R with the crag beside it. (119:Mc,51)

Totensteinwände:
✳ 06.00→21.00
(4−7b)(32)   FRANKENJURA [84]

There are two crags here, the above and FÜRTHER WAND, on the other side of the road. Both crags offer similar climbing in the middle grades. The largest by far is Totensteinwände which faces E. The *in situ* gear is varied [1−6].

Dir: 20km ESE of Bamberg. From Forchheim take the BS470 to Ebermannstadt, carry on just past then turn off L and go towards Heiligenstadt. Pass through Unterleinleiter and the crags are to the L and R as you enter the village of Veilbronn. (105:Mb,49)

Wachbergfelsen:
✶ 12.00→20.00
(6 – 8a)(32) FRANKENJURA [85]

A good large crag with some cracking routes. Bolts [1 – 4]. A lot of grade 7 routes here for the strong-fingered. A popular spot as well. Neighbouring crags are HAINBRONNER PFEILER to the W and SCHIFF which is in fact the R-hand end of the main wall. Definitely worth a detour.

Dir: 21km S of Bayreuth. Go S to the town of Pegnitz. Drive into the town and then out to the E and follow the road towards Auerbach. After 2km reach the village of Hainbronn. Go through the village then just after a track and path lead off to the L and the crags. (106:Md,50)

Weibenstein:
✶ 11.00→17.00
(5 – 7c)(33) FRANKENJURA [86]

A good roadside crag which is popular with evening climbers. Many of the routes are getting slippery. There are two parts to the crag, a small left side with some good easy to middle grade routes, and the right side with longer and steeper routes. A nice combination.

Dir: 34km S of Bayreuth. Take the A9 towards Nürnberg for 35km to the Plech turn-off. From Plech take the road towards Heuhaus. Pass through the village of Höfen then after 1km see a parking spot on the L. The crag is on the L as well, easy to find. (118:Md,51)

Wolkensteiner Wand:
(5 – 6c)(16) FRANKENJURA [87]

This crag has several grade 6 routes with *in situ* gear [1 – 4]. There is, however, plenty of scope for very hard routes indeed; watch press for details. Opposite, on the other side of the road, is the crag of SCHOTTERSMÜHLER WAND. This crag offers a handful of routes in grade 6 and is very pleasant.

Dir: 31km SE of Bamberg. From Forchheim take the BS470 to Ebermannstadt. Carry on towards Pottenstein but after 9km enter Muggendorf. Turn L and go to Doos, then turn R towards Beheringerstein. After 1km the crags are on the L and R of the road. (105:Mb,50)

Zehnerstein:
✶ 07.00→21.00
(4 – 7a)(15) FRANKENJURA [88]

A nice pillar of limestone offering some good long middle grade routes with *in situ* gear [1 – 4]. A few classics on the crag which will most probably become polished.

Dir: 34km SW of Bayreuth. See Richard Wagner Fels. (118:Mb,50)

Zimmerbergwände:
(4 – 7a)(20) FRANKENJURA [89]

This crag and its neighbour HAINKIRCHE, across the valley, offer small routes of not too great difficulty. Bolts [1 – 4]. The cliffs are a bit broken and scrappy but nevertheless do merit a trip if you are in the near area.

Dir: 38km ENE of Nürnberg, 12km ENE of Hersbrock. From Nürnberg take the A9 to the Lauf North turn-off, then the BS14 towards Sulzbach. After 16km turn L to Hohenstadt and carry on towards Neuhaus. Pass Vorra, then Artelshofen, 50m later turn R and follow the small road to Grünreuth. Carry on for almost 1km to a parking spot on the R. From here carry on straight then take the track which leads to the L and a path which leads to the crags. By following the road round towards Hartenstein the crag of HAINKIRCHE can be reached by taking a track to the R just beyond the crags. It lies due W of Zimmerbergwände. (118:Md,51)

South Frankenjura

This area has climbing similar to that of North Frankenjura. There are more crags than are listed here but due to insufficient info some have been excluded from this edition. The crags below are in the Altmuhl area and are quite popular with extreme climbers.

Kastlwand:
✳ Not a lot
(4 − 7c)(26)   FRANKENJURA [90]

The largest of the crags on the S side of the canal. Fair climbing and useful on a very hot day. There are about 5 other crags here but not that many routes. *In situ* gear [1 − 6].

Dir: 24km WSW of Regensburg. Take the BS16 in a SW direction but after 20km turn off R to Kelheim. From here go W to Essing. The crags are about 1km further, on the L side of the canal. Just before the village turn L over the canal and access can be made through the campsite on the R. This is a sensible place to stay if you are in the area. (132:Me,55)

Nusshausen:
✳ 10.00→18.00
(5 − 8a)(150)   FRANKENJURA [91]

This area has the largest concentration of crags. All the routes are single pitch with bolts [1 − 4]. There is not that much for the climber who has trouble with routes below 7a. For the harder climber it is a sunny summer paradise.

To the far end of the group of crags is the cliff PRUNNER TRUM, which is quite famous for its hard test piece climbs.

Dir: 26km WSW of Regensburg. Take the BS16 in a SW direction but after 20km turn off R to Kelheim. From here go W to Essing. Carry on for 4km and the crags are on the R overlooking the canal. (132:Me,55)

Schellneck Wand:
✳ Not a lot
(6c − 8b +)(30)   FRANKENJURA [92]

A very good area for the super climber. A good concentration of hard routes including Jerry Moffat's 'The Face'. Perhaps the most useful area in a hot summer for the top climber. If you don't cruise 7a − b then forget this area.

Dir: 23km WSW of Regensburg. Take the BS16 in a SW direction but after 20km turn off R to Kelheim. From here go W to Essing. The crags are just before the town on the S bank. Cross over the canal before the town and follow a track back down. (132:Me,55)

SOUTH GERMANY ─────────────
Schwäbische Alb

This is a very good limestone climbing area with plenty of routes across the grades and suited to a group of climbers of mixed ability. Most crags are three-season only; the area is quite far south, so in summer it can get very hot, as well as having a problem with the mosquitos in the evening. It is nevertheless a very beautiful spot. Apart from those listed, there are other crags in the area which look good from a distance but upon close inspection are loose and awful, and there are some other good crags missing from this guide because of lack of research into the area. However, there is enough info here to get you to the area and climbing and local details can be easily had. A topo for the area 'Donautalführer' is available from shops in Hausen where there is also a campsite which is used by most climbers. Climbing supplies are available here, including beer, more beer and even more beer.

Hausner Wande:
✳ Not a lot
(5 − 7c)(76)   SCHWÄBISCHE [93]

A very good series of crags in a quiet valley. All the climbs are single pitch and with bolts [1 − 4]. The climbing is in all grades with some fine hard routes. Crags of importance are LOCHELESFELS, FUCHSFELS, ZINNE, EIGERTRUM. Worth a visit, especially on a hot summer's afternoon.

Dir: 18km ENE of Tuttlingen, 12km W of Sigmaringen. Follow the road on the N side of the river Donau (Danube) towards Beuron. After 18km reach the town of Hausen, turn L under the railway and over the river towards the town of Kreenheinstetten. After 2km the road goes around a big LH bend, go on for 0.5km to a RH bend. Here a path leads up to the crags. Pass the crags of Vier Zinnen to reach the main section of Hausner Wande (153:Ka,60)

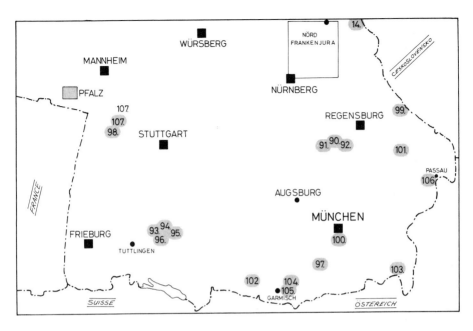

14. FICHTELGEBIRGE
90. KASTLWAND
91. NUSSHAUSEN
92. SCHELLNECK WAND
93. HAUSNER WANDE
94. SCHAUFELSEN
95. RABENFELS
96. VIER ZINNEN
97. BAD HEILBRUNN
98. BATTERAT
99. BAYERISCHER WALD
100. BUCHENHAIN
101. DEGGENDORF
102. FÜSSEN
103. KARLSTEIN
104. KOCHEL
105. OBERAU
106. PASSAU
107. SCHWARZWALD

Schaufelsen:
✳ 12.00→20.00
(5 – 8a)(100)   SCHWÄBISCHE [94]

A good large crag up to 120m high with lots of scope in the central section for hard routes. The cliff has traditionally been the best in the area and is now growing in popularity as the bolting continues. Most routes are geared up [1 – 6]. There is a lot of multi-pitch climbing here but even so the single pitch routes with an abseil back down are very popular. There are lots of good grade 7 routes here. Worth a visit. Impressive.

Dir: 21km ENE of Tuttlingen, 11km W of Sigmaringen. Take the road alongside the river Donau (Danube) towards Fridingen. After 10km pass the L turn to Gutenstein, after 2km pass the crag of Rabenfels on the R, carry on for another 5km and the crag is on the R before Neidingen. (153:Ka,60)

Rabenfels:
✳ 12.00→18.00
(6 – 8a)(23)   SCHWÄBISCHE [95]

Not to be confused with the other crag of the same name in the Frankenjura. A good hard limestone crag with single pitch hard climbs, *in situ* gear [1 – 4].

Dir: 21km NE of Tuttlingen, 7km W of Sigmaringen. From Sigmaringen take a road on the N side of the river Donau (Danube) towards Beuron, going W. After 7km pass the turn-off on the L to Gutenstein, then 2km later the crag is on the R. (153:Ka,60)

Vier Zinnen:
(5 – 8a)(43)   SCHWÄBISCHE [96]

One of the best crags in the area, if not *the* best, but unfortunately there is a restriction. No climbing here from 1 Jan to 30 June, because of birds nesting. After the restrictions have finished it is a very good crag with some of the hardest routes in the area. There are some easier routes here but not more than a handful outside grade 7. Some of the routes are single pitch and some double, *in situ* gear [1 – 4].

Dir: 18km ENE of Tuttlingen, 12km W of Sigmaringen. Follow the road on the N side of the river Donau (Danube) towards Beuron. After 18km reach the town of Hausen, turn L under the railway and over the river towards the town of Kreenheinstetten. After 2km the road goes around a big LH bend, on for half a km to a RH bend. Here a path leads up to the crags. The first set of crags reached are Vier Zinnen. This then leads to Hausener Wand then ALDERFELSEN directly overlooking Hausen to the North of the River. (153:Ka,60)

South

Bad Heilbrunn:
(4 – 7c)(27)   MÜNCHEN [97]

A small 40m sandstone crag. There is *in situ* gear [1 – 4] and good climbing to be found. The crag is an old quarry which is now quite popular. There is a topo to the crag which can be purchased locally.

Dir: 44km S of München, 4km W of Bad Tolz. From Bad Tolz take the BS472 towards Penzberg and after 6km reach Bad Heilbrunn. The crag is nearby. (170:Mc,62)

Batterat:
(4 – 7c)(400)   BADEN BADEN [98]

A good area with lots of routes in all grades. The rock is volcanic with quite a lot of the routes being just over 50m high. *In situ* gear varied.

Dir: The crags are in the Black Forest close to Baden Baden. For exact crags and details seek a climbing shop in Baden Baden for a local guidebook called *Kletterführer Batterat* by G. Gundermann.

Bayerischer Wald:
(4 – 8a)(300)   DEGGENDORF [99]

A good climbing area near the Czechoslovakia border. All the crags are volcanic of either granite or gneiss and routes vary from 30 – 60m high. The local guide is *Climbs von Regensburg bis Passau* by T. Stallinger, and can be purchased in climbing and book shops in Zwiesel, Deggendorf and Regensburg. There are three main crags which should not be missed: Falkenstein, Arberseewand and Kaitersberg. The area is popular for skiing in winter.

Dir: 36km NE of Deggendorf. From that town take the road to the NE which leads to Regen then the BS11 to Zwiesel. This is a good centre and most of the crags are within 30 mins from here, FALKENSTEIN to the NNE, and ARBERSEEWAND to the NNW. The area of Kaitersberg is 40km to the NW and best approached from near Kötzting. (135:0ab,54)

Buchenhain:
(Bouldering)   MÜNCHEN [100]

This area has been well recommended to me and has some very hard problems.

Dir: Not quite sure. Somewhere near Wolfratshausen, just to the S of München. (158)

Deggendorf:
(5 – 8a)(30)   DEGGENDORF [101]

A fair area with some warmer climbing than the exposed crags of the Bayerischer. The best spot in the area is the old granite quarry at Metten, 30m high with bolts [1 – 4]. A topo can be bought in Deggendorf.

Dir: 2km W of Deggendorf. Take the road up to the N bank of the Donau (Danube) for 2km then turn off to the R to Metten. Enquire locally for the quarry. (134.Nf,55)

Füssen:
(4 – 7c)(200)   FÜSSEN [102]

A good area which over the past few years has become more popular in pure rock climbing. Some of the crags have been bolted and as a summer area it should become popular. The longest routes are up to 90m. There is a guide to the area but look out for any new edition.

Dir: Füssen, 60km SW of München. (168:Le,63)

Karlstein:
(5 – 8a)(60)   SALTZBERG [103]

A good modern limestone crag with bolts [1 – 3]. There is a guide to the area, *Untterwegs in Sachen Fels* by W. Muller. A summer crag really.

Dir: 10km WSW of Saltzberg. From Saltzberg go W into Germany and to the town of Bad Reichenall. From here the E60 goes SW to Karlstein. The crag is nearby. (173:Ne,62)

Kochel:
(6 – 8a)(45)   MÜNCHEN [104]

A very good limestone crag with bolts [1 – 3]. The climbing is quite technical and there are not many routes in the lower grades. Not a winter crag.

Dir: 57km S of München, 18km SW of Bad Tolz. From Bad Tolz take the BS472 towards Mittenwald. This turns S into the BS11 after 10km which lead S to Kochel. A guide can be purchased locally. (170:Mc,63)

Oberau:
(5 – 8b)(17)   GARMISCH [105]

A very handy roadside crag with some very good hard routes. The longest routes are 40m but there are good shorter ones as well.

Dir: 7km NNE of Garmisch Partenkirchen. Oberau is on the BS2 which leads from the N down to Garmisch. The crag is near the town and a topo can be obtained locally. (169:Ma,63)

Passau:
(4 – 7b)(40)   PASSAU [106]

A small crag with routes up to 20m high in the middle grades. *In situ* gear [1 – 4].

Dir: 7km S of Passau. From Passau take the BS12 to the south. This leads after 12km to the town of Neuberg. From here the crag is nearby in the valley of the river Inn. (149:0c,58)

Schwarzwald:
(5 – 7b)(75)   ETTLINGEN [107]

A good sandstone outcrop up to 30m high with *in situ* gear [1 – 4]. There are various areas but the best is perhaps Falkenfalsen.

Dir: 24km S of Karlsruhe, 17km S of Ettlingen. From Ettlingen take a road going to Karlsbad then after a few km bear R and down S to Bad Herrenalb. Enquire locally for details. (125:Ic,56)

Switzerland

Climbing in Switzerland is largely affected by the poor weather the country suffers compared with the South of France, Spain and Italy. In summer, however, if it does stop raining the temperature is ideal for climbing hard routes, when it will be boiling at Buoux and sizzling at Saint Jeannet. The newer-developed areas are well protected with bolts and good crags on which to climb. The older crags, such as Handeg, still need many more bolts to become

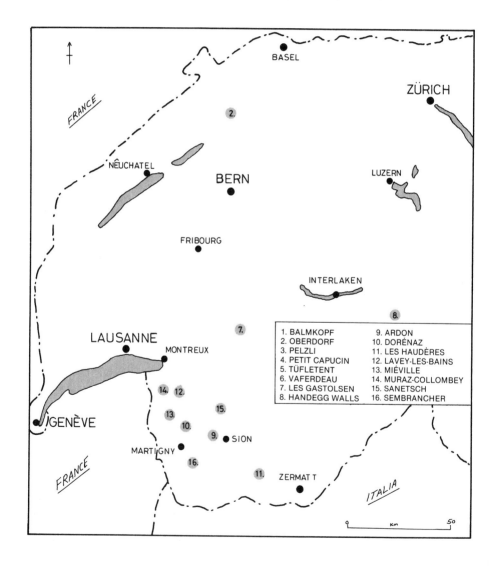

1. BALMKOPF
2. OBERDORF
3. PELZLI
4. PETIT CAPUCIN
5. TÜFLETENT
6. VAFERDEAU
7. LES GASTOLSEN
8. HANDEGG WALLS
9. ARDON
10. DORÉNAZ
11. LES HAUDÈRES
12. LAVEY-LES-BAINS
13. MIÉVILLE
14. MURAZ-COLLOMBEY
15. SANETSCH
16. SEMBRANCHER

thoroughly popular. The country is very beautiful − and very expensive. Facilities are superb but wet weather entertainment could prove costly.
There are more crags than listed here but good reliable information has not been forthcoming. The two areas listed of Jura Bâlois and Bas Valais have bolted limestone crags of good quality.

NORTH SWITZERLAND − JURA

Northern Switzerland is becoming ever more popular as a climbing area and new routes of high standard are common. There are various areas but the Jura Bâlois (to the SW of Basle) is very popular with hard climbers. A topo guide can be obtained from Eiselin Sports at Basle or at climbing shops in Bienne.

Balmkopf:
(6−7c+)(lots) JURA BÂLOIS [1]

A good crag with a lot of high grade 7 routes on.

Dir: Unknown.

Oberdorf:
✳ 09.00→19.00
(4−8a)(100) JURA SUD [2]

A very popular crag with good routes and *in situ* gear [1−4]. There are about 10 different crags in total offering all types of route. Worth a visit. Single pitch routes.

Dir: 4km NW of Solothurn, 30km N of Bern. From Solothurn take the high road towards Moutier. After 3km the road goes into Oberdorf. From the town carry on up to a ski lift station about 1km further on. Park here then as the road bends round to the R carry straight on up the track to the R of the river. Follow this until a path leads off to the R and the crags. 5 mins. (K:5)

Pelzli:
(5−7c+)(35) JURA BÂLOIS [3]

A popular crag in the area with some good routes.

Dir: Unknown.

Petit Capucin:
(6−8a) JURA BÂLOIS [4]

One of the major crags for new hard routes in grades 7 and 8.

Dir: Unknown.

Tüfletent:
(6a−7c+) JURA BÂLOIS [5]

A well established crag with some good hard routes on.

Dir: Unknown.

Vaferdeau:
(6−8a) JURA BÂLOIS [6]

A crag with some very hard routes on.

Dir: Unknown.

CENTRAL SWITZERLAND − FRIBOURG

Les Gastlosen:
✳ 12.00→21.00 (5−8b)(150)
BERNESE OBERLAND [7]

Some very high crags situated at 2,000m and only for summer on a fine day. There is a host of hard routes here with 5 grade 8s. There are about 15 different crags on a high ridge. Most of the routes have *in situ* gear [2−5]. Worth a trip.

Dir: 30km SSE of Fribourg. Exit the *autoroute* midway between Fribourg and Lausanne to the town of Bulle. Go to the S for 2km then turn L on to the mountain route to Thun via the Jaun Pass. After about 20km arrive at

Jaun/Bellegarde. Go in the direction of Ablänschen for 6km then take a road which leads off to the R and up to Chalet Grat. The road winds up the hill underneath the crags high up. Paths lead up the mountain from the obvious parking spots to the crags. (I:10)

Handegg Walls
✷ Sunny (5 – 7c)(60)
BERNESE OBERLAND [8]

These are famous granite slabs notorious for the long run-outs between bolts. With the invention of sticky rubber the routes have become less bolt but even so a steady head is of more use perhaps than actual finger strength. Not really a lot to occupy the high standard climber, all on the feet. A nice place to be when the sun shines in summer. Large crags up to 400m and *in situ* gear [2 – 6]. Very quick to get to from the car and dry quickly.

Dir: 35km ESE of Interlaken. Take the *autoroute* to Meiringen then take the road to the S and the Grimsel Pass. Arrive at the village of Handegg which lies on the N side of the pass. (0:10)

ELDORADO CLIFF, Handegg Walls, Switzerland. (Photo Simon Carr)

SOUTH SWITZERLAND

There is some very good climbing to be found in the area called Bas-Valais which is in the valley which runs down from Lac Léman to Martigny then up to Brig. This is a popular ski area in winter, and delightful summer pasture. There is a topo guide for the area by Eric Blanc which I presume will have been updated by time of publication, and is definitely worth getting. It is available locally in climbing shops.

Ardon:
✷ (5 – 8a)(38)   BAS-VALAIS [9]

A recently developed crag with some new hard routes. Bolts [2 – 4]. Limestone with routes up to 25m. Some of the sections are known as CLOS DE BALAVAUD and LENTELIÈRE.

Dir: 8km WSW of Sion. From Sion take the N9 towards Martigny. After 8km enter the village of Ardon. The crag is close by. (H:13)

Dorénaz:
✷   12.00→19.00
(4 – 8b)(60)   Bas-Valais [10]

Some good limestone climbing in the top grades to be found here. Routes from 10 – 40m high.

Dir: 7km NNW of Martigny. Take the main road towards Monthey. After 7km turn R and go over the river to the village of Dorénaz. The crag is nearby. (G:13)

Les Haudères:
✷ 12.00→20.00 (6b – 8b)(10)
BAS-VALAIS [11]

A good steep recently developed limestone crag with bolt [2 – 4] protected routes. Moulinettes are in place for abseil descents. Not a winter crag but good in the summer after it has dried out, situated at 1,600m.

Dir: 20km SSE of Sion. From Sion go S on either road which leads to the Arolla Valley. Follow this to the village of Les Haudères 8km before Arolla. From here turn L up the road leading towards La Sage. After 1km there is a parking place on the L. A path leads up to the R and the crag. There are two sections at present, on the main wall and on a tier up to the L. (K:14)

Lavey-les-Bains:
(6c)(2)   BAS-VALAIS [12]

A good couple of buttresses offering a couple of 25m limestone climbs. Worth doing if passing.

Dir: 8km SE of Monthey. Come off the *autoroute* at Lavey-les-Bains (1st exit going N after Martigny). Go towards the small village of Lavey, cross over the river to the W side, then take the road to St. Maurice. One crag is above a garage on the R then the other is just a bit further on to the R before you cross a canal. (G.13)

Miéville:
(5–8a)(22)   BAS-VALAIS [13]

Some good small crags in this area. Others are at LA BALMAZ, and VERNAYEZ. All offer similar types of hard limestone climbing bolted up [2–4].

Dir: 8km NNW of Martigny. From Martigny take the road running N up to W side of the *autoroute*. The towns all lie on the road — Vernayez, then Miéville and finally La Balmaz. The crags are close by. (G:13)

Muraz-Collombey:
(7a–c)(2)   BAS-VALAIS [14]

A crag above the road with a good couple of grade 7 routes on the upper tier. Limestone and moulinettes at the top.

Dir: 1km N of Monthey. From Monthey-Collombey take the road N towards Muraz. The crag is on the L above a factory. (G:12)

Sanetsch:
✳ 10.30→21.00
(6a–7b+)(5)   BAS-VALAIS [15]

This crag is sometimes referred to as FALAISE DE ROUA. A large limestone crag with routes up to 100m long, 3 pitches. Situated at 1,600m it does not come into condition until early May. Bolts [2–3]. A lovely spot.

Dir: 9km NNW of Sion. From the N side of town take the road up the mountainside to St. Germain then Chandolin. Carry on up towards Col du Sanetsch for another 10km where the road bends to the R and the crag can be seen up to the L. Carry on uphill and park before going through the short tunnel at the RH end of the cliff. A path leads back L to the main part of the crag and the climbs. (I:12)

Sembrancher:
(5–7b)(26)   BAS-VALAIS [16]

There are a couple of good limestone crags near the village, two of which are climbed on and bolted [2–4]. One is the VOLLEGES crag, and the other is LES TRAPPISTES, which has a mixture of climbs up to 100m and three pitches.

Dir: 7km ESE of Martigny. Take the N21 towards the Col du Grand St. Bernard. After 13km arrive at the village of Sembracher. Drive towards Volleges for one crag. For Les Trappistes follow the road towards Vens. On this road take a forestry track which leads off to the L. After a short while a path leads off to the R and the crag in 10 mins. (H:14)

France

The most important country in the world for rock climbing is undoubtedly France. It has a wealth of crags and access to the majority is quite straightforward. The sport has come of age in the 1980s, with thousands of bolts being placed and routes worked out, and standards have risen dramatically over the past 10 years from 7b to 8c all across France. There are a vast number of well-protected easy routes at most crags.

France has been split up into six geographical areas in this guide — 70 per cent of the climbing is to be found in the SE. Although there is very good climbing all over France, there is not very much of it. Nearly all the rock is limestone but in many different forms, from overhanging honeycomb to large flat slabs.

If you do not regard drinking as the major pastime to enjoy whilst in France, perhaps you

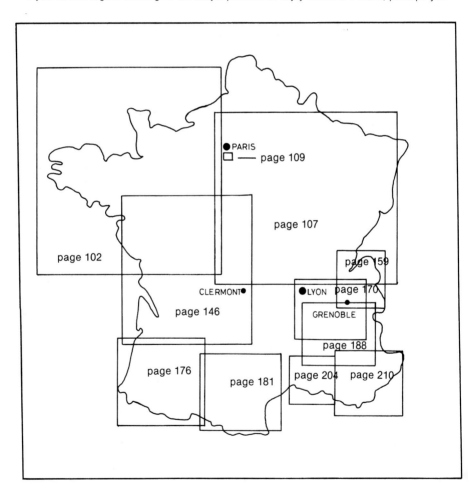

● PARIS
□ — page 109

page 107

page 102

page 159

CLERMONT ●   ● LYON   page 170

page 146   GRENOBLE

page 188

page 176   page 181   page 204   page 210

should think again. Without doubt France is the greatest imbibing country in the world, especially in the range and quality of wines available: fruity Beaujolais, nut crunchy Montrachet, earthy Châteaunef du Pape, pure velvet Margaux, eloquent St Emilion, full-bodied Beaune, majestic Champagne, serene Sancerre, sweet Sauternes, and of course great Cognacs to finish off the evening. To the climber this mixes so well; limestone soil is essential in the growing of great vines and the chalky deposits which create perfect lowland cliffs represent the final crucial factor in soil perfection. Testing personally is the only way to understand the merits of any particular wine. If you need help books are plentiful but as a starter I can recommend anything by Hugh Johnson and when it comes to sheer authority André Simion has no peer.

NORTH-WEST FRANCE

Manche – 50

This area is rather bizarre in the tradition of French climbing, because bolts were banned about 10 years ago and removed from the crags to encourage the use of nuts. The system has not really taken off, and as such the crags do not ever become busy. The climbing is good and the area consists of low rolling hills not that dissimilar to the south of England. Being close to the ports of Caen, Cherbourg and St Malo should see frequent visits from UK groups, especially families and those who prefer a relaxing few days in France sampling the excellent cuisine and doing the odd route to gain the necessary appetite.

La Brèche au Diable:
✳ 9.00→19.00 (4 – 6)(45)
MANCHE [1]

A small quartzite crag with easy routes up to 25m high. There are *in situ* bolts [1 – 2] and it is an excellent place for beginners.

Dir: 25km SSE of Caen, 9km N of Falaise. Take the N158 N from Falaise towards Potigny. After 6km turn R to Tassilly then at a T-junction turn L towards Ouilly. After 1.5km the crag is on the L. (32:B2)

La Fosse Arthour:
(Grade 5)(70)   MANCHE [2]

A brilliant crag for beginners with all top-roping bolts [1 – 2] in place. The crag is quartzite 15 – 25m high in a slabby form. Quite popular at weekends. If you want to lead routes at present bring nuts (this may well change).

Dir: 26km SSE of Vire, 10km WNW of Domfont. From Domfont take the D907 towards Mortain but after about 13km at St Georges-de-Rouelley turn R. After 400m fork R and carry on for 2km where the crag is signposted from the restaurant. (31:F4)

Mortain:
(23.25.18.4.0)(70)   MANCHE [3]

This crag is quartzite towers up to 30m high and has been very popular now for a number of years. The bolts [1 – 2] are quite recent and the routes have superb climbing in the lower to middle grades. There are two areas; PETITE CASCADE and LA MONTJOIE.

Dir: Overlooking Mortain; 30km E of Avranches. There are signs in the town to the crags. (31:E4)

Calvados – 14

Clécy:
✳ 10.00→18.00 (24.25.44.2.0)(93)
CALVADOS [4]

An excellent crag of pudding stone which is perfect for the lower grade climber. The routes have plenty of holds but are quite steep and

well bolted up [1 – 2]. A hot crag in summer but the river down below offers excellent swimming and canoeing. Very popular at weekends so arrive early if you want to park in the shade. Routes up to 100m but for the most single 55m pitches are best so bring a spare rope to lower off. To the S about 15km there is

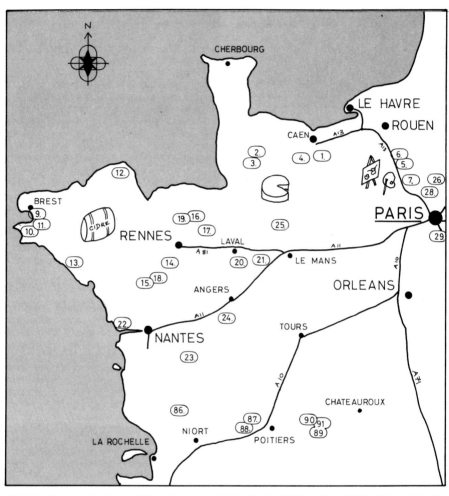

1. LA BRÈCHE AU DIABLE	10. PEN-HIR	19. VIEUX-VY-S-COUESNON	29. FONTAINEBLEAU
2. LA FOSSE ARTHOUR	11. ROC'H NIVELEN	20. ENTRAMMES	86. MERVENT
3. MORTAIN	12. PLOUMANACH	21. SAULGES	87. BEAUVOIR
4. CLÉCY	13. QUIBERON	22. LE CROISIC	88. BERUGES
5. CONNELLES	14. LE BOEL	23. LE MANYS	89. LA DUBE
6. LA ROQUE	15. L'ILE AUX PIES	24. PIERRE BECHERELLE	90. LA GUIGNOTRIE
7. VERNONNET	16. MÉZIÉRS SUR COUESNON	25. SAUT DE SERF	91. RIVES
8. HALOUZE	17. LE SAUT ROLAND	26. SAINT-VAAST	
9. L'IMPERATRICE	18. SAINT-JUST	28. ISLE-ADAM	

a campsite on a farm 2km E of Athis which is quite excellent, and sells home-made cider.

Dir: 31km SSW of Caen, 8km S of Thury-Harcourt. Midway between Thury and Condé-s-Noireau on the D562 turn-off to Clécy. From the town go down to the bridge across the river at Le Vey. Immediately before the bridge is an excellent bar-café with a garden by the river. Cross over the bridge and turn R on to a track which leads to the crag, 1km on the L and very obvious. (32:A3)

Eure – 27

Connelles:
✷ 11.00→19.00
(11.27.45.8.0)(91)   EURE [5]

A 30m crag very similar to La Roque but offering a lot more climbing in the lower grades. Chalk embedded with sharp flints (watch ropes). *In situ* pro [1] being replaced in 1990 – 91. Lovely setting.

Dir: 28km NNE of Evereux, 10km NE of Louviers. From Louviers take a small road going E towards the Seine, over the motorway and follow signs to St Pierre-du-Vauvray. Cross over the Seine to Ande, turn L on to the D11 to Herqueville, then the D19 to Connelles. Carry on for another 2km to see the crag. (34:B1)

La Roque:
✷ 19.00→15.00
(0.4.22.54.5)(85)   EURE [6]

A crag of quite but not really solid chalk. The *in situ* pegs [4 – 6] are being replaced and in the future should be reliable. The rock is very flinty and climbing is predominantly on the exposed faces. The setting is beautiful and worth visiting if *en route* to Paris from Le Havre. A very traditional and long-established French climbing ground.

Dir: 30km NNE of Evreux, 6km W of Les Andelys. From Les Andelys take the D313 N along the bank of the Seine to Le Thuit. It is best to park here in the village and then take a footpath along the river to the crags 10 mins downstream. (34:B1)

Vernonnet:
(4 – 7b)(21)   EURE [7]

A small limestone crag with *in situ* gear [1 – 4], single pitch routes. Just upstream on the same side of the river are the house and gardens of Claude Monet at Giverny. Definitely worth a visit if in the area.

Dir: 1km NE of Vernon, 66km WNW of Paris. At Vernon cross over to the N bank of the river Seine and the crag is obvious above the road (D313). (34:C2)

Orne – 61

Halouze:
✷ 9.00→18.00 (Bouldering)
ORNE [8]

Finistère – 29

L'imperatrice:
(3 – 7b)(22)   FINISTÈRE [9]

A largish quartzite crag but only single pitch climbs up to 50m. *In situ* gear [2 – 4] and quite popular at weekends.

Dir: 6km E of Brest. From Brest take the main road over the bridge (Elorn) towards Daoulas and Quimper, see the crags over to the L. Exit the main road and go over N towards the E part of Brest and to a hamlet called Passage. The crag is obvious. (26:C3)

Pen-Hir:
✷12.00→22.00
(13.52.59.7.0)(131)   FINISTÈRE [10]

The French call this an 'adventure crag'. It is quartzite and up to 50m high, set at sea level and gets the full force of the Atlantic waves blowing in. The *in situ* gear [6] is worthless and corrodes so fast that nuts are essential. There are routes in all grades and the area is very picturesque and pleasant in summer. Great for those who combine climbing with windsailing or sea fishing. The easy routes are very accessible and non-tidal – good for even the most frail of Diff leaders.

Dir: 9km W of Crozon, 17km SW of Brest (swimming only). From Crozon on the S side of the Brest estuary take the D8 to Camaret then a smaller road to Pointe de Penhir. The cliffs are below the road. (26:B4)

Roc'h Nivelin:
(3–6b)(32) FINISTÈRE [11]

Some good quartzite crags, very popular with climbers from Brest. *In situ* gear [2–4].

Dir: 6km ESE of Brest. From the town cross over the river Elorn towards Quimper but very shortly turn R before you reach Plougastel and head around it to the S where the crags are. (25:C3)

Côtes-du-Nord – 22

Ploumanach:
✳ 07.00→22.00
(Bouldering) Côtes-du-Nord [12]

Not the best area in France to say the least, but about 100 granite boulders which are very rounded and give some excellent friction and mantelshelf problems. Worth a few hours if working in the area. The area is a top spot for tourists, however, they rarely frequent the more rugged terrain. Good leisure spot.

Dir: 4km NW of Perros-Guirec. From the horrible holiday town drive to Ploumanach and take the small road down to the village and beach. Park if possible and the boulders are obvious. (27:F1)

Morbihan – 56

Quiberon:
✳12.00→22.00
(Bouldering)(15) MORBIHAN [13]

Some very nice granite up to 15m with good middle grade routes which do not have any *in situ* protection. An excellent family spot.

Dir: 30km SSE of Lorient, 30km SW of Auray. From Auray take the D768 towards the town of Quiberon. From arriving on the peninsula take the second turn on the R towards the Pointe du Percho and the crag. (62:A3)

Ille et Vilaine – 35

Le Boel:
08.00→21.00 (1.1.9.5.0)(16)
ILLE-ET-VILAINE [14]

Not one of the best-known crags in France and this is perhaps just as well. The crag is of volcanic schist and climbs at their longest are all 25m. The rock is not very solid and at the moment most of the routes are just being equipped and are mostly in an aided state. Keep an eye on the press for details.

Dir: 14km SSW of Rennes. Take the D177 out of Rennes towards Redon. 8km after the ring road turn L to Pont Réan. Go through the village and shortly after turn L to Le Boel. There are cliffs on either side of the Vilaine river. (48:B4)

L'ile aux Pies:
(3b–6b)(45) ILLE-ET-VILAINE [15]

A very good granite crag around 25m high. The gear is all cemented in pegs [4]. There seems to be a slight access problem here as the crag is on private land, so it is best to tread cautiously and not abuse the privilege of enjoying this very pleasant setting.

Dir: 7km N of Redon overlooking the Canal de Nantes. Leave Redon on the D873 towards La Gacilly. After about 6km there is a turn-off on the R (D60) to Bains-s-Oust. Go past this for 100m and turn L towards Croix de Penlhuer. After a while go R to Groulais Farm where you can park and take the footpath to the crag in a few minutes. (63:F2)

Mézières sur Couesnon:
✳ 9.00→16.00 (4b – 6b)(30)
ILLE-ET-VILAINE [16]

An excellent 15 – 20m granite crag in a very pleasant setting by a river. The routes are easy but a bit broken in places. There are cemented pegs [4 – 6] in many parts. Nowhere is the rock any steeper than nice slabs and in general the climbing approach here is very relaxed.

Dir: 30km NE of Rennes, 18km W of Fougères. From St Aubin almost midway between the two towns on the N12 take the D794 to Mézières. From the village carry straight on towards St Ouen on the D102. After about 2km the road dips down into the Couesnon valley. Cross over the bridge and turn L down a track to the crag in about 300m. (49:D2)

Le Saut Roland:
(18.12.10.0.0)(40)
ILLE-ET-VILAINE [17]

An excellent quartzite crag which has been recently equipped with bolts [2 – 3] and offers great fun for all. There is also some bouldering here. The crag varies from 7 – 20m high and demands an athletic approach on many of the routes.

Dir: 42km ENE of Rennes, 12km SSE of Fougères. From Fougères take the D798 towards Laval and after 12km the crag is signposted on the L. (49:E3)

Saint-Just:
(3 – 7b)(35)
ILLE-ET-VILAINE [18]

A small pudding stone crag which rarely exceeds 10m in height. Good climbing and quite technical in parts. *In situ* gear [1 – 4]. Quite good as an introduction to climbing for beginners.

Dir: 14km NNE of Redon, 39km SSW of Rennes. From Redon take the D177 towards Rennes. Pass around Renac after 12km, carry on for another 5km then turn L to St-Just. Go through St-Just and carry on towards Bourg. Just before the hamlet park and take a path on the R which leads up the R side of the lake and to the crag. (63:F1)

Vieux-Vy-s-Couesnon:
✳ 11.00→17.00 (3 – 6c)(15)
ILLE-ET-VILAINE [19]

A granite crag very similar to its neighbour at Mézières. All single pitch climbs. *In situ* gear unknown.

Dir: 30km NNE of Rennes. Take the N175 N to St Aubin, carry on towards Romazy but after about 12km turn R to Vieux-Vy. Arrive in the village centre and turn L on to the D97 which goes towards Chauvigné. After 1.5km the road goes down sharp bends to the river Couesnon. Cross on to the other side then take the path leading off to the L to the crag. (48:C2)

Mayenne – 53

Entrammes:
(4 – 7b)(33) MAYENNE [20]

A crag of little interest unless stuck in the area for any length of time. Single pitch climbs on volcanic rock. A bit damp and gloomy in the winter.

Dir: 8km SSE of Laval. Take the N162 S towards Château-Gontier. Pass the airport on the R, carry on to Entrammes, instead of turning L into the village turn R on to the D103 towards Nuillé-s-Vicoin. After 1km turn R and take this small road to a track which leads to the crag by the river. (49:F4)

Saulges:
✳ 07.00→21.00
(16.22.25.9.0)(72) MAYENNE [21]

An excellent crag of a mixture of limestone in a very pleasant setting. The crag is up to 25m high and consists of slabs, walls and very flat walls. Overhangs for good measure as well. *In situ* bolts [1 – 3]. There are a few hard routes to entertain but no longer than an afternoon. The crag is primarily suited to intermediate climbers. Camping at the bottom by the river. The crag is situated in a small gorge and is very sheltered from the wind, and there are many sections so you can always climb in the sun or shade. Worth a visit.

Dir: 44km W of Le Mans, 31km ESE of Laval. From Vaiges just S of the A81 on the N157 between Laval and Saulges take the D24 S to Chémeré, then turn L to Saulges (2km). Go through Saulges on to the D235 towards St Pierre-s-Erve. After 1km the Grotte is signposted to the L. (50:B4)

Loire Atlantique – 44

Le Croisic:
✳ 10.00→21.00 (Big Bouldering)(40)
LOIRE ATLANTIQUE [22]

There are some good quality crags and boulders here up to 20m high. There are no reports of *in situ* gear and apparently the tops of the routes are a bit loose, so that bouldering is more the order of the day.

Dir: 26km W of St. Nazaire. Drive to Le Croisic but just before the town turn L to Port-Lin on the coast road. Carry on towards the point and the crags are obvious. (63:D4)

Maine-et-Loire – 49

Le Manys:
✳ 10.00→17.00 (12.18.15.0.0)(45)
MAINE-ET-LOIRE [23]

A lovely crag for climbers in the lower grades. Granite up to 45m high and mainly pinnacles which all lead to one very prominent summit – out there, man. Soloing here is one of life's great experiences, however, 'below in the pastoral setting snakes have been spotted swimming in the river! Notwithstanding, the crag offers excellent entertainment for the lower grade climber. Bolts [1–4].

Dir: 15km WSW of Cholet, 3km ESE of Le Longeron. From Cholet drive S on the N160 to Mortagne-s-Sevre, turn R on to the N149 towards Nantes. After at least 3km there is a turn-off on the R (D202) towards St Christophe. Turn L instead on to the D53. After 1km turn R on to a small road towards Le Longeron (if you end up down by the river then you've gone too far). Carry on the road for 2km then turn L to the small hamlet of Le Manis. Park almost at the farm; a path leads off from the back garden of the farm down to the crag which overlooks the river. (80:A2)

Pierre Becherelle:
(3–6c)(25)
MAINE-ET-LOIRE [24]

A small 20m crag of pudding stone. Bolts [1–2]. A good crag to visit if sampling the delicacies of Sancerre, etc.

Dir: 10km SW of Angers near the Loire river. In Angers cross over the Maine river on the N23 (dual carriageway) going towards Nantes. Just over the bridge take the first exit and go L over the road. This leads down to Pruniers and Bouchemaine. Carry on for 2km on this road near the river to the crag. (65:F4)

Sarthe – 72

Saut du Cerf:
(Bouldering) **SARTHE** [25]

A small area of sandstone boulders from 10–20m high in the very soothing surroundings of the Forest de Sillé. Not a serious crag obviously.

Dir: 31km NW of Le Mans. From the NW edge of town on the A11 and A81 interchange take the D304 towards Mayenne. After 27km at Sillé turn R on to the D310 towards Fresnay. After 6km turn L into the forest then at the T-junction turn R on to a forest road which leads to near the crag. (50:C3)

NORTH-EAST FRANCE

Oise – 60

Saint-Vaast:
✶7.00→20.00
(Bouldering)(40)   Oise [26]

Hardly the most brilliant crag in the world but nevertheless worthy of inclusion. Limestone of the softer kind up to 10m high with top-rope rings [1–2] *in situ* at the top of all the routes. There is little here for the expert; more a crag for the grade 5–6 climber. The routes are marked with grades, no need for a topo.

Dir: 47km N of Paris, 11km NNW of Chantilly, 6km WNW of Creil. From Creil go to the district to the W of Montataire, then take the D123 towards Mello. After 4km turn R at Saint-Vaast (5-ton sign). Park after about 250m and then take a path into the forest and boulders. 10 mins. (36:A1)

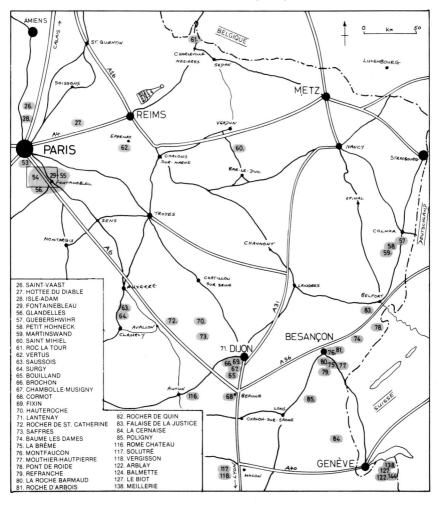

26. SAINT-VAAST
27. HOTTEE DU DIABLE
28. ISLE-ADAM
29. FONTAINEBLEAU
56. GLANDELLES
57. GUEBERSHWIHR
58. PETIT HOHNECK
59. MARTINSWAND
60. SAINT MIHIEL
61. ROC LA TOUR
62. VERTUS
63. SAUSSOIS
64. SURGY
65. BOUILLAND
66. BROCHON
67. CHAMBOLLE-MUSIGNY
68. CORMOT
69. FIXIN
70. HAUTEROCHE
71. LANTENAY
72. ROCHER DE ST. CATHERINE
73. SAFFRES
74. BAUME LES DAMES
75. LA BRÊME
76. MONTFAUCON
77. MOUTHIER-HAUTPIERRE
78. PONT DE ROIDE
79. REFRANCHE
80. LA ROCHE BARMAUD
81. ROCHE D'ARBOIS

82. ROCHER DE QUIN
83. FALAISE DE LA JUSTICE
84. LA CERNAISE
85. POLIGNY
116. ROME CHATEAU
117. SOLUTRÉ
118. VERGISSON
122. ARBLAY
124. BALMETTE
127. LE BIOT
138. MEILLERIE

Aisne – 2

Hottee du Diable:
✳ 9.00→19.00
(Bouldering) AISNE [27]

Some sandstone boulders in the forest very similar to Fontainebleau but not as extensive. There are about 200 problems and a centre block up to 8m on which a rope is useful. A very popular *boules* spot with the locals.

Dir: 17km NNE of Château-Thierry, 87km ENE of Paris. From C – T take the D1 going N towards Oulchy, after about 10km enter the village of Rocourt-St Martin and turn R on the D310. Pass through Coincy towards Fere-en-Tardenois. About 2km after Coincy a track leads off to the L into the woods and the rocks, park in the woods. (37:E1)

Val d'Oise – 95

Isle-Adam:
✳ 10.00→16.00 (7.8.8.4.0)(27)
VAL D'OISE [28]

A small 8m crag of a very gritty limestone. Top-roping is the order of the day here and I suggest that you bring an old rope. The climbing is quite gymnastic and there are trees which shade the crag well in summer. A topo is hardly necessary since the names and grades are painted at the bottom of each route. Bolts [1 – 2].

Dir: 26km NNW of Paris. Take the N1 out of Paris (St Denis exit from the *périphérique*). Pass Maffliers on the L then take the turn-off on to the D9 into the Forêt L'Isle-Adam and towards Mériel. After the traffic lights turn L and take a track up to Club Hippique and park. Take the track Pontoise à Beaumont which leads to a trail marked with red and black which leads to the top of the crag in 20 mins. (35:F2)

Seine-et-Marne – 77

Fontainebleau:
✳ 05.00→22.00 (*See* sections)(3000)
SEINE-ET-M[29]

It is most important to have a layout guide to the climbing areas of Fontainebleau. As the climbing is in the forest it is just about impossible to find the particular areas without a map, so this guidebook sets out to help you navigate perfectly. Some areas are more popular than others, and you should bear this in mind. The local map of the area is well worth buying if you are spending some time in the area – 401 FORÊTS DE FONTAINEBLEAU ET DES TROIS PIGNONS, 1:25,000 Cartes IGN, (Institut Géographique National). It marks all the climbing areas on it, as well as approach footpaths, roads, campsites, forested areas and parking spots. A camping spot which can be recommended is at Gres-Sur-Loing to the S of the forest and river Loing. It is close to the village which has a good bar in the centre.

The crags at Fontainebleau are often referred to as 'Bleau' and are made up of hundreds of sandstone boulders. Rarely do they ever exceed 5m and even at the highest they are only 8m with very good sandy landings. There are many areas catering for various standards of climbing. Circuits have been worked out, whereby a particular standard of problem is given a colour with a tiny spot of paint at the bottom, then at the top there is a coloured arrow in the direction of the next problem. By no means have they covered the rocks with paint or made it look unsightly and in some cases finding the next problem proves to take quite a while (to the relief of throbbing fingertips!) There are, of course, many problems which are not part of circuits and among the 2,000 or so recognised problems there must be 1,000 or so variations.

The weather is one advantage of Bleau; in winter the trees have no leaves and the sunlight warms the rock very quickly because of its dark colour, while in the summer the trees shade the rock well but let in enough light to make climbing very pleasant. Its one drawback is that it is near Paris and consequently hordes of climbers descend upon the crag; still, it's fun. The French are addicted to it.

On the problems and climbs each colour represents a standard of difficulty, as listed below:

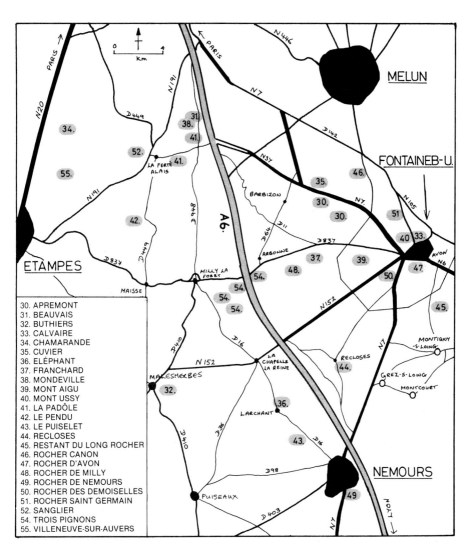

30. APREMONT
31. BEAUVAIS
32. BUTHIERS
33. CALVAIRE
34. CHAMARANDE
35. CUVIER
36. ELÉPHANT
37. FRANCHARD
38. MONDEVILLE
39. MONT AIGU
40. MONT USSY
41. LA PADÔLE
42. LE PENDU
43. LE PUISELET
44. RECLOSES
45. RESTANT DU LONG ROCHER
46. ROCHER CANON
47. ROCHER D'AVON
48. ROCHER DE MILLY
49. ROCHER DE NEMOURS
50. ROCHER DES DEMOISELLES
51. ROCHER SAINT GERMAIN
52. SANGLIER
54. TROIS PIGNONS
55. VILLENEUVE-SUR-AUVERS

Yellow	[F]	Facile (2)
	[PD]	Peu difficile (3)
Orange	[AD]	Assez difficile (4)
Green	[AD +]	Assez difficiles plus (5c)
Blue	[D]	Difficile (6a – 6b)
Red	[TD]	Très difficile (6c – 7a)
Black	[ED –]	Extrêmement difficile (7b +)
White	[ED +]	Extrêmement difficile plus (7c +)

Some of the grades overlap and many climbers will find that these grades are not exactly correct for them, but they do offer a good starting point. Good climbers should find up to blue easy; red, all possible on sight; and white, quite hard indeed.

Picnics in the forest abound and a visit here nearly always gives great fun and enjoyment. It is perhaps better to visit the area on the way down to the south, since sandstone boulders after say, Ceüse or Verdon will often be an anti-climax.

If a number is given after a colour it suggests the approximate number of problems in the circuit. The number in square brackets is the number given to the crag so it can be located using the maps included.

Apremont:
FONTAINEBLEAU [30]

This is one of the main areas of Fontainebleau. It is very spread out and must consist of well over 1,000 different boulders. Plenty here for everyone. There are four main areas which are classified as separate but neighbour each other quite closely. It is close to the very popular Cuvier, but a better bet at weekends if you want to avoid the crowds. These are:

APREMONT BIZONS
Blue, D ▶ 17 [1]
Blue, D − ▶ 49 [2]

GORGES D'APREMONT
Green, AD ▶ 11 [3]
Red − White, TD ▶ [4]
Blue, TD + ▶ 35 [5]
Blue, D ▶ 44 [6]
Orange, TD − ▶ 74 [7]
White, ED ▶ 14 [8]
Blue, D + ▶ 41 [9]
Orange, AD + ▶ 28 [10]
Squashed Strawberries, TD − ▶ 27 [11]
Green, AD ▶ 14 [12]
Red, ED − ▶ 46 [13]
Yellow, PD + ▶ 42 [14]
Bright Red, AD − ▶ 30 [15]

ENVERS D'APREMONT
Yellow, PD ▶ 26 [16]
Orange, AD ▶ 45 [17]
Red, TD − ▶ [18]

DÉSERT D'APREMONT
Yellow, PD ▶ 50 [19]
Yellow, PD ▶ 19 [20]
Orange, AD ▶ 23 [21]
Orange, AD − ▶ 26 [22]
Orange, AD + ▶ 24 [23]

Beauvais:
FONTAINEBLEAU [31]

Quite a large area but rather spread out with boulders that tend to be small. The area stays damp after rain, so reserve it for a hot spell. It is not worth visiting in the mid seasons.

CIRCUITS
Red, TD ▶ 26 [24]
Red, TD ▶ 34 [25]
Orange, AD + ▶ 41 [26]
Orange, AD − ▶ 80 [27]
Yellow, PD + ▶ 50 [28]
Red, TD ▶ 25 [29]
Blue, D − ▶ 69 [30]

Buthiers:
FONTAINBLEAU [32]

This area, also known as MALESHERBES, has some very good climbing. There are two groups of boulders. Malesherbes Canard to the NW has high climbs; it is well worth bringing a rope along as the routes do tend to collect lichen and slipping off is very easy indeed. Buthiers to the SE is exposed but slightly smaller and offers a very good hard circuit which dries quickly after rain.

MALESHERBES CANARD
Blue, D + ▶ 80 [30]
Yellow, F/PD − ▶ 29 [31]
Green, AD + ▶ 40 [32]
Black, ED ▶ 18 [33]

BUTHIERS
Pink, TD + ▶ 36 [34]
Green, AD ▶ 50 [35]
Blue, D + ▶ 42 [36]
Black, ED ▶ 57 [37]

Calvaire:
FONTAINEBLEAU [33]

A good area very close to the town of Fontainebleau just near the Croix du Calvaire. There are some good overhangs and traverses here which will test your complete fitness to the full.

CALVAIRE
Yellow, PD − ▶ 36 [38]
Orange, AD ▶ 20 [39]
ED ▶ Various [40]

Chamarande:
FONTAINEBLEAU [34]

A small area with four circuits on boulders. The boulders are quite exposed and reasonably high giving good long problems. All circuits are in close proximity to one another with a new Extreme circuit. There is also a small group of slabs nearby.

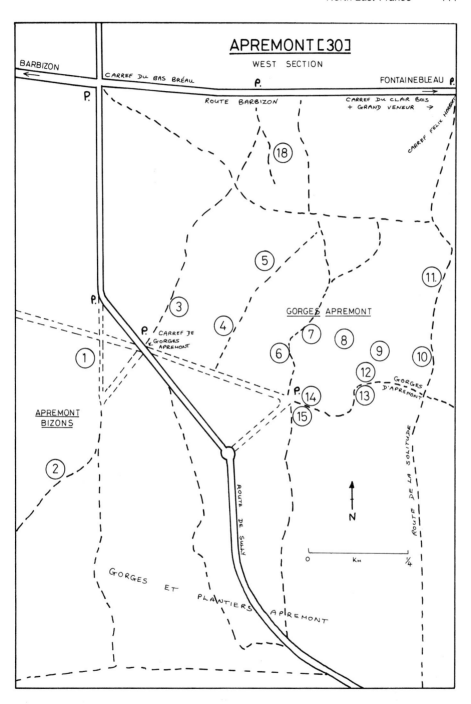

APREMONT [30]
WEST SECTION

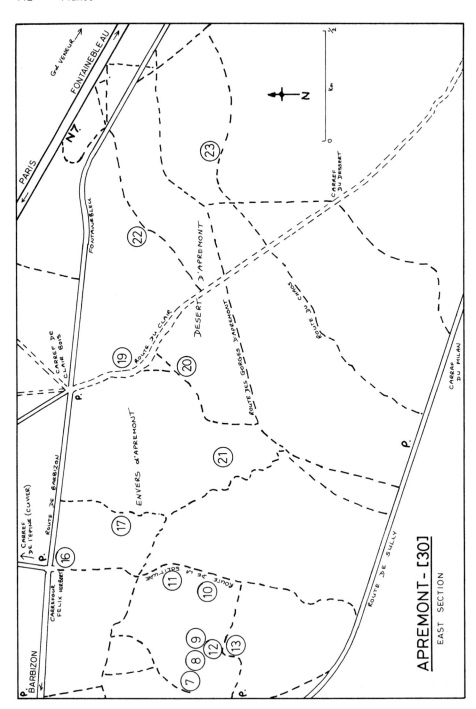

APREMONT - [30]

EAST SECTION

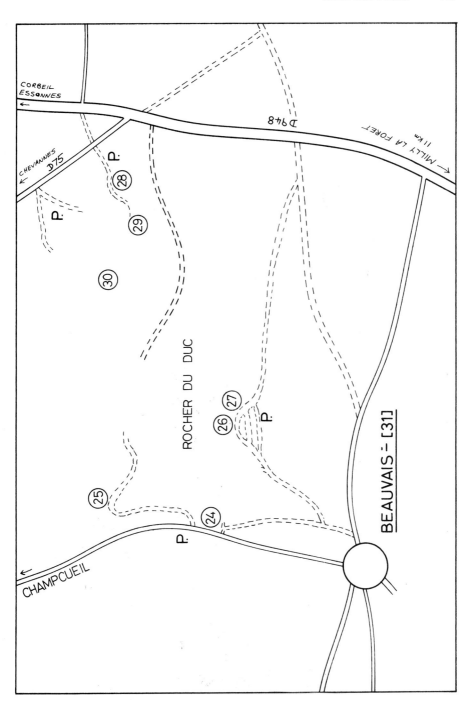

CORBEIL ESSONNES

D 948

MILLY LA FORÊT 11 Km

CHEVANNES D75

P.

(28)

P.

(29)

(30)

ROCHER DU DUC

(27)

(26)

P.

BEAUVAIS - [31]

(25)

(24)

P.

CHAMPCUEIL

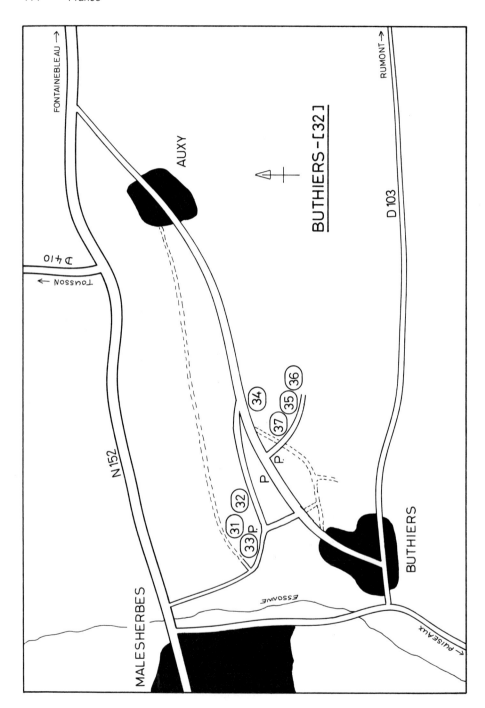

BUTHIERS - [32]

FONTAINEBLEAU →

RUMONT →

AUXY

D 410

TOUSSON ←

D 103

N 152

34

35

36

37

P

P

32

31

33 P.

ESSONNE

BUTHIERS

MALESHERBES

PUISEAUX →

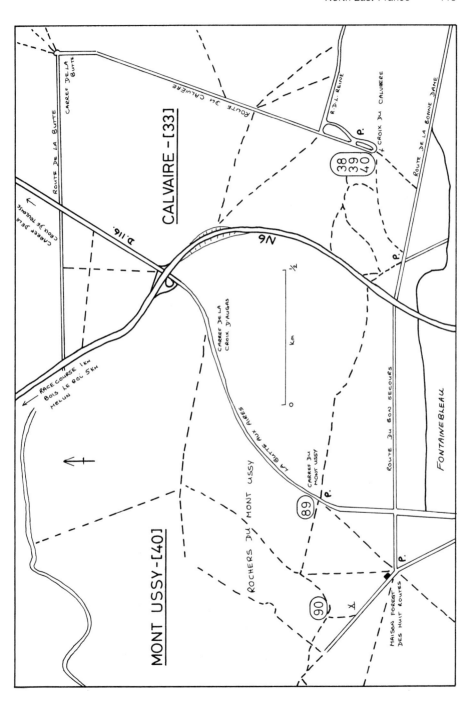

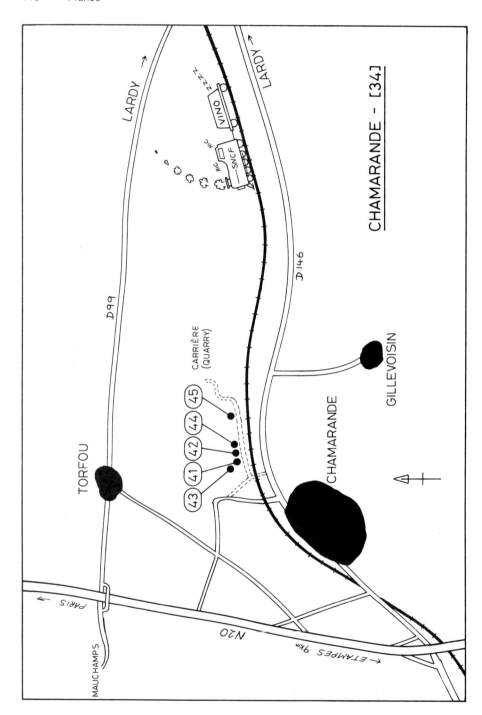

CHAMARANDE – [34]

CHAMARANDE
Red, D ▶ 25 [41]
Orange, AD − ▶ 33 [42]
Green, AD ▶ 25 [43]
White, ED ▶ 26 [44]
Slabs, [45]

Cuvier:
FONTAINEBLEAU [35]

If you have not heard of Cuvier then you are out of touch, I'm afraid. It is perhaps the most famous of all the outcrops around Font-ainebleau and rightly so. The extreme circuit was known throughout the 1970s and early 80s as having the hardest climbing in France, if not the world. Admittedly now Buoux makes it look like a country walk but the routes never get easier and flashing a white problem is still very much a rarity. The circuits are good, although not very high or complex. Pleasant landings and quite shaded. Gets extremely busy on weekends. There are two sections which join each other; to the W is Bas-Cuvier, and to the E is Cuvier-Rempart.

BAS-CUVIER
White, ED + ▶ 16 [46]
Black, ED − ▶ 28 [47]
Red, TD + ▶ 42 [48]
Blue, TD − ▶ 48 [49]
Orange, AD − ▶ 53 [50]
Orange, AD + ▶ 20 [51]
Blue, TD − ▶ 30 [52]

CUVIER-REMPART
Black, ED − ▶ 47 [53]
Yellow, D − ▶ 13 [54]
Red, AD − ▶ 16 [55]

Eléphant:
FONTAINEBLEAU [36]

There are three groups of rocks here that offer the highest climbing in the area, up to 15m. Beginners will find a rope here quite necessary and even grade 8 climbers have been known to bottle out of some climbs. To the N is the group of pinnacles that form Rocher de Dame Jouanne. These stay in the shade in the summer and, providing that the mosquitos don't get you, it makes a great spot. To the E from here, only a few minutes' walk, is Maunoury which is exposed, sunny and very good for beginners and lower grade climbers; worth remembering. The most famous of the

outcrops is Eléphant just to the S of these. Again, large boulders offering a very large range of circuits. A demanding place by virtue of the actual distance climbed during a day here.

DAME JOUANNE
Mauve, AD + ▶ 76 [56]
Yellow, PD ▶ 110 [57]
Red, TD − ▶ 46 [58]

MAUNOURY
Green, AD − ▶ Lots [59]
Blue, D − ▶ 71 [60]
Blue/Green, AD ▶ Lots [61]

ELÉPHANT:
Orange, AD ▶ 48 [62]
Green, TD ▶ 30 [63]
Blue, D ▶ 84 [64]
Black, ED − ▶ 44 [65]
Yellow, PD − ▶ Lots [66]
Red, TD ▶ Lots [67]

Franchard:
FONTAINEBLEAU [37]

This area is normally split into three, but the second two are just seconds apart and only a track separates them. Franchard Cuisinière has a lot of hard climbing and is a good place to work out. Franchard 'Isatis has many more easier climbs and has the benefit of being quick to dry after rain.

FRANCHARD CUISINIÈRE
Orange, F + ▶ 6km of route [68]
Orange, AD ▶ 18 [69]
Red, D + ▶ Lots [70]
White, ED ▶ 60 [71]
Red, D + ▶ 30 [72]
Black/White, TD ▶ 123 [73]

FRANCHARD L'ISATIS
Yellow, PD − ▶ 15 [74]
Blue, D − ▶ 58 [75]
Red, TD ▶ 80 [76]
White, ED ▶ 92 [77]

FRANCHARD SABLONS
Yellow, PD + ▶ 30 [78]
(Hautes Plaines)
Yellow, PD − ▶ 17 [79]
Orange, TD + ▶ 41 [80]
Red, D ▶ 53 [81]

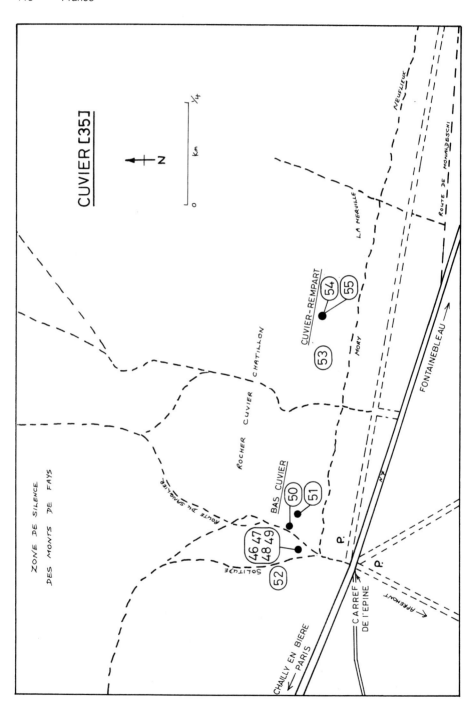

CUVIER [35]

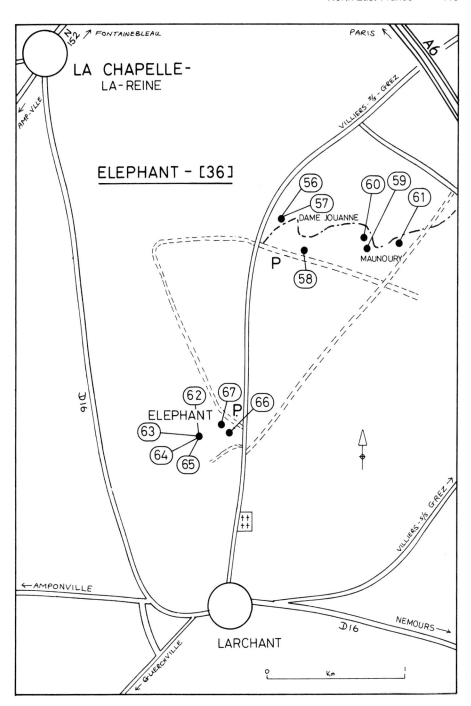

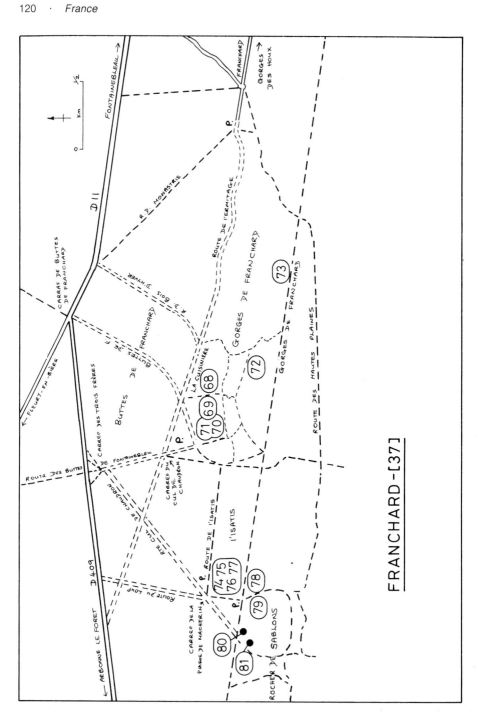

FRANCHARD-[37]

Mondeville:
FONTAINEBLEAU [38]

One of the more discreet spots to boulder near Paris, mainly because the area stays lichenous and damp in the shade. Not a popular area, nevertheless worthy of a mention. Each circuit offers interesting parts if visited during a very long hot spell, the Red in particular.

MONDEVILLE
Yellow, PD − ▶ Lots [82]
Green, AD − ▶ Lots [83]
Red, D + ▶ 38 [84]

Mont Aigu:
FONTAINEBLEAU [39]

There are two areas of climbing to be found here − boulders to the S and a beginners' circuit at the Gorges du Houx. All climbing typical of the area.

MONT AIGU
Orange, AD ▶ 35 [85]
Yellow, PD − ▶ 26 [86]
Blue, TD − ▶ 56 [87]

GORGES DU HOUX
Yellow, PD − ▶ 21 [88]

Mont Ussy:
FONTAINEBLEAU [40]

A couple of circuits in this very dense part of the forest.

MONT USSY
Yellow, PD ▶ 50 [89]
Yellow, PD − ▶ 35 [90]

La Padôle:
Fontainebleau [41]

A good spot high on a south-facing hill, quite exposed and open to the elements. The circuits are close together and complementary to one another. There is also another area within a couple of km. I suggest you drive, since walking is extremely hazardous (or beneficial) to your health, and you might catch the dreaded disease of 'Rambling'!

LA PADÔLE
Yellow, PD ▶ 46 [91]
Orange, AD/AD + ▶ 47 [92]
Orange, AD + ▶ 34 [93]
Blue, TD ▶ 25 [94]

VIDELLES-LES-ROCHES
White, PD ▶ Lots [95]
Orange, AD + ▶ 55 [96]

Le Pendu:
FONTAINEBLEAU [42]

A very good small area well worth visiting. Away from the hordes and excellent for middle grade climbers.

LE PENDU
Yellow, PD ▶ 24 [97]
Orange, D + ▶ 27 [98]

Puiselet:
FONTAINEBLEAU [43]

A good area with some quite high boulders. There are many N-facing problems which become greasy in the winter, however, there are also W-facing ones which warm to winter sunshine. A good spot for the hard climber in a hot summer. The circuit has some recent very hard additions on quite small holds. Worth a visit, bring a rope as well.

PUISELET
Orange, AD ▶ 20 [99]
Black, ED ▶ 42 [100]
Black, D + ▶ 36 [101]

Recloses:
FONTAINEBLEAU [44]

A small vegetated outcrop of little importance but with a circuit for the enthusiastic.

RECLOSES
Orange, AD ▶ Various [102]

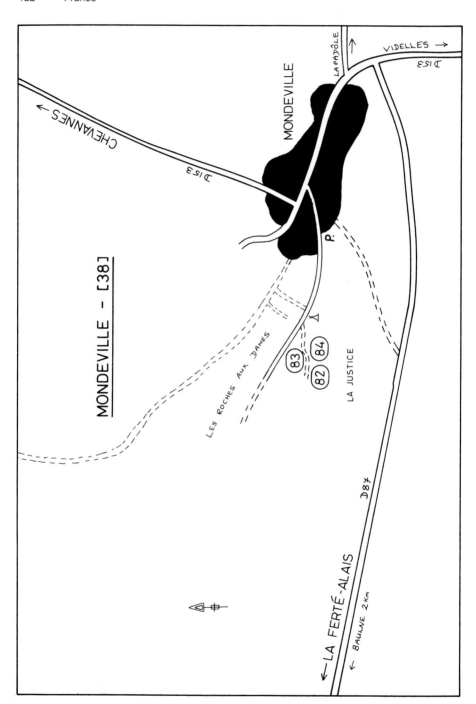

MONDEVILLE – [38]

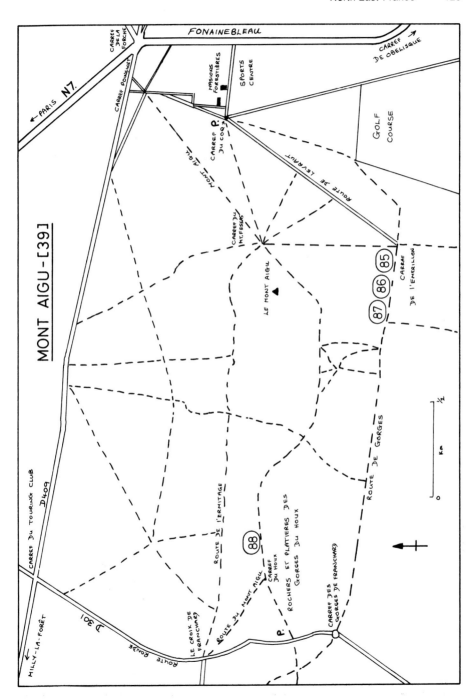

MONT AIGU-[39]

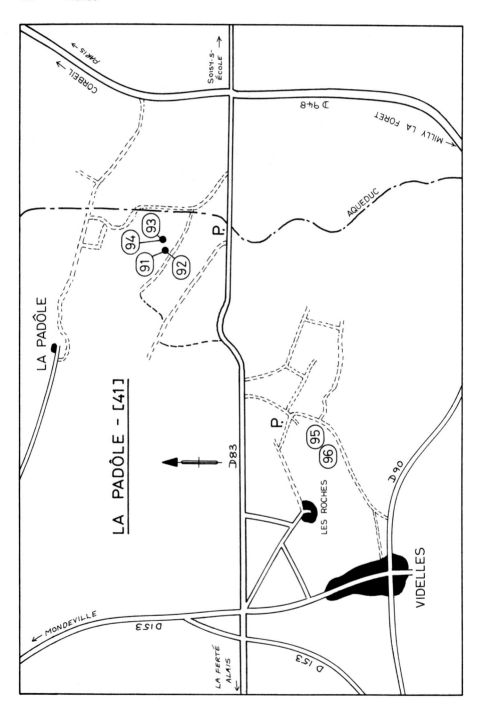

LA PADÔLE – [41]

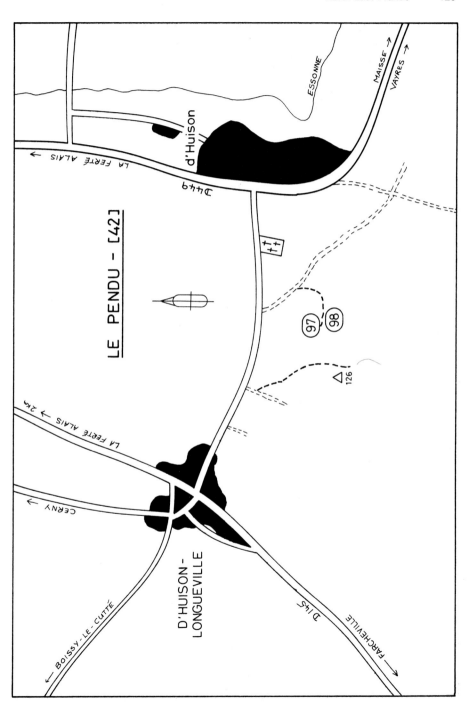

LE PENDU – [42]

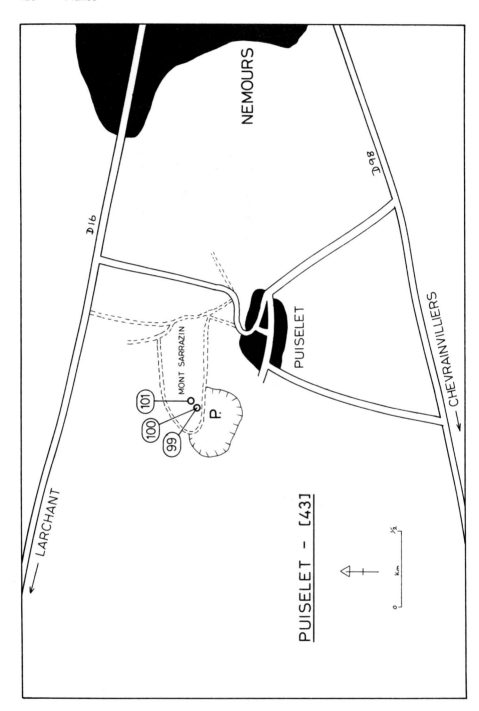

PUISELET – [43]

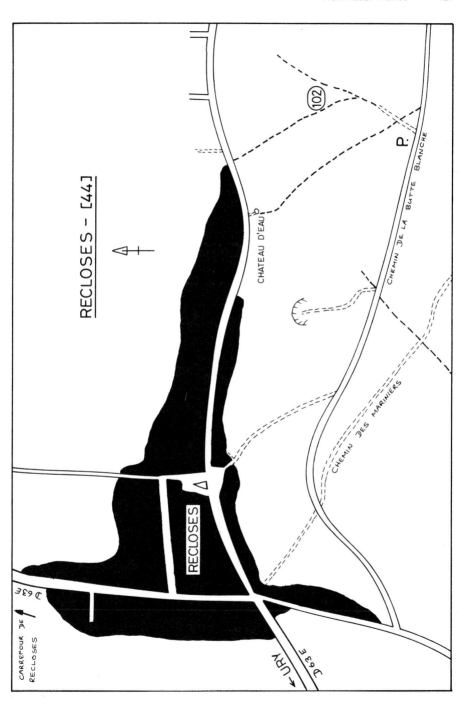

RECLOSES – [44]

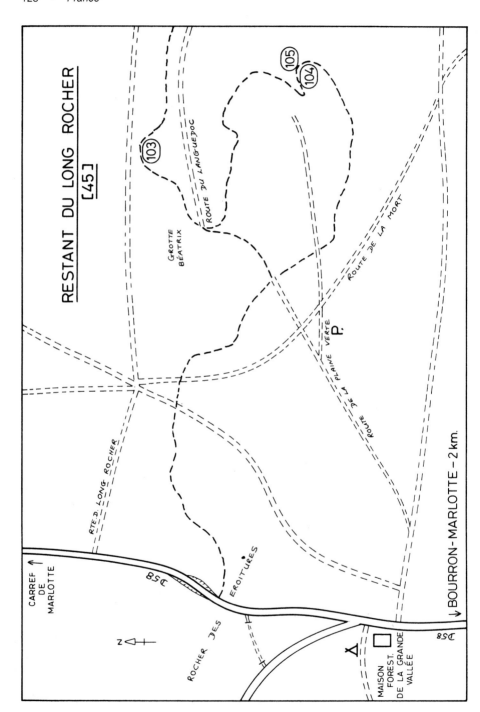

RESTANT DU LONG ROCHER

[45]

GROTTE BÉATRIX

ROUTE DU LANGUEDOC

103

105
104

ROUTE DE LA MORT

ROUTE DE LA PLAINE VERTE

P.

RTE. D. LONG ROCHER

CARREF
DE
MARLOTTE

D58

ROCHER DES EROITURES

N

MAISON
FOREST.
DE LA GRANDE
VALLÉE

D58

→ BOURRON-MARLOTTE – 2 km.

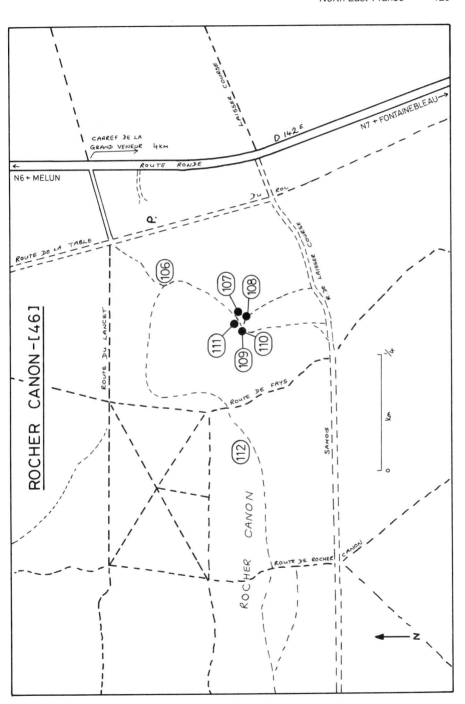

Restant du Long Rocher:
FONTAINEBLEAU [45]

A very fine group of boulders in this lovely forest close to Bourron-Marlotte. A good range of climbing in the middle grades. The rocks tend to stay quite damp in winter and into late spring. Summer and autumn are the best times to visit.

RESTANT DU LONG ROCHER
Orange, AD ▶ 33 [103]
Green, AD ▶ 12 [104]
Red, TD − ▶ 38 [105]

Rocher Canon:
FONTAINEBLEAU [46]

Another one of the famous areas and very popular since it is the nearest outcrop to the town of Melun. There is plenty of climbing here in all grades with the addition of a new White circuit in recent years. The only drawback with the area is that it does take a long time to dry out, and the mosquitos come out in full force. Visit in a hot spell in spring.

ROCHER CANON
Blue, D ▶ 48 [106]
Light Blue, D + /TD − ▶ 40 [107]
Red, TD + ▶ 56 [108]
Green, AD + ▶ 31 [109]
Yellow, PD ▶ 40 [110]
White, ED ▶ 20 [111]
Yellow/Orange, PD − ▶ Lots [112]

Rocher d'Avon:
FONTAINEBLEAU [47]

A small outcrop with some good easy circuits. A fine view of Fontainbleau for those scenically inclined.

ROCHER D'AVON
Yellow, PD ▶ 10 [113]
Orange, AD − ▶ 20 [114]
Blue, AD ▶ 10 [115]

Rocher de Milly:
FONTAINEBLEAU [48]

A good area away from the crowds and in a very peaceful spot.

ROCHER DE MILLY
Yellow, F + ▶ 27 [116]
Blue, D + ▶ 38 [117]

Rocher de Nemours:
FONTAINEBLEAU [49]

A small circuit hardly worth a mention unless you find yourself here for some other reason.

ROCHER DE NEMOURS
Green, AD ▶ Various [118]

Rocher des Demoiselles:
FONTAINEBLEAU [50]

Only one circuit here but worth the trip entirely. On a hot summer's day most of the problems are in the shade and not too hard. Quite a long circuit and one not to be missed for the middle grade climber.

ROCHER DES DEMOISELLES
Orange, AD − ▶ 20 [119]

Rocher Saint Germain:
FONTAINEBLEAU [51]

A popular area, with good reason. Two circuits of quite easy problems which are good fun to do and are in the shade in summer. Les Bumblières are ever present here. Worth a visit.

ROCHER SAINT GERMAIN
Yellow, PD + ▶ 60 [120]
Green, AD + 52 [121]

Sanglier:
FONTAINEBLEAU [52]

A fair bouldering spot in the lower grades with three circuits. The circuits have been overgrown in the past and some of the landings are poor; several days of good strong sun are needed to dry out after a wet period.

SANGLIER
Yellow, PD ▶ 38 [122]
Orange, AD ▶ 28 [123]
Blue, TD − ▶ 55 [124]

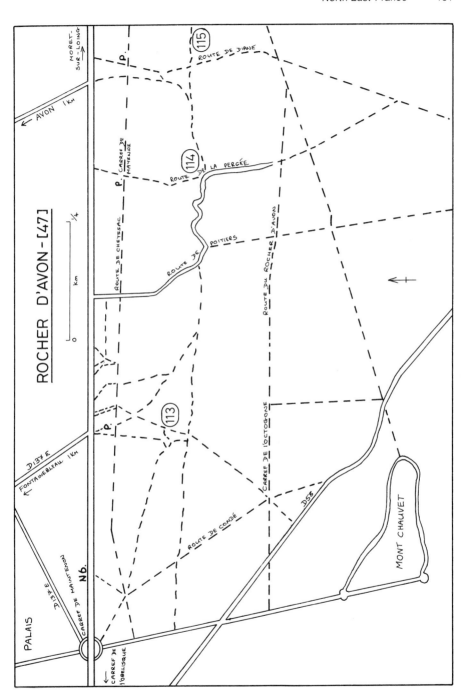

ROCHER D'AVON - [47]

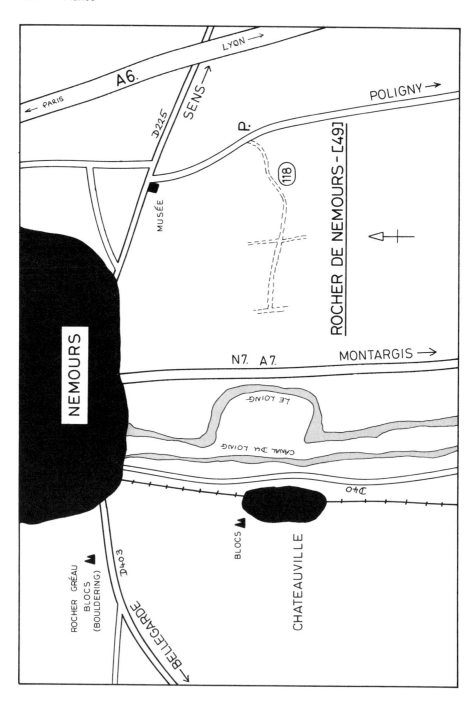

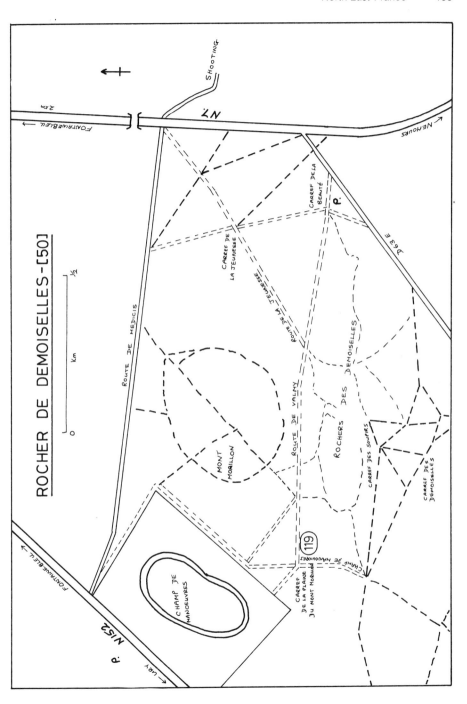

ROCHER DE DEMOISELLES -[50]

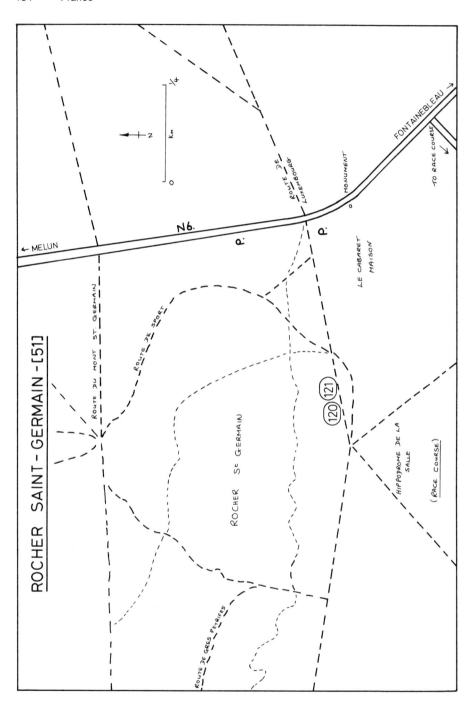

ROCHER SAINT-GERMAIN - [51]

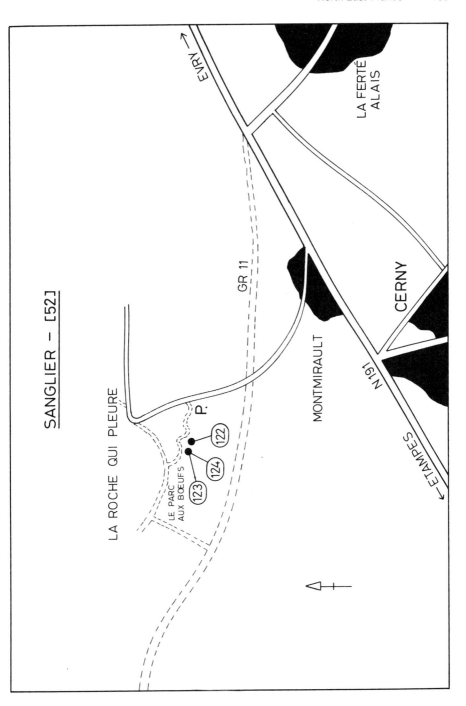

SANGLIER – [52]

La Troche:
FONTAINEBLEAU [53]

This area is different from most of the areas in the Paris sandstone region. The crag is unnatural and consists of a once quarried wall which curves around in a horseshoe. The climbs face S, N and E, with the entrance being from the W. It is popular with beginners and up to 6m high. The flatter walls offer very good tiny holds for hard pebble problems.

For access drive to the Paris suburb of Palaiseau which is approx 14km SSW of the *périphérique* and 2km W of the A10. From here go to the town where the quarry lies just to the S of a cycle track.

LA TROCHE
Orange, D/D + ▶ 20 [125]
Red, TD − /TD ▶ 10 [126]

Trois Pignons:
FONTAINEBLEAU [54]

This is the largest area of concentrated circuits and one of the best. There are so many areas about which you could write a page of compliments. Cul de Chien is the most famous and always worth a trip; Gros Sablons is a quick-drying spot with an excellent ED circuit; 95.2, with its rather bizarre name, gives very good hard fingery problems. Most of the crags are worth visiting.

DREI ZINNEN
Red, D + ▶ 24 [127]

ROCHER DE LA REINE
Yellow, PD + ▶ 48 [128]
Blue, D + ▶ 52 [129]
Orange, AD ▶ 37 [130]
Blue, D + ▶ 33 [131]

CANACHE AUX MERCIERS
Yellow, PD − ▶ 41 [132]
Orange, AD ▶ [133]
Blue, D + ▶ 42 [134]
Blue, D ▶ 41 [135]

CHATEAUVEAU
Yellow, PD + ▶ 17 [136]
(A rope can be useful on this circuit.)

PIGNON POTEAU
Yellow, PD − ▶ [137]

GROS SABLONS
Orange, AD ▶ 43 [138]
(Exposed and quick to dry.)
Orange, AD + ▶ 43 [139]
Blue, D + ▶ 65 [141]
Black/White, ED ▶ 35 [142]
95.2: Yellow, PD + ▶ 41 [143]
Orange, AD + ▶ 50 [144]
Blue, D ▶ 38 [145]
Red, TD − ▶ 61 [146]
White, ED ▶ 45 [147]

ROCHERS DES POTETS
Yellow, PD − ▶ 20 [148]
Orange, AD ▶ 36 [149]

JEAN DES VIGNES
Red, AD + ▶ 35 [150]

ROCHER FIN
Yellow, PD ▶ 13 [151]
Blue, D ▶ 51 [152]
Red, TD + ▶ 34 [153]

CUL DE CHIEN
Blue, D − ▶ 35 [154]
Green, AD ▶ Lots [155]
Yellow, PD + ▶ 58 [156]
Red, TD ▶ 36 [157]
91.1 Green, AD − ▶ 37 [158]
Orange, AD + ▶ 50 [159]
Red, TD − ▶ 47 [160]

ROCHE AUX SABOTS
Yellow, PD ▶ 25 [161]
Blue, D ▶ 44 [162]
Red, TD + ▶ [163]

ROCHER DU GÉNÉRAL
Yellow, PD ▶ Various [164]
(71,1) Green, D + ▶ 30 [165]

DIPLODOCUS
Green, PD ▶ Lots [166]
Yellow, PD ▶ 28 [167]
Orange, AD + ▶ 31 [168]
Blue, D ▶ [169]

LA GRANDE MONTAGNE
Green, AD + [170]

ROCHER DU POTALA
Green, AD ▶ 36 [171]
(Vallée de la Mée) Blue, D ▶ 57 [172]
Light Blue, TD ▶ 21 [173]

POTALA-SUD (96,2)
Green, PD + ▶ Lots [174]

J.A. MARTIN
Yellow, PD − ▶ 28 [175]
Green, AD ▶ Lots [176]
Green, AD ▶ Lots [177]
Green, AD + ▶ 30 [178]
Light Blue, D − ▶ 41 [179]
Blue, D + ▶ 43 [180]
Red, TD + ▶ 48 [181]

ROCHER GUICHOT
Yellow, AD − ▶ 34 [182]
Red, TD + ▶ 32 [183]

Villeneuve-sur-Auvers:
FONTAINEBLEAU [55]

A more popular spot with the lower grade boulderers. A high quarried face up to 8m high. The circuits are varied with quite different problems. The shaded pine trees make this a popular picnic spot in summer.

VILLENEUVE
Yellow, PD − ▶ 37 [184]
Green, AD + ▶ 31 [185]

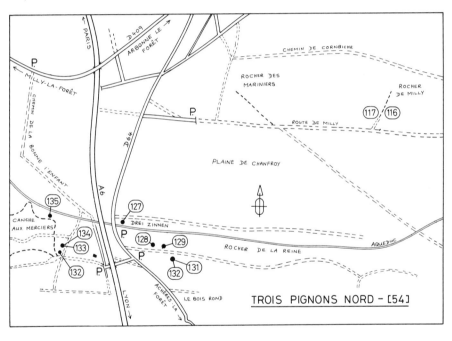

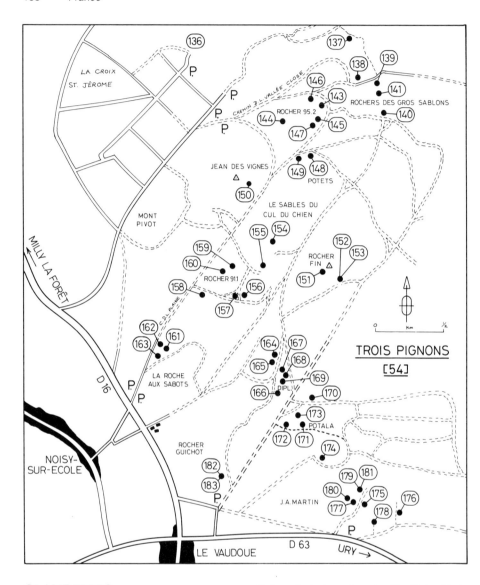

GLANDELLES:
✶ 09.00→15.30
(3−6c)(25) FONTAINEBLEAU
[56]

A pudding stone crag of softish quality in the very southern end of the Fontainebleau region. Mostly slabs with a few steep parts and slight overhangs. Worth a trip for the lower grade climber. A single wall up to 10m high with *in situ* gear [3−4]. Very near the road and not bad.

Dir: 20km S of Fontainebleau, 6km SSE of Nemours. From Nemours take the N7 S towards Montargis. After 7km at Glandelles turn L on the small road towards Poligny. After about 1km the crag is on the L. (54:C3)

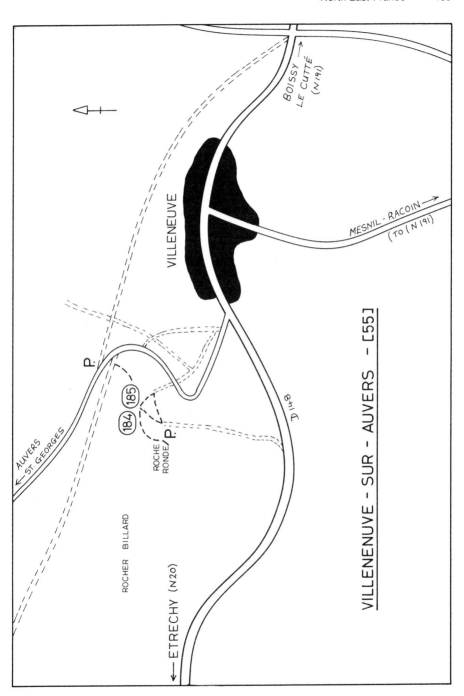

VILLENENUVE - SUR - AUVERS - [55]

VILLENEUVE

BOISSY LE CUTTÉ (N 191)

MESNIL - RACOIN → (TO (N 191)

AUVERS ← ST. GEORGES

P.

(184) (185)

ROCHE RONDE P.

D 148

ROCHER BILLARD

← ETRECHY (N20)

Haut-Rhin – 68

Guebershwihr:
✳ 08.00→14.00 (50.60.40.30.0)(180) HAUT-RHIN [57]

A sandstone crag quite similar to that found at Fontainebleau but not as extensive. Most of the routes tend to be short problems but a rope is useful for some of the longer routes to 25m. Climbing all year round but the crag is set at 300m altitude and is best in summer.

Dir: 12km SSW of Colmar. The N83 goes S from Colmar, take this and after 4km the village of Guebershwihr is signposted to the R. Drive into the village, then turn R on to the small road which goes up to St. Marc Convent and Osenbuhr. The crag is in the forest on the R and the L. Reached by foot in 5 mins. (61:D4)

Petit Hohneck:
✳ 9.00→19.00 (Bouldering) HAUT-RHIN [58]

A good area of granite boulders offering many problems. Some are quite high indeed. Worth a visit if passing.

Dir: 24km WSW of Colmar. Midway between Munster and Gérardmer is the Col de la Schlucht. From here take the D430 S (Route des Crêtes) for 4km and then turn L to the summit of Hohneck. From here a path leads to the W and the area in about 15 mins. (60:C4)

Martinswand
✳ 10.00→15.00 (10.20.20.10.0)(60) HAUT-RHIN [59]

Quite a good crag but old-fashioned granite cracks. At 1200m, definitely summer only or, God forbid, ice climbing! 50–70m high with little bolting as yet. A crag for Macho Mountain Muncherzzz.

Dir: 24km WSW of Colmar. Midway between Munster and Gérardmer is the Col de la Schlucht. From here take the D430 S (Route des Crêtes) for 2.5 km. Park by a sign and then take the path to the SE. A guide and topo for the crag can be obtained from CAF de Mulhouse, 8 rue de la Bourse, 68100 Mulhouse. (60:C4)

Meuse – 55

Saint Mihiel:
Bouldering MEUSE [60]

Good hard, steep limestone by the side of the road. All year round climbing with little in the easier grades. *In situ* gear situation at present unknown.

Dir: 15km SSE of Verdun. Take the D964 S from Verdun towards St Mihiel. There are about 6 outcrops on the L side of the road. (40:B23)

Ardennes – 08

Roc La Tour:
(15.10.12.4.0)(41) ARDENNES [61]

A quartzite crag, 25m with *in situ* cemented pitons [4]. Good for the lower grade climber or family.

Dir: 16km NNE of Charleville-Mézières. From here drive N to Monthermé on either the D1 (picturesque) or D988 and D989 (quicker). From the town take the D31 going E towards Viesse for 1km where a thin road on the L leads up to a car park at Roc La Tour in 3km. Here a footpath leads to the crag in 10 mins. (21:E1)

Marne – 51

Vertus:
✳ 8.00→15.00 (10.10.7.6.4.0)(37) MARNE [62]

A very good small limestone crag for the middle grade climber. 20m with lots of pockets for all 4 fingers. Never less than vertical but all good holds and *in situ* gear [3–4]. Overlooking the Champagne vineyards. Recommended routes: Pol Roger, Taittinger, Pommery to start with; Krug and Bollinger are worth taking time over.

Dir: 16km S of Epernay. Take the road S to Vertus. The crag can be seen in the trees up and to the W of the town. Drive up into the vineyards with care where a path leads up to the crag. (38:B3)

Yonne – 89

Saussois:
✳ 12.00→20.00
(32.80.180.110.8)(410)   YONNE [63]

One of the most popular cliffs in France. There are four major areas on which to climb: ROCHE CENTRALE, GRANDE ROCHE, RENARD and ROCHERS DU PARC. Bolts are very good indeed, which is necessary since many of the routes are very polished. Steep limestone with pockets, 50m. Very good overhangs and some good long sustained pitches, and many routes with 2 pitches. Can get crowded at weekends. There are some very good grade 8 routes here, the work of J.B. Troubat, which means they should be quite easy! Definitely on the crag list for any climber in the universe. All *in situ* gear [1–4]. Topos can be bought locally in the Café des Roches.

Dir: 26km S of Auxerre, 21km WNW of Avallon. From Auxerre take the N6 S towards Vermenton, at the bypass to Vincettes take the D100 on the R to Bazarnes. Carry on going S and cross the river after 9km to Mailly-la-Ville. Carry on down the D100 towards Châtel Censoir and after 5km there is Rochers du Parc on the L. Carry on for another 4km and the main crag is on the L just past the hamlet of Le Saussois. (72:A3)

DUDULE VARIANT, 7a +, Saussois. (Climber Ed Stone, Photo Dave Turner)

Nièvre – 58

Surgy:
✳ 05.00→17.00
(30.39.175.65.5)(330)   NIÈVRE [64]

A group of very good limestone crags 10–40m high. Situated by the river Yonne and not a bad choice for a good winter's day. There are five major listed areas but all are within 60 seconds' walk so explore at will. The routes are polished but this is of no real consequence since the holds are quite sharp and pocketed, and climbing is quite delightful. A must for the lower grade climber. The crag appears steep but in fact is rarely even vertical and offers only a small amount in the harder grades. Saussois further up the valley is a better choice. The *in situ* bolts [1–2] are a result of recent re-equipping. Some of the routes are up to 50m high so bring a spare rope to de-equip routes. Most of the routes are in the shade in the afternoon except for about 30 of the easier routes. There is a topo to the crag which should be available locally.

Dir: 34km SSW of Auxerre, 2km NNW of Clamecy. From the S go to Avallon (N6), then to Vézelay (D957), Clamecy (D951), then take the D144 down along the W bank of the Yonne towards Surgy. Pass through La Forêt, under the narrow railway bridge, and reach the crag after 2km and before Surgy. From the N approach from Auxerre take the N151 S through Courson-les-Carrières to Coulanges-s-Yonne. Then take the small road through Surgy

towards Clamecy and the crag is 1.5km after Surgy. (71:F3)

Côte d'Or – 21

Bouilland:
✳ 10.00→15.00
(25.40.70.60.4)(199) CÔTE D'OR [65]

This limestone crag is very good in most parts and is one of the best in the area. It varies from 14–40m high, dries out very quickly and has some cracking routes including After Eight, needless to say not easy. Most types of routes with some good overhangs. *In situ* gear [1–3] on most routes. A very beautiful setting. Some of the tops of the routes have loose flakes and care should be taken. The area to the S of the cliff, overlooking Bouilland and the Combe à la Vielle, has birds of prey nesting and there is to be no climbing there from 15 Feb until 15 June.

Dir: 28km SW of Dijon, 13km NNE of Beaune. From the N of Beaune take the D18 and D2 to Savigney-lès-Beaune. Carry on up the D2 to the village of Bouilland passing Combe à la Vielle. From the village drive up to the top and the crag. (88:A2)

Brochon:
✳ 10.00→17.00
(30. 50.30.20.0)(130) CÔTE D'OR [66]

The smaller of the good crags in the area. Limestone walls and cracks 10–25m, good for mid grade climbers and beginners. The best climbing is to be found on the S-facing part of the crag. *In situ* gear [1–2]. Worth a look. A topo can be purchased locally from Bar La Dame Blanche.

Dir: 12km SSW of Dijon. Take the D122 S out of Dijon which runs parallel to the N74 on the Route de Grand Crus. Pass through Fixin and into Brochon. Take the 1st R up into the village and follow the road up to the Combe. Walk up to the crag. Camping at Chamboeuf. (88:B1)

Chambolle-Musigny:
✰ 10.00→17.00 (3–7c)(50) CÔTE D'OR [67]

A good limestone crag up to 25m high. The routes are on smooth walls with cracks and face holds. *In situ* gear [1–2]. The crag gets the sun but there is shade from the trees all morning. Very good in spring and autumn. Worth a visit.

Dir: 16km SSW of Dijon. Take the N74 S towards Nuits St Georges. After 16km turn R at the village of Chambolle Musigny, pass through the centre and take the road in the direction of Chamboeuf and find a parking spot. The crag is 10 mins from the road. (88:B1)

Cormot:
✳ 10.00→16.00
(20.30.30.10.0)(90) CÔTE D'OR [68]

Quite a large crag but very old-fashioned limestone giving plenty of horizontal strata breaks and holds. 50m and no water pockets. Very good for the middle grade climber. *In situ* gear [1–4]. Routes are polished but this remains a popular crag in a nice setting. For the imbiber, however, this crag is an absolute must since the town of Puligny Montrachet is only a couple of km away and worth a good week's visit in its own right. A visit to Marquis de Laguiche and Domaine Baron Thénard should set you back several thousand francs at least.

Dir: 16km WSW of Beaune. From Beaune, hic, take the N74 for a few km towards Meursault, hic, turn R on to the D973 to Rochepot, then carry on to Nolay. From the N of the village a road leads to the D111 and Vauchignon. Follow the road to the R and sign Bel Air. At the top of the hill take the track on the R for a few hundred metres and then walk to the crag. The crag can be reached by a very steep path from the village of Cornot le Grand. (87:F2→3)

Fixin:
✳ 12.00→19.00
(7.42.76.52.3)(180) CÔTE D'OR [69]

A very good crag indeed for the area. Not many hard routes but the grade 6s are really good. 30m natural limestone giving walls in the main with a few large overhangs for good measure.

There is an area as yet undeveloped which will eventually have about 15 grade 8s. Watch the mags for details. There are very few shaded areas. Near to the towns of Gevrey Chambertin, simply excellent wine. Bolt [1]. A very nice campsite at Chamboeuf 8km W of Gevrey Chambertin.

Dir: 11km SSW of Dijon. Take the N74 S towards Beaune and after 10 or so km turn L up the D122E to Fixin. Carry straight on and take the road which winds up to a small parking and picnic area. Here take the path leading off to the R which goes up the valley and to the crag. Go right up to the Col and then work back along the crag to ensure that you find the best bits. Don't get put off by the very steep wall near the col (grade 8 routes). (88:B1)

Hauteroche:
✳ 12.00→18.00
(3−7c)(80)
CÔTE D'OR [70]

A very organised 35m limestone crag but unfortunately the tops are loose and there are no lower-off points at 25m. This may be amended in due course. Good routes in all grades especially 4s and 5s. The crag has recently been equipped with new bolts [1−3].

Dir: 48km E of Avallon, 12km NNE of Vitteaux. From Vitteaux take the D26 E to Villey-en-Auxois then turn L on to the D9 to Jailly-les-Moulins. Pass through the village and after about 4km take the small road to Hauteroche (1km). At the village go SE up a hill to the plateau where parking at the top of the hill. Here a footpath marked with orange leads to the crag in a few minutes. (73:E3)

Lantenay:
✳ 10.00→18.00
(5.14.18.20.4)(60)   CÔTE D'OR [71]

Sometimes known as Combe du Mammouth. A very good small crag consisting of some 10−20m limestone pillars with excellent climbs around grade 6, 7 and 8. Shade or sun can be found nearly all day; all bolts [1]. A very peaceful and quiet crag. Watch out for the snakes in the undergrowth in summer on the approach.

Dir: 15km W of Dijon. Take the *autoroute* A38 coming off at Jtn Fleury Sur Ouche which is just to the N. From the village take the D104 to Lantenay (4km). At the top of the village a small path leads off into the woods going W. After about 15 mins the path goes uphill and leads to the crag quite easily. Views from the plateau above are beautiful. (74:A4)

Rocher de St. Catherine:
✳ 11.00→20.00
(15.20.14.12.0)(65)   CÔTE D'OR [72]

This granite crag is sometimes called VIEUX CHÂTEAU. A very beautiful crag on a river bend. Slabs on one side and vertical walls on the other. In the summer it gets too hot to climb in the sun. *In situ* pro [2−4], and the climbs are superb. Very good for the grade 5−6 climber.

Dir: 8km E of Avallon, 1.5km S to Toutry. From Avallon take the N6 towards Saulieu. After 14km enter Ste. Magnance, nearly leaving turn L and follow signs to Vieux Château. Go through the village and take the road towards Toutry. After 100m there is a track on the L which is signposted to the top of the crag. People often camp here but be warned for once I had my tent run over by a car. (72:C3)

Saffres:
✳ 11.00→17.00
(18.32.64.54.5)(170)   CÔTE D'OR [73]

A very large crag of quarried and natural limestone, 5−35m. Steep and very sustained. Routes here for all the family. The main walls in the middle have some very hard routes on indeed. The crag is surrounded by trees and shelter from the sun can often be found. The village of Saffres below has a café which sells topos. A superb crag but generally busy every day of the year. Bolts [1−2] everywhere. Even though the crag is S-facing there is plenty of tree shade to allow climbing on summer's days.

Dir: 50km ESE of Avallon, 4km SE of Vitteaux. From Vitteaux take the D905 S towards Sombernon but after 4km turn L to the village of Saffres. Carry along through the village and up the hill with the crag in the trees on the L. 2 mins. (73:E4)

Doubs – 25

Baume les Dames:
(6.7.14.8.3)(38) DOUBS [74]

A good limestone crag with routes from grade 4 to 8 inclusive. There have also been a lot of bolts [1–3] placed recently as well as the addition of Souriez Braves Gens, 8b +.

Dir: 26km ENE of Besançon. Take the *autoroute* or N83 to Baume les Dames. Take the N83 back towards Briancon towards Champvans-les-Baumes. The cliff can be found on the side of the river. (76:A4)

La Brême:
✳ 10.00→22.00
(30.40.50.50.10)(180) DOUBS [75]

One of the best crags in the area. Routes in all grades up to 8b on very good limestone 20–50m high. Bolts [1–3] but the easier routes tend to have less gear. A topo for the crag can be obtained in the bar Le Pêcheur at Ornans. Worth a visit, very good aspect. Will get popular; a lot of routes polished already.

Dir: 3km WNW of Ornans, 16km SSE of Besançon. From Ornans take the D67 for 3km towards Besançon to a small road leading off to the L and where the rivers Loue and Breme meet. A path leads from the road to the crag. (90:A1→2)

Montfaucon:
(10.22.71.69.2)(170) DOUBS [76]

A recently developed and recently bolted [2–3] limestone crag offering very good climbing up to 7c. Very handy for Besançon and now quite popular in the evenings. 20–40m high. Worth a visit.

Dir: 5km E of Besançon. Take the N57 towards Pontarlier then after 5km turn L to the village of Montfaucon, signposted. (90:A1)

Mouthier-Hautpierre:
✳ 10.00→16.00
(2.2.4.5.1)(14) DOUBS [77]

A very good large limestone crag with good wall climbing with pockets. 60–100m. The crag although facing S is at 650m high and can be quite a cold place on a windy day. The views are fantastic though. Re-equipping [1–2] has gone on. Routes are quite polished though. Topos can be obtained from the CAF at Rue Luc Breton in Besançon.

Dir: 30km SE of Besançon near the village of Mouthier-Hautepierre. Take the N57 S out of Besançon then after a few km take the D67 to Ornans. Carry on through Montgesoye, Vuillafans, Lods and to Mouthier-Hautepierre. Then turn L onto the D244 which goes up to Hautepierre le Châtelet. The crag can be seen and takes 5 mins to walk to. (90:B2)

Pont de Roide:
✳ 10.00→18.00
(20.30.48.56.9)(163) DOUBS [78]

A good hard compact limestone crag, 10–20m high. The crag is about 1km long and is still being developed with a possible 100 more routes in the harder grades. New topos will be around by publication date, enquire locally. New bolts [2–3].

Dir: 15km S of Montbéliard. Take the D437 S to the village of Pont-de-Roide. The road goes over a bridge on to the E side of the river Doubs, here a small road leads off to the L along the N bank of the river. After about 250m take the turning on the R (D124) which goes up the valley for 3km to some parking. Take the footpath to a sign 7, then take the footpath to the R and the top of the cliffs. (76:D4)

Refranche:
(6.7.7.8.0)(28) DOUBS [79]

Birds are nesting here and there are specific restrictions from 15 Feb till 15 June. Please enquire locally or climb outside these periods. Very strict. Not a very developed crag but lots of potential I hear. Limestone with bolts [2].

Dir: 24km S of Besançon in the hills. From the S of Besançon take the B473 S through the towns of Epeugney, Cléron to Amancey. Here turn R on to the D103E to Eternoz. (This can also be reached via Nans-sous-St Anne and Salins-les-Bains.) From Eternoz take the D15 which after 6km arrives at Refranche. Park by a purple bollard and walk to the crag. (89:F2)

La Roche Barmaud:
(20.30.53.60.12)(175) DOUBS [80]

One of the best crags in the immediate area with all climbs worth doing. Good steep, rough limestone 25–45m with modern bolts [2–3]. The crag topo guide can be obtained at Ornans in the bar Le Pêcheur. Here the rock stars can try 8bs. A beautiful area. Keep away!

Dir: 16km SSE of Besançon. Take the N57, then the D67 to Ornans. Take the small road from the centre of the town D241 towards Chassagne St Dennis (past a campsite). After 2.5km there is a bend and parking where two footpaths lead off from the road. Take the path on the R to the crag. (90:A2)

Roche d'Arbois:
(Some)   DOUBS [81]

A little-known crag but recent report of a grade 8 climb here.

Belfort – 90

Falaise de la Justice:
(1.2.3.2.0)(8)   BELFORT [83]

I know little of this crag except that it is in the Belfort region and the routes noted above have new bolts [2].

Dir: 5km E of Besançon. Take the N57 towards Pontarlier then after 5km turn L to the village of Montfaucon. The crag is situated a little lower down than Montfaucon crag. (90:A1)

Rocher du Quin:
(5–8b+)(40)   DOUBS [82]

A limestone crag with much current development. A good handful of grade 8 routes.

Dir: Unknown; watch press for details.

Dir: Near Belfort, 56km W of Basel. Seek local info in Belfort. (76)

Jura – 39

La Cernaise:
(0.2.3.7.1)(13)   JURA [84]

There are probably more routes here than this but it is not certain. A high-level limestone crag with single pitch routes. *In situ* gear [3–4].

Dir: 24km NW of Genève, 6km SE of St. Claude. From St. Claude take the road through the Gorges du Flumen then turn R on to the D25 towards Les Moussières. The road passes the belvédère and the crag. (104:A→B2)

Poligny:
✶ 12.00→18.00
(10.10.20.15.2)(57)   JURA [85]

An excellent roadside limestone crag which has been equipped with the latest bolt

protection [1–2]. A very nice area with good views at about 500m high. Camping at Poligny. Apparently the Lac de Chalain is worth visiting which is 16km to the SSE through the forest of Poligny.

Dir: 55km SSW of Besançon, 20km NW of Lons le Saunier. Take the N83 to Poligny. Then go SW into the village and take the N5 towards Champagnole. This winds up a steep hill for 3km and a sign 'Trou de la Lune' is seen. Park and walk to the crag in 5 seconds. (89:E3)

CENTRAL WEST FRANCE

Vendée – 85

Mervent:
✻ 12.00→21.00
(5–7b)(35) VENDÉE [86]

Some gneiss crags which have recently been equipped with bolts [1–2] and provide excellent climbing. There are a few crags but the main outcrop is called PIERRE BLANCHE and has the above listed routes on. The cliffs are up to 35m high. By now there should be a topo in circulation and available locally.

Dir: 34km NW of Niort, 8km NNE of Fontenay-le-Comte. Take the D938 N out of Fontenay towards Châtaigneraie. After 6km pass the Mervent turn-off then take the next R which leads down to the river after 2.5km. The crags are beside the river. (93:E1)

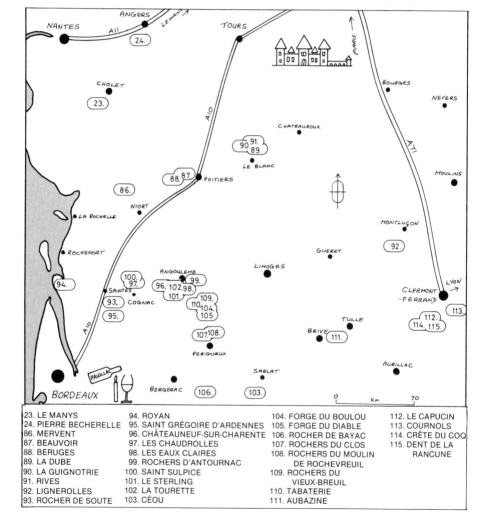

23. LE MANYS	94. ROYAN	104. FORGE DU BOULOU	112. LE CAPUCIN
24. PIERRE BECHERELLE	95. SAINT GRÉGOIRE D'ARDENNES	105. FORGE DU DIABLE	113. COURNOLS
86. MERVENT	96. CHÂTEAUNEUF-SUR-CHARENTE	106. ROCHER DE BAYAC	114. CRÊTE DU COQ
87. BEAUVOIR	97. LES CHAUDROLLES	107. ROCHERS DU CLOS	115. DENT DE LA
88. BERUGES	98. LES EAUX CLAIRES	108. ROCHERS DU MOULIN	RANCUNE
89. LA DUBE	99. ROCHERS D'ANTOURNAC	DE ROCHEVREUIL	
90. LA GUIGNOTRIE	100. SAINT SULPICE	109. ROCHERS DU	
91. RIVES	101. LE STERLING	VIEUX-BREUIL	
92. LIGNEROLLES	102. LA TOURETTE	110. TABATERIE	
93. ROCHER DE SOUTE	103. CÉOU	111. AUBAZINE	

Vienne – 86

Beauvoir:
✳ 11.00→16.00
(8.53.54.18.2)(154)   VIENNE [87]

A small but very good crag in a very pleasant setting. The crag is quite popular and being so close to Poitiers it gets busy on most summer evenings. 7–20m limestone with lots of good pockets and flints in, occasionally giving quite a varied climbing style. There are three main buttresses – the hard routes on the L, easy ones in the middle and the grade 6s to the R. There are plenty of trees to shade the routes, even so in the summer it can get very hot if there is no breeze blowing. A very pleasant spot for a day, and good for a family day out. The campsite at Poitiers is the pits!

Dir: 7km WNW of Poitiers. Leave the city on the N149 in the direction of Nantes and Vouillé. After 5km at the village of Moulinet turn L on to the D87F in the direction of Vouneuil. In 200m turn R towards Beauvoir and then at the cross turn R and go down to a farm. Park here please; a track leads off down to the R and the crag is visible from the parking spot, 5 mins. (95:E1)

Beruges:
(6.7.28.11.0)(52)   VIENNE [88]

A small crag with recently bolted [1–3] routes. The limestone is very good and has good walls, slabs and very good overhangs. There are three sections with all being single pitch routes. There is good scope for harder routes and the 8as might well have been put up by now. The crag is on private property so please respect this.

Dir: 10km W of Poitiers. From the ring road on the E side of town take a small road over the motorway signposted to Beruges. Enquire locally for exact crag location. (95:D1)

La Dube:
✳ 12.00→20.00
(4.8.18.14.1)(46)   VIENNE [89]

This crag is directly on the side of the road and in the past has been very popular. The routes in many cases are very polished but nevertheless are superbly technical and worth doing on a cool day. 10m–30m with very good bolts. Limestone without pockets. Quite a deceptive crag with some of the routes being paths and others desperate. Great for those who like belaying from inside the car.

Dir: 42km ENE of Poitiers. 30km ESE of Châtellerault. From Ct. take the D14 to Vicq-sur-Gartempe then the D5 to Angles-sur-l'Anglin. At the village triangle turn L and take the D2 towards Le Blanc. After 4km at Fournioux turn R on to the D50 which goes to Mérigny, after 2km pass through Rives, carry on for another 3km by the river and the crag is beside the road on the R. (82:C4)

La Guignoterie:
✳ 8.00→14.00
(3.8.39.36.5)(100)   VIENNE [90]

This is one of the best crags on the W side of France. Although there are not that many routes, nearly all are worth doing once, if not twice. Steep, smooth, pocketed limestone offering very sustained routes. 10–30m with the short routes involving powerful moves. The crag is in the shade all afternoon, making it a

HARMONIUM, 7b, Guignotterie. (Climber Le Frog, Photo David Jones)

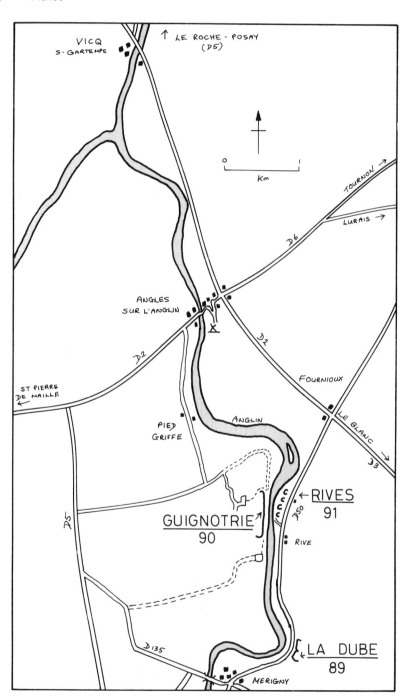

VICQ
S-GARTEMPE

↑ LE ROCHE - POSAY
(D5)

TOURNON →

LURAIS →

D6

ANGLES
SUR L'ANGLIN

D2

FOURNIOUX

ST PIERRE
DE MAILLE →

D2

LE BLANC

D3

PIED
GRIFFE

ANGLIN

← RIVES
91

GUIGNOTRIE
90

D50

RIVE

D5

D135

LA DUBE
89

MERIGNY

Km

good summer crag. Fully bolted up and good for falling off. The central wall offers eight 7c climbs in a row, all of which are brilliant.

Dir: 42km ENE of Poitiers, 30Km ESE of Châtellerault. From Ct. take the D14 to Vicq-sur-Gartempe then the D5 to Angles-sur-l'Anglin, cross over the river then carry on the road (D2) towards St Pierre. Before actually leaving Angles take a small road on the L towards Pied Griffe. After about 3km at a T-junction turn L, carry on for 0.5km then turn R and follow the road around seemingly into a farm and then turn L (signpost Les Rochers). Here you can park in a field. A path carries on and down to the R on to a track which if followed to the R leads to the crag in 5 mins. There is a very pleasant campsite in Angles. (82:C4)

Rives:
✳ 13.00→20.00
(2.5.5.11.1)(28) VIENNE [91]

A small group of crags very close to the main outcrop of La Guignoterie on the opposite side of the river. The climbs are only 7–10m high, but offer good sport in the distance. The easier climbs tend to be quite polished but good nevertheless. All routes are steep and quite powerful. There are two crags of ROCHER ST. BERTHAMS, easier and DU MOULIN, harder. The crag is also in the shade in the morning and offers routes of a more similar nature to those of La Guignoterie than La Dube.

Dir: 42km ENE of Poitiers, 30km ESE of Châtellerault. From Ct. take the D14 to Vicq-sur-Gartempe then the D5 to Angles-sur-l'Anglin. At the village triangle turn L and take the D2 towards Le Blanc. After 4km at Fournioux turn R onto the D50 which goes to Mérigny, after 1.5km and before you reach Rives (Guignoterie opposite) turn R on to a track which leads to the crags on the R about 0.5km apart. (82:C4)

Allier – 03

Lignerolles:
(8.6.15.12.3)(45) ALLIER [92]

A fair crag with most routes being 45m long except the harder ones. The rock is a bit of a mixture but mainly it is gneiss. There are parts with a texture very akin to granite. Very solid indeed and all *in situ* pro. A nice area and very much a weekend and evening crag. A topo is available for the crag from Michel Bonnefoi, École Victor-Hugo 22, 03100 Montlucon.

Dir: 8km SSW of Montlucon. From the town take the D993 S towards Evaux-les-Bains. After 5km turn L on to the D605 towards Lignerolles, following signs to the gare (station). Park here by a railway bridge. A path leads to the crag in 10 mins. (99:D3)

Charente Maritime – 17

Rocher de Soute:
✳ 13.00→22.00
(6.4.2.0.0)(12) CHARENTE-MAR [93]

A superb 10m limestone crag which offers good prospects all year round. The crag is used quite a lot by beginners. There are about 30 routes in all grades and a good few in the higher 6 and 7 grades. For some reason these have not been equipped as yet, however top-roping I'm sure can be arranged. Worth a detour after visiting Cognac and on the way to the Château of Margaux and St Estephe.

Dir: 2km W of Pons, 19km SSE of Saintes. Take the bypass around Pons and in between the N137 and the D732 turn-off on to the D142 towards Tesson. After 1km stay on the road turn L by a bridge then R towards Soute and park 300m further on. A footpath leads to the rocks below. (107:D3)

Royan:
✳ 11.00→22.00
(Bouldering) CHARENTE-MAR [94]

There are several sea cliff bouldering and traversing spots in the local area. Areas known to be frequented are to the N at SAINT PALAIS-

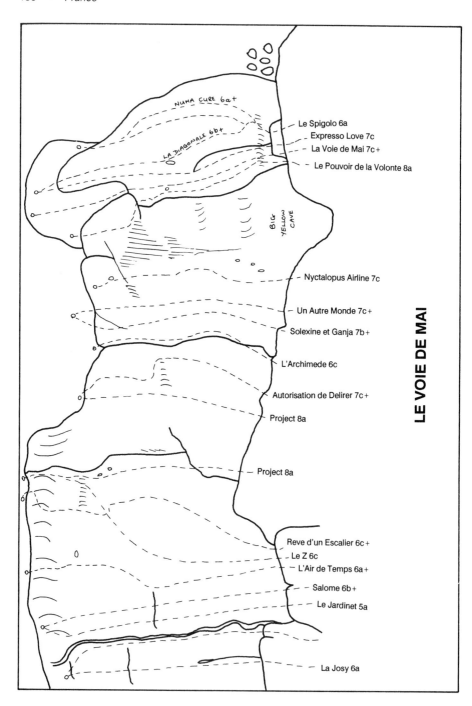

NUMA CURE 6a+

LA DIAGONALE 6b+

Le Spigolo 6a
Expresso Love 7c
La Voie de Mai 7c+
Le Pouvoir de la Volonte 8a

BIG YELLOW CAVE

Nyctalopus Airline 7c

Un Autre Monde 7c+

Solexine et Ganja 7b+

L'Archimede 6c

Autorisation de Delirer 7c+

Project 8a

Project 8a

Reve d'un Escalier 6c+
Le Z 6c
L'Air de Temps 6a+

Salome 6b+

Le Jardinet 5a

La Josy 6a

LE VOIE DE MAI

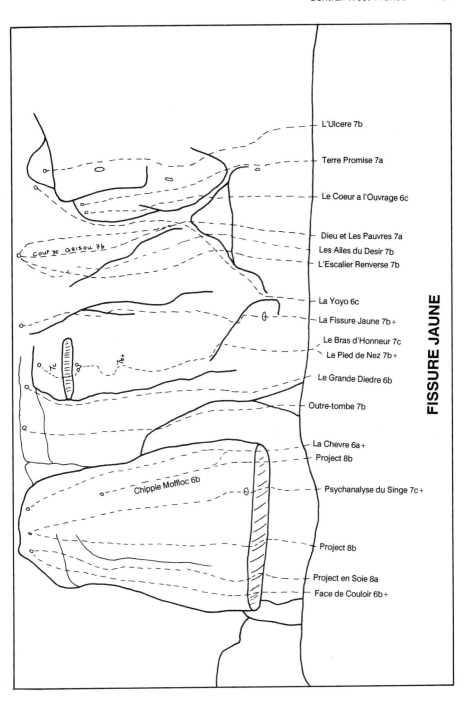

L'Ulcere 7b

Terre Promise 7a

Le Coeur a l'Ouvrage 6c

Dieu et Les Pauvres 7a
Les Ailes du Desir 7b
L'Escalier Renverse 7b

COUP DE GRISOU 7b

La Yoyo 6c
La Fissure Jaune 7b+
Le Bras d'Honneur 7c
Le Pied de Nez 7b+

7c   7b+

Le Grande Diedre 6b

Outre-tombe 7b

La Chevre 6a+
Project 8b

Chippie Moffloc 6b   Psychanalyse du Singe 7c+

Project 8b

Project en Soie 8a
Face de Couloir 6b+

FISSURE JAUNE

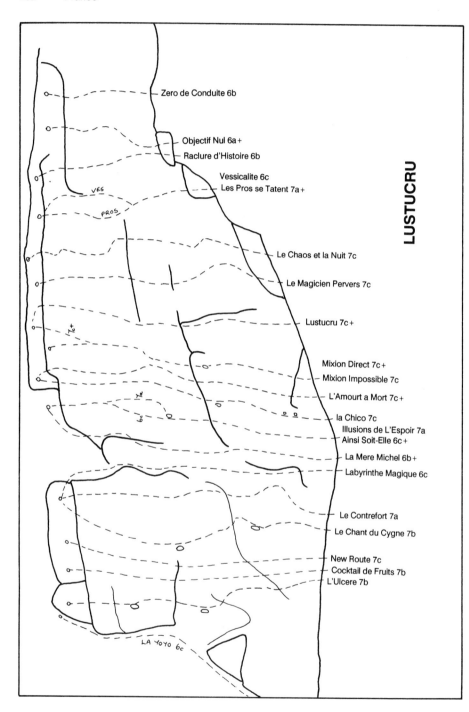

LUSTUCRU

Zero de Conduite 6b

Objectif Nul 6a+
Raclure d'Histoire 6b

Vessicalite 6c
Les Pros se Tatent 7a+

VES

PROS

Le Chaos et la Nuit 7c

Le Magicien Pervers 7c

Lustucru 7c+

7c+

Mixion Direct 7c+
Mixion Impossible 7c

L'Amourt a Mort 7c+

7a

6c

la Chico 7c
Illusions de L'Espoir 7a
Ainsi Soit-Elle 6c+

La Mere Michel 6b+
Labyrinthe Magique 6c

Le Contrefort 7a
Le Chant du Cygne 7b

New Route 7c
Cocktail de Fruits 7b
L'Ulcere 7b

LA YOYO 6c

S-MER, and at the S end of SAINT GEORGES DE DIDONNE.

Dir: St Palais is 5km NW of Royan, and St Georges is 3km to the SE of Royan. (106:B23)

Saint Grégoire d'Ardennes:
(3 − 6c)(20) CHARENTE-MAR [95]
A small 20m crag with some good little routes and worth a visit if passing.

Charente − 16
A topo for the area can be purchased from Igloo Sports at Bordeaux.

Châteauneuf-sur-Charente:
✳ 10.00→16.00
(15.53.56.21.0)(144) CHARENTE [96]

A limestone crag of excellent quality from 5−15m high with plenty to keep you occupied. The crag does suffer from intense heat in the summer months, when I suggest you go to the seaside instead.

Dir: 19km WSW of Angoulême, 2km W of Châteauneuf. From the town of C. take the D84 in a S direction towards Eraville. After going 1km take a turning on the R to Haute Roche and after a short distance the rocks are above on the R and are reached in only a couple of minutes. (108:A3)

Les Chaudrolles:
(6.21.22.11.0)(70)(40) CHARENTE [97]

A small limestone crag with a nice range of bolted [1−4] routes. All are single pitch. (*See* also St. Sulpice.)

Dir: 8km NW of Cognac. Leave the town on the D731 towards St Hilaire, and after about 6km enter the small village of Les Chaudrolles. I presume the crag is to the R in the direction of Saint Sulpice but I recommend that you enquire locally for exact crag location. (107:E2)

Les Eaux Claires:
✳ 10.00→20.00
(19.44.92.69.30)(254) CHARENTE [98]

Short, sharp and hard is the best description for this crag. An excellent crag and the best

Dir: 30km SSE of Saintes, 8km S of Pons. From Pons take the D142 S towards Jonzac but after 8km at the village of Marignac turn R to St Grégoire-d'Ardennes. Enquire locally for exact location of crag. (107:D3)

bouldering spot in France west of Fontainebleau. All routes here seem to be hard. The easy ones are steep and polished, and the hard routes tend to be boulder problems, powerful moves on small holds. The pockets are very shallow and the rock overhangs in most places. 5−10m high, pocketed limestone. Good bolts. The crag is made up of about 20 small buttresses. Climbing in or out of the shade can usually be found, although it is usually very hot at midday in summer.

Dir: 5km SSE of Angoulême. From the town go S to the 'suburb' of Puymoyen (quite a dreadful ruined village). There doesn't seem to be a town centre but go past the open area and just after the road starts to narrow, and 100m past the church, take a R turn towards Vallée des Eaux Claires and Charsé. This goes down a hill, and at the bottom turn R and the crag begins on the R. A white track leads all the way along the crag to each of the buttresses, not too bad for the car. (108:B3)

Rochers d'Antournac:
✳ 12.00→20.00
(2.16.36.17.1)(70) CHARENTE [99]

A good limestone crag with routes up to 12m high. The crag has quite a few high trees also so in the summer it is shaded well which can often be a blessing. Lots of types of routes from cracks to walls and overhangs. Bolts [1−3] and lowering-off rings. Worth a look. A topo guide for the crag can be obtained at Shoot Sports in Angoulême or Le Refuge at Bordeaux.

Dir: 5km E of Angoulême. Take the D939 going SE out of the town towards Dignac, at the outskirts of town is a turn-off to Soyaux. Pass this and take the second turn off to Soyaux. Pass the town keeping R and after 1.5km turn R and the rocks are on the R side of the valley. (108:B2)

Saint Sulpice:
(10.10.10.6.1)(39) CHARENTE [100]

A limestone crag offering some good short routes. Previously semi-bolted but I would imagine by now the local trend of placing bolts [1] will have been adopted.

Dir: 8km NNW of Cognac. From the town take the D731 towards St Hiliare but after 8km turn R on the D55 to St. Sulpice. Enquire in the town but I would imagine that the crag is slightly to the S. (107:E2)

Le Sterling:
✳ 10.00→16.00
(4−7a)(15) CHARENTE [101]

A good small limestone crag 5−15m high and compact with good boulder type moves; very similar to Les Eaux Claires.

Dir: 7km SSW of Angoulême. From Angoulême take the D674 to Voeuil-et-Giget to the S. From here take the D41 towards Couronne, pass through the hamlet of Le Sterling and the crag is on the R. Park just a bit further on. (108:B3)

La Tourette:
✳ 10.00→16.00
(4a−7a)(10) CHARENTE [102]

A small good limestone outcrop much frequented in the evenings by local climbers, however, it is worthy of inclusion because of the merit of the climbing available. Up to 10m high and climbing similar to that of Les Eaux Claires.

Dir: 4km S of Angoulême. From Angoulême take the D674 S in the direction of Montmoreau, pass the D104 on the L, carry on down the hill to the Eaux Claires valley, go up the hill and then take the turning on the R which is signposted to Cothiers. Opposite the racecourse at Tourette, turn L on to a dirt track which after 300m leads to the top of a small group of crags. For the crag, from Angoulême take the D674 for 8km to Voeil-et-Giget. Turn R towards Couronne. After the village of Le Sterling the road goes along the bottom of the crag. Park a couple of hundred metres on. (108:B3)

Dordogne − 24

The whole of the Dordogne is scattered with so many small limestone crags of great quality that eventually it will become a classic area of its own. There are very few really big crags, except perhaps Céou, but nevertheless there are so many undeveloped crags that keeping an eye on the press over the next few years will be time well spent. The area is beautiful, so stay well away from the horrible tourist centre of Sarlat and find out what else is on offer − great friendly local villages and unspoilt countryside. It is a very hot area in the summer and climbing in the sun is completely out of the question, so think carefully when planning a trip. A swim in the Dordogne river even on a scorching June day is still about 8a. This is an area worth visiting, especially with a small group.

The crags in the Périgord Blanc area have parts which are often in shade so it is worth looking around at the various outcrops to find cool places if necessary.

Céou:
✳ 10.00→18.00
(7.25.51.44.2)(139) DORDOGNE [103]

A superb 50m limestone crag in a fantastic position. Do not confuse with the other Ceuse; it's not that great. The crag catches the sun for most of the day which is a real nuisance in the summer but a blessing in the winter. The crag is really open and often a good cool wind blows. The limestone is very varied, from walls of medium quality to absolutely brilliant. The main developed area is the R of the two high cliffs above the campsite. Some of the routes in the big caves are fantastic. All the bolts are

[1 – 3], and friction for the feet is unusually good for limestone. The routes in many cases have to be split into two pitches, or better still bring a spare rope to tie together to lower off easily. The view at the top is great, but so is the chance of severe sunburn; relaxed belaying in the shade, swimming pool down below at the campsite in summer. A guide can be bought at the campsite which has been updated and now for 40FF looks very good value. Most routes have grades and names painted at the bottom.

Dir: 60km E of Bergerac, 10km SSW of Sarlat-la-Canéda. From Sarlat take the D57 towards Beynac, just before the town turn L (before the railway bridge) and go over the Dordogne to Castelnaud. Turn L and take the D57 down the valley towards St Cybranet. After half a km turn down a lane on the L which after 1 km leads to the luxurious campsite below the crag. (You have to pay to park here all day so it is worth camping here and at least getting that free.) A topo can be bought at the camp shop. To reach the crag, walk around the side of the farm and cross direct to a path beneath the crag which zig-zags up in 20 mins. Further up is a high path which leads across to the LH crag. (123:F4)

Forge du Boulou:
☀ 10.00→16.00
(4 – 8a)(80)   DORDOGNE [104]

One of the very good limestone crags in the Périgord Blanc area. This area has had many quite recent developments and is perhaps less polished than the other areas but will I'm sure become like glass in the future. Good pocketed rock offering well protected routes.

Dir: 48km SE of Angoulême, 8km WSW of Brantôme. From Brantôme take the D78 to Bourdeilles, cross over the river and take the D106 for about 4km then turn R and go towards Paussac-et-St-Vivien. After nearly 1km before a new house there is a white track on the R. Take this down into the valley with a small river and the crag, approximately 1km from the road. (109:D4)

Forge du Diable:
☀ 12.00→19.00
(4 – 7c)(30)   DORDOGNE [105]

Another limestone area, one of the smaller outcrops but still offering good climbing.

LES EAUX CLAIRES, 7c + . (Climber David Jones, Photo Jeff Odds)

Dir: 50km SE of Angoulême, 5km SW of Brantôme. From Brantôme take the D78 towards Bourdeilles and after about 6km and before Valeuil take the D106 instead of crossing over the river. After 1.5km turn R towards Gueyzat and the crag is about 50m away on the R. (109:D4)

Rocher de Bayac:
☀ 10.00→16.00
(2.3.7.3.0)(15)   DORDOGNE [106]

An excellent limestone crag up to 20m high. Good bolts everywhere on walls and some demanding quite large overhangs. More scope for new routes also but in the upper grades. The overhang routes are apparently worth a detour. Good crag.

Dir: 21km ESE of Bergerac, 3km NNW of Beaumont. Take the D660 from Bergerac going E almost to Lalinde. Turn R on to the D660 towards Beaumont. After 6km turn R and go past the Château Bannes, continue for 1.7km from the main road then take a track on the R which descends into a valley. Park just before the bottom where the crag lies 200m further on. (123:D4)

Rochers du Clos:
✳ 10.00→16.00
(5 − 7c +)(30)   DORDOGNE [107]

Some 5 outcrops offering a host of polished problems and routes on smooth but pocketed rock. Great for a few hours' finger wreaking. A must.

Dir: 19km NW of Périgueux, 12km SW of Brantôme. From Brantôme take the D78 through Bourdeilles, and on for about 5km (not as far as Lisle) and then turn R on to the D2 towards St Just. After 1km cross over the river and take the road immediately on the L. The crags are close to Vieux-Breuil. (122:C3)

Rochers du Moulin de Rochevreuil:
✳ 09.00→14.00
(5a − 7b)(40)   DORDOGNE [108]

Some quite small limestone cliffs up to 8m high but nevertheless offering superb climbing with lots of variations.

Dir: 19km NW of Périgueux, 11km SW of Brantôme. From Brantôme take the D78 through Bourdeilles, and on for about 5km (not as far as Lisle) and then turn R on to the D2 towards St Just. After 1km cross over the river and take the road immediately on the L. The crags are on the side of the road. (122:C3)

Rochers du Vieux-Breuil:
✳ 10.00→16.00
(4c − 8a)(110)   DORDOGNE [109]

Some excellent limestone crags up to 50m high offering superbly protected routes on steep pocketed rock. A lovely setting and the major crag in the PÉRIGORD BLANC area. *See also* the other crags in this region.

Dir: 44km SE of Angoulême, 10km W of Brantôme. From Brantôme take the D78 to Bourdeilles, cross over the river and take the D106 for about 4km then turn R and go (3km) to Paussac-et-St-Vivien. From the village take the D93 in a N direction towards Léguillac, after 2km pass Le Breuil on the L, and the crag is on the right in just over 1km. (109:D4)

Tabaterie:
✳ 10.00→16.00
(6b − 7c)(20)   DORDOGNE [110]

Another good limestone crag in the area offering some very good and well-protected routes. *In situ* bolts are fab.

Dir: 45km SE of Angoulême, 7km W of Brantôme. Drive to Paussac-et-St-Vivien (if you have no map *see* other crags in the area for details). From the village take the road going N towards St-Julien-de-Bourdeilles. After 2km turn L opposite the road to Puy Fromage. After 1km take the first white track on the L which after 300m gets you to the rocks. (109:D4)

Corrèze − 19

Aubazine:
✳ 10.00→16.00
(4a − 6c)(73)   CORRÈZE [111]

A group of three gneiss crags situated by a canal. The routes are either wall, corners or cracks. In most parts there are *in situ* pegs and various pro but on many of the cracks this is a bit lacking. In due course the crags might get bolted up but if you can, bring along some nuts just in case. Situated at 600m it is climbable on good sunny winter days, but on a hot day in August forget it. There are routes ranging from 5 to 50m with the majority being 25 − 30m long. There are also some more climbs at SAUT DE LA BERGÈRE of a similar nature. Local topos can be obtained at the *boulangerie* at Aubazine.

Dir: 12km E of Brive-la-Gaillarde. Take the N89 towards Tulle but after 10km turn R and go to Aubazine. From the village take the D48 in the direction (E) of Chastang. After 1km park on the R for Aubazine or by the restaurant for Saut de la Bergère. From here a footpath leads beside the canal to the cliffs. (124:C2)

Puy-de-Dôme – 63

The Mont Dore area in the Auvergne is a superb area to visit – a ski area in the winter and simply beautiful hills in the summer, with temperatures that are much more bearable than those on the Cote d'Azur. The climbing is hardly in the Verdon or Ceuse class, but it nevertheless does offer good scope for the middle grade climber and is ideal for the family on holiday in France. The only hindrance is that all school holidays are in August, so you can't expect it to be empty. A topo for the area can be purchased locally at Le Buron de Tame Tartine, Route du Sancy, Le Mont Dore, Puy-de-Dôme (tel: 73 65 05 22) or buy the *Topo du Massif du Sancy*, from François Palandre, BP 30, 63500 Issoire for 50FF.

Le Capucin:
✲ Not a lot (5.7.35.10.0)(62) PUY-DE-DÔME [112]

A 80m basalt crag situated up at 1,500m. The crag has recently been modernised and you stand very little chance of ever coming to harm here, even so the cracks have been left free for nut placing masochists (they should have just filled them up with cement to make excellent face routes). There is much varied climbing here which does make it a very good place to visit.

Dir: 33km SW of Clermont Ferrand, 2km W of Le-Mont-Dore. From the town take the D213 towards La Tour d'Auvergne. After 3km turn left opposite the Golf Auberge to the parking for the Salon du Capucin ski lift. The crag can be reached in 10 mins. (112:C3)

Cournols:
✲ 9.00→21.00 (Bouldering) PUY-DE-DÔME [113]

A very popular and good bouldering spot for climbers of Clermont Ferrand.

Dir: Take the N9 S out of Clermont then turn off at the second exit on to the D213 towards St Amant. Stay on the main road towards Ponteix but 2km before that town turn L to the village of Cournols. The boulders are close by. (113:D3)

Crête du Coq:
✲ 10.00→16.00 (6.9.23.0.0)(38) PUY-DE-DÔME [114]

A 130m dark basalt tower offering some very good middle to lower grade routes. The pro is excellent and well organised on all the routes. There are slabby routes as well as a large overhanging section on the L side of the crag. Definitely worth a visit.

Dir: 32km SW of Clermont Ferrand, 5km SE of Le-Mont-Dore. *See* Dent de la Rancune. (112:C3)

Dent de la Rancune:
✲ 05.00→22.00 (0.1.20.7.0)(28) PUY-DE-DÔME [115]

The Resentment Tooth, a pretty impressive volcanic crag of mainly basalt. 90m high and very well bolted with 10mm heavyweight bolts. The crag consists of slabs, walls and overhangs giving some gymnastic moves. Situation about 1,500m and being a pinnacle it faces in many different directions. There are good abseil points at the top of all of the 1st pitches, and of course on the top of the pinnacle. Definitely worth a visit, but not in winter unless you like ice climbing. The crag will sometimes be referred to as VALLÉE DE CHAUDEFOUR, but even so there are other crags in the area.

Dir: 32km SW of Clermont Ferrand, 5km SE of Le-Mont-Dore. Take the D36 over the Col de la Croix St Robert from Le-Mont-Dore, down through Monaux to the bottom of the Chaudefour valley. Turn R up to St Anne and park at the 'Buron', a shepherd's hut. Walk to the crag in about 30 mins. (112:C3)

Saône et Loire – 71

Rome Château:
✳ 09.00→17.00
(30.35.40.20.0)(120) SAÔNE ET LOIRE [116]

A very good limestone crag, with most of the routes being around 20m but larger routes to be found. Plenty in all grades and a wonderful aspect. Bolts [1–2]. Smaller than Cormot and often a lot less busy; wonderful for mid-week ambling and quietness.

Dir: 24km E of Autun, 20km SW of Beaune. Drive to Nolay almost midway between the two towns. From here drive S to Créot in 4km then continue on the D1 to Mazenay. Turn L to St Sernin. Here a road on the L leads up to Mt de Rome Château and the crag. (87:F3)

Solutré:
✳ 10.00→16.00
(10.30.10.0.0)(50) SAÔNE ET LOIRE [117]

A limestone crag which is particularly suited to beginners and holiday climbers. Good *in situ* gear, routes 20–25m high, and friendly in

angle of inclination. Topos can be bought in the local café in Solutré. The crag is dangerously close to Pouilly Fuissé, a real treat for Mâconnais imbibers. If you are feeling a bit peckish one lunch-time I can recommend that you take a trip about 20km S to Fleurie and dine at the Auberge du Cep; absolutely excellent.

Dir: 9km W of Macon. From Macon take the N79 E over the *autoroute* then shortly after turn L on to a smaller road to Davaye. From here follow signs to Solutré.

Vergisson:
✳ 10.00→16.00 (14.25.10.2.0)(41) SAÔNE ET LOIRE [118]

An ideal crag for the lower grade climber. Limestone up to 40m high with *in situ* gear which was replaced in 1987. Very similar to Solutré. Topo can be purchased at the café at Solutré.

Dir: 9km W of Macon. From Macon take the N79 E over the *autoroute* then shortly after turn L on to a smaller road to Davaye. From here take the D177 to Vergisson and the crag.

CENTRAL EAST FRANCE

Loire – 42

Roche Corbière:
(1.7.17.4.0)(29) LOIRE [119]

Not a large crag but it has been equipped with bolts [2–3] over the past few years on a number of routes.

Dir: 6km SE of St. Etienne. Leave the city on the D8 towards Le Bessat on the SE corner of town (rue Fauriel). After 5km reach the village of Rochetaillée. Here turn R on to a small R which leads to the Dam of Gouffre d'Enfer and the crag. (115:E4)

Haute-Savoie – 74

The guidebook to this area is called *Les Carroz-Cluzes* but it will soon be out of date since there is quite a lot of activity going on. Information to the area near Lac Léman can be obtained from *Chroniques de Chablais*, by Daniel Pirret-Jeanneret, Le Lyaud, 74200 Thonon.

Anthon:
✳ 11.00→19.00
(Unknown) HAUTE-SAVOIE [120]

A limestone crag with quite a few routes from 4b to 8b. All are single pitch 25m routes. The bolts [2–6] have been renewed recently. Busy at weekends and summer holidays.

Dir: 28km ESE of Genève, 9km NE of Bonneville. Take the D907 from Annemasse towards Taninges. The road bypasses St Jeoire; carry on for 5km on the way to Mieussy to reach the junction with the D226 which goes to Quincy. The crags are here overlooking the Gorge du Giffre. (105:D3)

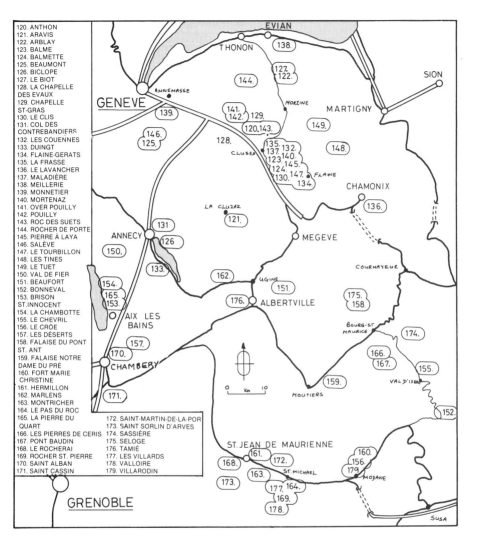

120. ANTHON
121. ARAVIS
122. ARBLAY
123. BALME
124. BALMETTE
125. BEAUMONT
126. BICLOPE
127. LE BIOT
128. LA CHAPELLE
DES EVAUX
129. CHAPELLE
ST-GRAS
130. LE CLIS
131. COL DES
CONTREBANDIERS
132. LES COUENNES
133. DUINGT
134. FLAINE-GERATS
135. LA FRASSE
136. LE LAVANCHER
137. MALADIÈRE
138. MEILLERIE
139. MONNETIER
140. MORTENAZ
141. OVER POUILLY
142. POUILLY
143. ROC DES SUETS
144. ROCHER DE PORTE
145. PIERRE À LAYA
146. SALÈVE
147. LE TOURBILLON
148. LES TINES
149. LE TUET
150. VAL DE FIER
151. BEAUFORT
152. BONNEVAL
153. BRISON
ST.INNOCENT
154. LA CHAMBOTTE
155. LE CHEVRIL
156. LE CRÔE
157. LES DÉSERTS
158. FALAISE DU PONT
ST. ANT
159. FALAISE NOTRE
DAME DU PRÉ
160. FORT MARIE
CHRISTINE
161. HERMILLON
162. MARLENS
163. MONTRICHER
164. LE PAS DU ROC
165. LA PIERRE DU
QUART
166. LES PIERRES DE CERIS
167. PONT BAUDIN
168. LE ROCHERAI
169. ROCHER ST. PIERRE
170. SAINT ALBAN
171. SAINT CASSIN

172. SAINT-MARTIN-DE-LA-POR
173. SAINT SORLIN D'ARVES
174. SASSIÈRE
175. SELOGE
176. TAMIÉ
177. LES VILLARDS
178. VALLOIRE
179. VILLARODIN

Aravis:

✴ 08.00→16.00
(6.7.20.10.2)(45)   HAUTE-SAVOIE
[121]

A good 25m limestone crag, a good range of routes bolted [1–3]. Home of the classic Le Toit de Gilbert Ogier. At 1,500m, not so hot in winter. More development is going on. Worth a detour. A topo can be purchased from P. Gallay, Le Nojak, 74220 La Clusaz.

Dir: 4km SE of La Clusaz, 26km E of Annecy. From La Clusaz take the D909 towards Flumet. This takes you up the col; on the way there is a chalet by a bend with a sign 'Rochers d'Escalade'. Park here and walk to the crag in about 15 mins. (118:C1)

Arblay:
✳ 10.00→16.00
(7b – 8b)(15)   HAUTE-SAVOIE
[122]

A very high standard crag which has been well bolted [3 – 4]. All single pitch limestone terrors. Those who have weak fingers or are overweight shouldn't bother coming. The classic test piece is Ici-Mêmec (Menestrel).

Dir: 41 km ENE of Genève, 16km SE of Thonon. Take the D902 S from Thonon to La Baume; here turn L on to the D32 up to Le Biot, carry on up to the top of the Col do Corbier. On the L is a track which goes to the Chalets de l'Arblay; follow this past the chalets to a footpath which cuts back up to the crag. 5 mins. (105:E2)

Balme:
✳ 10.00→18.00
(6a – 7c)(12)   HAUTE-SAVOIE
[123]

A large limestone crag reaching up to over 200m. The routes are long and quite demanding, including a powerful style of climbing. Nothing very easy here; the rock is very good, giving some 'out there' routes. Bolts [1 – 3]. Situated low down at 700m. Definitely worth a visit.

Dir: 41km ESE of Genève, 4km SE of Cluses. Take the N205 from Cluses in the direction of Chamonix. After 4km turn L on to the D6 towards Flaine, shortly reach Balme and the crag is obvious. Park beneath the crag. (105:E4)

Balmette:
✳ 13.00→22.00
(5c – 7c)(20)   HAUTE-SAVOIE
[124]

A very good limestone crag with superb walls of water pockets and finger-wreaking holes. There is quite a lot of development going on here and nearly all of the routes are fairly new. Please be careful when abseiling. Bolts [1 – 3].

Dir: 41km ESE of Genève, 4km SE of Cluses. Take the N205 from Cluses in the direction of Chamonix. After 4km turn L on to the D6 towards Flaine, shortly reach Balme. Carry on to the second bend under the crag. (105.E5)

Beaumont:
✳ 14.00→22.00
(5c – 6c)(15)   HAUTE-SAVOIE
[125]

A good limestone cliff with three pitch routes up to 100m high. Good slab climbs with *in situ* gear [1 – 3], very quick to dry after rain. A lot of the routes are polished so bring a good supply of chalk in summer. The crag is covered in the same guide to Salève.

Dir: 12km SSW of Genève. Take the D18 or the N201 going S out of Genève. Where they meet is the village of Le Châble. At the village turn L and take the small road to Beaumont and the crag is obvious. Walk to the crag. 10 mins. (104:B4)

Biclope:
✳ 11.00→19.00
(24.65.70.32.4)(195)   HAUTE-SAVOIE [126]

A large limestone crag which is very polished. In fact, most of the routes are very hard for their grade because of the slippery nature of the rock. *In situ* bolts, 50 per cent [1], 20 per cent [2 – 3], 30 per cent [6]. There are some very good grade 8 routes here with very technical steep climbing on rather small holds. Many of the routes have the first bolt an alarming distance up above a bulge, so be careful. Sheltered from cold winds and a good sun trap. Not really worth more than a passing glance if you climb below grade 7.

Dir: 4km SE of Annecy. From the desperate traffic system in Annecy take the D909 towards Tallories to the E. Pass through Chavoires and then the crag is on the L just before the sign to the village of Veyrier-du-Lac. The cliff is easily visible and is 5 mins walk away. (118:B1)

Le Biot:
✳ 08.00→15.00
(5c – 8b)(208)   HAUTE-SAVOIE
[127]

The major crag in the area, also known as PAS DE L'OURS. There are very few routes in the lower grades here. There are many different styles of route, with most of the routes having been re-equipped [1 – 3] recently.

Dir: 40km ENE of Genève, 16km SE of Thonon. Take the D902 S from Thonon to La

Baume. Here turn L on to the D32 up to Le Biot, carry on up towards the Col do Corbier. There is a sign to the L on the route marking Pas de l'Ours. A footpath leads to the crag in about 5 mins. (105:E2)

La Chapelle des Evaux:
✳ 13.00→22.00
(1.5.8.6.0)(20) HAUTE-SAVOIE [128]

A limestone crag up to 30m situated at 750m. There are some good wall routes here. *In situ* gear [2−6].

Dir: 26km SE of Genève, 5km SSW of Bonneville. From Bonneville go S to the town of St Pierre-en-Faucigny. Here take the D12 into the Gorges des Evaux towards le Petit-Bornand. After entering the gorge take a small road on the L which leads to the bottom of the cliff. There are two obvious sections. (105:D4)

Chapelle St Gras:
✳ 13.00→19.00
(0.6.22.6.0)(34) HAUTE-SAVOIE [129]

A 50m limestone crag with bolts [1−2] on most of the routes. There are more areas of the cliff under development and this will give more routes in the future. The rock is good and the climbing is mainly on steep walls. An all year round crag.

Dir: 30km E of Genève, 4km WNW of Taninges. From Taninges take the D907 towards Mieussy, after 3km take the small road on the R signposted to Chapelle St Gras. Take this to the crag. (105:D3)

Le Clis:
✳ 13.00→19.00
(6a−7c)(20) HAUTE-SAVOIE [130]

A limestone cliff with some very good climbs on. Various reports have given this crag an excellent write-up. Situated at 900m it is sometimes referred to as ROCHERS DES GÉRATS. The cliff itself is up to 200m high but most of the climbs are single pitch with good abseil points [1−3].

Dir: 44km ESE of Genève, 7km SE of Cluses. From Cluses take the N205 towards Chamonix.

and at Balme take the D6 up towards Flaine. At Les Carroz locate a purifying plant of Carroz. From here go down to the bottom of the fields where a footpath goes off to the L and to the crag in 15 mins. (105:D4)

Col des Contrebandiers:
✳ 16.00→22.00(10) HAUTE-SAVOIE [131]

A good mountain limestone crag with 25m routes from grade 5 upwards. All the routes are new, and well equipped, and there will be many more put up over the next few years. Watch the press for details.

Dir: Check locally for exact details or try: 5km E of Annecy. Go to the Annecy-le-Vieux part of town, locate the Zone Industriale des Glaisins where a road (signposted) leads to the forest and up to the Col des Contrebandiers (smugglers). The crag takes about 5 mins to reach. Best of luck. (118:B1)

Les Couennes:
✳ 11.00→20.00
(5c−7c)(15) HAUTE-SAVOIE [132]

A good limestone crag situated at 850m with some nice wall routes. Bolts [1−3].

Dir: 40km ESE of Genève, 5km SE of Cluses. Leave Cluses on the N205 in the direction of Chamonix. After 4km at Balme turn L on to the D6 up towards Arâches. Take this winding road up the hill to just past a hamlet called L'Arberroz. Take a track which leads past the Ferme du Sangle and to the top of the cliff. Abseil rings. (105:E4)

Duingt:
✳ 12.00→20.00
(8.22.20.0.0)(40) HAUTE-SAVOIE [133]

A 25m limestone cliff with steep slabs offering good delicate climbing and worth a visit. Situated at 450m it can even be fair game on a very warm winter's day. Bolts [2−4].

Dir: 11km SSE of Annecy. Leave Annecy on the N508 and follow it S along the lake to Duingt. At the village there is a cycle track by the lake. Park by this and walk to the crag which is obvious. (118:B1)

Flaine-Gérats:
✳ 10.00→16.00
(4 − 7b +)(29) HAUTE-SAVOIE
[134]

A 25m limestone crag at 1600m. Good quality climbing with *in situ* bolts [2 − 4] but in places some of the bolts tend to be quite widely spaced. There is some easier climbing near here at a waterfall. Enquire locally.

Dir: 46km ESE of Genève, 11km SE of Cluses (an hour's drive sometimes). Take the N205 from Cluses in the Chamonix direction, after 4km at Balme turn L and take the D6 and then the D106 up to Flaine. Go to a Norwegian hamlet before you get to the golf course. Here a path leads to the Col de Cou. Take this then follow the red markers on the left to the crag. (105:E4)

La Frasse:
✳ 10.00→16.00 (20) HAUTE-SAVOIE [135]

A good S-facing limestone crag up to 70m high. A good crag for the lower grade climbers with most routes being from grade 3 to 6; in fact, it is a good spot for beginners. At just under 1,000m it is quite a sun trap and gets hot in the high summer months. Bolts [1 − 3].

Dir: 41km ESE of Genève, 4km E of Cluses. From Cluses take the N205 towards Chamonix, past the motorway exit, on for 2km then turn L on to the D6 to Arâches. At the village turn L and continue to La Frasse. Go through the village on the way to St Sigismond continuing for 200m to arrive at the crag. (105:E4)

Le Lavancher:
✳ 10.00→1900 (1.2.6.3.0)(12)
HAUTE-SAVOIE [136]

There are two crags here, both are granite and quite large, up to 80m. Very much summer crags, and autumn if the weather permits. DALLE DE L'ARVEYRON and DÔME DU CHAPEAU. The *in situ* gear [4 − 6] is varied and sometimes spaced. Altogether nice crags in a splendid position at the foot of the Mer de Glace. Worth a visit in summer.

Dir: 4km NE of Chamonix. Take the N506 towards Argentière. After 4km turn R up to Le Lavancher, go through the village and carry on

up the road to some parking. From here a path leads up to Le Chapeau. Follow this for about 15 mins and the slabs can be seen to the R in the forest. For the Dôme du Chapeau carry on the footpath for 10 mins but turn down to the R before you reach the Buvette du Chapeau. The path leads down to the summit of the crag in 5 mins. (105:F4)

Maladière:
✳ 11.00→20.00 (6a − 7c)(27)
HAUTE-SAVOIE [137]

A large limestone crag with all the routes being multi-pitch up to 10 pitches. The climbing is on good pocketed rock with *in situ* bolts [1 − 3]. A great crag if you're going around 6c, also offering some entertaining overhanging sections. Situated at around 1,100 − 1,300m.

Dir: 41km ESE of Genève, 4km ENE of Cluses. From Cluses take the N205 towards Chamonix, past the motorway exit, on for 2km then turn L on to the D6 to Arâches. At the village turn L and continue to La Frasse, go through the village on the way to St Sigismond. Carry on to the Col de la Croix Verte and locate the forestry track to Chalets de Chevran. Pass them, through some fields to a wood at the edge of the cliff. The crag is best reached from above. (105:DE4)

Meillerie:
✳ 15.00→22.00
(3 − 8a)(30) HAUTE-SAVOIE [138]

A good 35m limestone crag on the side of Lac Léman. All the routes are single pitch except for a couple which are two pitch. The cliff offers good technical climbing and still is under development. Bolts [2 − 6].

Dir: 50km ENE of Genève, 9km E of Evian-les-Bains. From Evian take the N5 along the lake for 9km to Meillerie. Park in the village then walk 200m to the crag. (105:E2)

Monnetier:
✳ 15.00→22.00
(5c − 8a)(40) HAUTE-SAVOIE [139]

This crag is sometimes referred to as MORNEX. A limestone crag with mainly single pitch routes but all in the upper grades. Gear *in situ* [1 − 3], and a good choice of route type.

Dir: 6km SE of Genève. From Annemasse take the D2 going S for a short while then turn off to the R on to the D41 to Monnetier-Mornex and park near the church. A footpath is marked with white markers. For 'Canape', take the no through road Pas de l'Echelle, cross the bridge at the end on the L, go L again and take a footpath between two fenced areas; 10 mins. For 'The Château', take the no through road again but turn R after La Chaumière. Other areas are on the W slope of Petite Salève to the N of the village. (104:C3)

Mortenaz:
✳ 16.00→22.00
(5c – 7c)(40) HAUTE-SAVOIE [140]

A good limestone crag with some cracking long pitches which do require good finger strength. Bolts are being replaced on the hard routes [2 – 6].

Dir: 40km ESE of Genève, 5km SE of Cluses. Leave Cluses on the N205 in the direction of Chamonix. After 4km at Balme turn L on to the D6 up towards Arâches. Take this winding road up the hill to just past a hamlet called L'Arberroz. Here a sign indicates the way to the crag which is reached in 5 mins by footpath. (105:E4)

Over Pouilly:
✳ 08.00→15.00
(6a – 7b)(20) HAUTE-SAVOIE [141]

Smaller than its neighbour, good limestone and varied, offering slabs, walls, overhangs and roofs. Worth a visit.

Dir: 25km ESE of Genève, 9km NNE of Bonneville. Take the D907 to St Jeoire, then turn up the valley on to the D26 towards Bellevaux. After 2km enter the hamlet of Pouilly. Carry on up the valley to the start of the gorge. The crag is then on the L and only 5 mins walk away. (105:D3)

Pouilly:
✳ 10.00→16.00
(5 – 8a)(30) HAUTE-SAVOIE [142]

This crag and Over Pouilly are sometimes referred to as SAINT JEOIRE. Quite a large crag with 3 pitch routes but many of the harder routes are just single pitches. Steep limestone wall climbing predominates, bolts [1 – 3] with some good technical problems. Situated at 750m.

Dir: 25km ESE of Genève, 9km NNE of Bonneville. Take the D907 to St Jeoire, then turn up the valley on to the D26 towards Bellevaux. After 2km enter the hamlet of Pouilly. The crag is obvious, and reached in a few minutes. (105:D3)

Roc des Suets:
✳ 13.00→21.00
(0.0.4.7.1)(12) HAUTE-SAVOIE [143]

A 30m limestone crag with some very hard routes up to 8a plus, but most around 7b. There is more development going on so by 1992 expect a few more routes here. The rock is excellent and consists of good leaning walls. Bolts [1 – 2]. The crag is at 950m and if the weather holds is often climbable in the winter months.

Dir: 32km E of Genève, 2km WNW of Taninges. Take the D907 from Taninges towards Mieussy. After 3km take the road on the R signposted to Chapelle St Gras. After a short distance take the R fork signposted to Briffes. From the hamlet descend into a small valley on the R and a path through the woods opposite to the crag. 5 mins. (105:D3)

Rocher de Porte:
✳ 10.00→16.00
(4c – 8a)(70) HAUTE-SAVOIE [144]

A good 80m limestone crag situated at 1,000m. Quite a lot of double and triple pitch routes. The *in situ* gear is a weird array of equipment [3 – 5]. Good rock, offering walls with bulges and cracklines.
Dir: 30km ENE of Genève, 16km SSE of Thonon-les-Bains. Go to Bellevaux on the D26 from either Thonon or St Jeoire, take the D26 S towards the Col de Jambaz, then follow signs to Route du Lac de Vollon. Park beneath the crag. (105:D3)

Pierre à Laya:
✲ 12.00→19.00
(5c – 8a)(70) HAUTE-SAVOIE
[145]

A 50m limestone crag with good routes in all grades. The rock is excellent with good walls which have cracks and water pockets. Worth a visit. Bolts [2 – 3].

Dir: 42km ESE of Genève, 5km ESE of Cluses. Take the N205 towards Chamonix from Cluses, then turn L at Balme on to the D6 to Arâches. Park near the church in the village. The crag is below the village about 15 mins' walk away. (105:E4)

Salève:
✲ 13.00→22.00
(30.64.146.80.2)(322)
HAUTE-SAVOIE [146]

One of the big French climbing areas with lots to occupy anyone. The crag is in various sections and sun or shade can be found at most times. There are routes up to 200m and plenty of shorter ones for good measure. The area has been popular for a long time and trade routes are very polished; even so, it is a good place to go. On the longer routes double ropes can be very useful for the abseil descents. The area has a good topo which can be purchased at the local café and is well worth buying. Bolts [1 – 5].

Dir: 8km S of Genève. From the S part find the N206, cross over this and the *autoroute* to Collonges then bear S to the small village of Le Coin. The crag is quite obvious. (104:C3)

Le Tourbillon:
✲ 10.00→16.00
(4 – 6a)(11) HAUTE-SAVOIE [147]

A small 25m limestone crag which proves excellent for lower grade climbers. It consists of slabs interspersed with small overhangs. There is some artificial climbing which will no doubt go free soon, once it is developed with the usual cement holds. Watch press for details. Situated at 1,250m.

Dir: 43km ESE of Genève, 7km SW of Cluses. Take the N205 S towards Chamonix and after 3km turn L at Balme on to the D6 towards Flaine. After 6km pass through Les Carroz then start up the hairpin bends to Flaine. At the second bend a footpath leads down to the R and the crag. Park further on up the road in a layby. (105:E4)

Les Tines:
✲ 17.00→22.00
(3c – 8a)(40) HAUTE-SAVOIE
[148]

A 90m limestone crag with some wonderful steep face climbing on, up to 3 pitch routes. Quite technical in unpositive holds which are very tiring to the forearms. Bolts [1 – 3] are correctly spaced. Even in the rain parts stay completely dry and in the hot summer the crag is in the shade for most of the day. At the moment the routes are not polished but this will only be a matter of time. Worth a good visit. Situated at 800m. Sometimes referred to as GORGES DES TINES.

Dir: 50km ESE of Genève, 5km SE of Samoëns (11km S of Morzine). From Morzine take the D907 up the valley towards Sixt-Fer-à-Cheval. About 1km before Sixt the Gorge is on the R. There is a path which leads to the Gorge from beside the metal bridge, signposted. (105:E4)

Le Tuet:
✲ 11.00→19.00
(4 – 7c)(40) HAUTE-SAVOIE [149]

A large limestone crag with routes up to 5 pitches and 120m high. Situated at just over 1,000m. There is more development going on but in the summer months it can get quite hot, especially in the afternoon. Snakes have been seen here, so watch out. A good crag, nevertheless. Bolts [2 – 6].

Dir: 47km E of Genève, 11km S of Morzine. Go to Samoëns then from the far E part of the village a road leads N up the valley towards Les Allamands. In about 300m there is parking. From here follow the obvious path to the crag in 20 mins. (105:E3)

Val de Fier:
✲ 10.00→16.00
(0.5.24.12.0)(41) HAUTE-SAVOIE
[150]

A limestone crag of very high quality, mountain-type rock and up to 250m high. The best routes are around 6b−7a; wall climbing demanding balance and technique as opposed to sheer finger strength. Pitches can be quite long and it is standard to carry about 15 tie-offs. Please respect the natural flora and do not remove more than is necessary. The crag dries very quickly after rain and is only at 450m high. A very worthwhile crag. Bolts [1−2].

Dir: 22km W of Annecy, 9km NW of Rumilly. From Rumilly take the D910 to Vallières, then turn L on to the D14 which leads to St André. Carry on to the Gorge and the crag is on the R. A footpath leads to the cliff in 15 mins. The nearest town to the N is Seyssel. (118:A1)

Savoie − 73

An area more known for its skiing than for the climbing. In the summer months take advantage of the great facilities at Les Arcs and Tignes, with golf, tennis, canoeing and windsurfing. There is a topo guide to the Bourg-St Maurice − Isère valley, *Topo de la Vanoise*, which is hopefully as accurate as possible, but because of the Winter Olympics here in 1992 a large road building operation is in progress, with many new roads and bypasses planned, so a new map of the area is worth buying. The crags should still be easy to find as there is little chance of the small roads to the villages being affected.

Beaufort:
✳ 10.00→16.00
(3−6c)(30)   SAVOIE [151]

A 25m gneiss crag with routes mainly in the lower grades. The rock is very good and hard but *in situ* gear [6] is poor at present; it will hopefully be renewed. Situated at 750m. Bring nuts just in case. This is also the home of one of the greatest cheeses ever made.

Dir: 16km ENE of Albertville. Take the D925 towards Beaufort. About half a km before the town, park and the crag is obvious beside the road. (119:D2)

Bonneval:
✳ 10.00→16.00
(Bouldering)   SAVOIE [152]

Some good bouldering to be found on these gneiss boulders up to 10m high. The climbing is quite gymnastic. Situated at nearly 2,000m and definitely a summer crag only.

Dir: 12km SE of Val d'Isère, 8km NE of Lanslebourg-Mont-Cenis. From Lanslebourg take the D902 up to Bessans, continue past and on up to Bonneval-s-Arc. Carry on up further to the hamlet of Lenta and the crag is obvious. (119:F4)

Brison St Innocent:
✳ 12.00→21.00
(4−8a)(40)   SAVOIE [153]

A 120m limestone crag with some very good routes which have been recently equipped with modern bolts [2−3]. Not that many routes but situated at 300m and a good crag in the moderate seasons.

Dir: 2km NNW of Aix-les-Bains, 81km E of Lyon. From the N end of Aix near the lake take the D902 lake road to St Innocent where the crag is near the railway and obvious. A popular crag in the evenings. (118:A2)

La Chambotte:
✳ 12.00→20.00
(4−8b)(250)   SAVOIE [154]

This is by far the best limestone crag in Savoie and offers climbing of fantastic quality. The routes vary from single pitch to 130m. The *in situ* gear at present is not as good as you might hope for: bolts 10 per cent [1−2], 50 per cent [3], 10 per cent [4−6], 30 per cent not there yet. The style of the cliff is impressive − a huge escarpment situated at 700m and overlooking the lake. The only real problem is the fact that the crag faces W and is quite low down but very exposed to winds. In winter it is very cold, and on summer afternoons too hot. Anyway, the cliff is 30 seconds from the car. Very good bouldering here on the overhanging starts to the central routes [8a−b]. Worth a visit. There are a few very peaceful compsites in the valley behind of St Germain, and windsurfing on the lake below, and it is also a lovely walking area.

Dir: 9km NNW of Aix-les-Bains, 81km E of Lyon. From Aix take the N201 going N towards Albens and Annecy. Turn off L beforehand at La Biolle and go to St Germain. Here take the winding D991 up to La Chambotte. Do not go up to the *belvédère* but straight on, through the tunnel and park by the bend on the L. The crag is evident to both sides of the road. (118:A2)

Le Chevril:
(4 − 7c)(50 +)   SAVOIE [155]

A good hard limestone crag up to 50m with some good butch routes. Summer only though, at 1,800m. There is a topo to the crag which I presume can be bought locally.

Dir: 19km SE of Bourg-St. Maurice. From that town take the D902 towards Val d'Isère. Just after the Tignes turn off at the *belvédère*, park (before any of the tunnels next to the lake). From here take the track up to the hamlet of Le Chevril where the crag is to the R and close by. (119:E3)

Le Cröe:
✳ 09.00→19.00
(Bouldering + Routes)(100)
SAVOIE [156]

A crag of mixed boulders around 10 − 15m high and cliffs up to 50m high with new bolts [1 − 3]. The crag is of a black limestone and offers technical climbing. Route info can be found in the village. Situated at 1,400m, so not a winter crag.

Dir: 6km ENE of Modane. 78km E of Grenoble. From Modane take a high road out of the town to the N (D215) which leads up to Aussois. The crag is down a track to the L of the village (E) upon arriving. (133:E1)

Les Déserts:
✳ 07.00→17.00
(3 − 4)(10)   SAVOIE [157]

A limestone crag which is superb as an introduction to climbing on a warm day. Slabs at about 40 degrees for the 1st pitch 30m, then a bit steeper second pitch. Situated at 800m with *in situ* bolts [1 − 3]. Very good beginner's crag.

Dir: 10km ENE of Chambéry, 13km SE of Aix-les-Bains. From Chambéry take the D912 to St Jean-d'Arvey. Carry on up the hill to Les Déserts and the crag can be seen from the road. Do not confuse this town with another of the same name 13km to the S of Chambéry. (118:AB2)

Falaise du Pont St. Antoine:
✳ 11.00→19.00
(6a − 7c)(20)   SAVOIE [158]

A crag with a mixture of limestone and quartz up to 30m high and situated at 1,600m. The crag is a real sun trap in the afternoon. Good for the harder climber as most of the walls are overhanging and bolted [1 − 3].

Dir: 52km ESE of Annecy, 8km NNW of Bourg-St Maurice. From B-St Maurice take the D902 from the N end of town (nearest Val d'Isère) up towards Cormet de Roseland. After 11km pass the hamlet of Crêt Bettex, carry on for a couple of km to the St Antoine bridge. Park here and walk to the crag. 5 mins. (119:E2)

Falaise Notre Dame du Pré:
✳ 09.00→19.00
(3 − 7a)(80)   SAVOIE [159]

A limestone crag situated at 1,600m with routes for the middle grade climber. Bolt [1 − 3] protected climbs up to 30m long.

Dir: 8km ENE of Moûtiers. From the town take the N90 in the direction of Bourg-St Maurice. After 4km just past the village of Pomblière turn R on to the D88 and take the hairpin bends up to Notre Dame due Pré. From here a path leads to the crag. (119:D3)

Fort Marie Christine:
✳ 11.00→19.00
(3 − 7c)(60)   SAVOIE [160]

A limestone crag with routes up to 50m high and situated at 1,400m. The routes are equipped with *in situ* bolts [1 − 3]. Great views from the crag.

Dir: 6km ENE of Modane, 78km E of Grenoble. From Modane take a high road out of the town to the N (D215) which leads up to Aussois. On entry to the village take the road on the R signposted to the Fort. The crag is just above and easily seen. (133:E1)

Hermillon:
✳ 11.00→18.00
(4 – 7a)(20)   SAVOIE [161]

A 30m granite crag offering some, good energetic climbing in the lower to middle grades and protected by *in situ* gear [2 – 4]. Situated at 700m.

Dir: 2km NE of St Jean-de-Maurienne. Go N on the small road by the railway then turn R to Hermillon and the crag is beside the road. (118:C4)

Marlens:
✳ 07.00→21.00
(15.23.32.12.2)(85)   SAVOIE [162]

This limestone crag is in four different sections, each crags of their own importance: LE ROCHER DE MARLENS, the most important and up to 50m high with the majority of routes; LE ROCHER DES TORCHES, slightly smaller but still with a couple of good routes; LE DIPLODOCUS, and LE PETIT CHARVIN, both smaller cliffs with routes that are very good for beginners. All *in situ* gear [2 – 5]. A topo for the crag can be purchased at Stéphane Sport, Albertville.

Dir: 11km NNW of Albertville, 24km SE of Annecy. From Albertville take the N212 to Ugine then the N508 towards Faverges. Halfway there turn off the Moulin de Marlins. Park 100m further on. From here a footpath leads to the crag in 15 mins. (118:C2)

Montricher:
(3 – 7b)(15)   SAVOIE [163]

A small 20m pudding stone crag offering a handful of well-equipped routes. Situated at just under 700m. Bolts [1 – 3].

Dir: 7km SE of St Jean-de-Maurienne. From the town take the D road to the S which joins the N6 before it becomes a dual carriageway. At this point as the road goes over the railway turn L on to a small road to Montricher-Albanne. Carry on fo Montricher where the crag is obvious. (132:C1)

Le Pas du Roc:
✳ 11.00→19.00
(4 – 8a)(100)   SAVOIE [164]

A limestone crag with routes from 15 – 200m high. A lot of the routes are quite new and protected with recently placed bolts [2 – 3]. Indeed, the harder routes are very good indeed and the crag will become quite popular. The French regard it as a very fashionable crag. Worth a visit.

Dir: 1km SE of St Michel-de-Maurienne, 12km ESE of St Jean-de-Maurienne. Take the N6 from St Jean to St Michel, carry on to the railway bridge and the crag is just after on the L. Also a steep path leads from the parking spot to the second section of the crag. (133:D1)

La Pierre du Quart:
(5 – 8a)(30)   SAVOIE [165]

A 35m limestone crag situated up at 700m, bolted up [2 – 3] but a bit of a walk. Most of the routes here are in the higher grades. Reports of cars being broken into are not uncommon here.

Dir: 7km N of Aux-les-Bains, 81km E of Lyon. From Aix take the D991 going N towards Ruffieux. After passing some cliffs at Brison (tunnel), take a track on the R. Park some way up this then take a footpath going off to the L which leads to the crag in about 10 mins. (118:A2)

Les Pierres de Ceris:
✳ 10.30→19.00
(Bouldering)(120)   SAVOIE [166]

Some bouldering on volcanic rock up to 20m high with bolts [2] on the summits of the boulders.

Dir: 8km S of Bourg-St Maurice. 5km before B-St maurice on the N90 from Moutiers take a road S which goes to Landry. From here carry on up the valley to the small quaint village of Peisey Nancroix and reach the crag just before the village. (119:E3)

Pont Baudin:
✳ 10.00→19.00
(3 – 7a)(25)   SAVOIE [167]

A volcanic crag consisting of two faces, one steep and the other a very nice grade 5 slab. The routes are half on each. Bolts [3 – 4]. The valley is very quiet and catches the sun for the best part of the day. Situated at 1,500m and up to 70m high but suffers quite a lot from drainage in the spring-time. A popular spot for winter cross country skiing.

Dir: 10km S of Bourg-St Maurice. 5km before B-St Maurice on the N90 from Moutiers take a road S which goes to Landry. From here carry on up the valley to the small village of Peisey Nancroix, then continue past Le Moulin, Nancroix, La Chénarie to 1km before Les Lanches. Stop at the Pont Baudin next to the campsite at La Laverie. The crag is obvious on the L side of the road. (119:E3)

Le Rocherai:
✳ 17.00→21.00
(3 – 7c)(60)   SAVOIE [168]

A large granite crag situated at 650m with routes varying from single pitch to 110m monsters. A good crag all round with cemented pegs [4] and a couple of areas for beginners.

Dir: 3km NNW of St Jean-de-Maurienne, 43km SE of Chambéry. Leave St Jean on the N6 towards Aiguebelle. After 3km go L over the bridge of Hermillon and the crag is obvious on the L bank of the river Arc. The crag is reached by footpath in 15 mins. (118:C4)

Rocher St Pierre:
✳ 12.00→22.00 (4 – 6)(30)
SAVOIE [169]

A 30 – 50m limestone crag situated at 1,500m with a mixed assortment of *in situ* gear [2 – 5].

Dir: 14km SSE of St Jean-de-Maurienne. From St Jean take the N6 towards St Michel then turn R on to the D902 over the Col du Télégraphe to Valloire. From the village take a track to the L of the small church which leads to the crag and is obvious. (132:C1)

Saint Alban:
✳ 12.00→20.00 (4 – 7)(30)
SAVOIE [170]

A small limestone crag 10 – 15m high with bolts [1 – 2]. Situated at 300m and best for the middle grade climber.

Dir: 3km NE of Chambéry. From the town go NE crossing over the bypass on to the D8 towards Verel. After a couple of km reach the village of La Clusaz. Park here and take a footpath to Gollet. 20 mins. (118:A3)

Saint Cassin:
✳ 10.00→20.00
(Bouldering)(100)   SAVOIE [171]

Some limestone boulders 2 – 10m high and situated at 500m. Some of the larger boulders have new bolts [1 – 2] on the summit for top-roping and it is planned to re-equip further. There are about 200 problems but the area stays damp after a rain shower. Even so, it does remain popular, especially in the evenings.

Dir: 5km SSW of Chambéry, 85km ESE of Lyon. Take the N6 out of the Cogin part of Chambéry in the S towards St Thibaud. After 3km turn L to St Cassin and the boulders are signposted (to the SE of the railway line) 'Ecole d'Escalade'. (118:A3)

Saint-Martin-de-la-Porte:
✳ 11.00→17.00
(4 – 8b)(30)   SAVOIE [172]

A limestone crag with only a handful of easy routes. Routes from single pitch up to 130m triple pitch easier routes. The crag is situated at 1,000m and is close to the road. *In situ* gear [2 – 6] is varied but on the harder routes the bolts [2 – 3] are newer.

Dir: 8km ESE of St Jean-de-Maurienne. From the town take the N6 towards Modane. After going through an arch turn L on to the D219 to St Martain. In the village park by the new church on the L. The crag is obvious. (132:C1)

Saint Sorlin d'Arves:
✳ 05.00→9.00
(3 – 6c)(12)   SAVOIE [173]

A gneiss crag up to 60m which offers routes best suited to the beginner. Situated at 1,500m.

Dir: 11km SW of St Jean-de-Maurienne. Leave the town on the D926 towards Croix de Fer. After about 20km enter the village of Saint Sorlin d'Arves. Here take a track which leads to the crag in about 10 mins. (132:C1)

Sassière:
✳ 10.00→16.00
(4 – 6c)(12)   SAVOIE [174]

A volcanic crag from 30 – 70m high with bolts [3 – 4]. Situated at nearly 1,500m and very much a summer crag.

Dir: 14km E of Bourg-St Maurice. From the town take the N90 then the D902 towards Val d'Isère. Just after the small village of St Foy turn L up to Les Masures then Le Crôt. Carry on up towards La Sassière and park. The crag is 5 mins away. (119:E2)

Seloge:
✳ 10.00→16.00
(4 – 7a)(20)   SAVOIE [175]

A good crag for the middle grade climber. A slabby crag of volcanic mountain rock which starts at 1,750m and goes up to nearly 2,000m. *In situ* gear [2 – 3].

Dir: 14km N of Bourg-St Maurice. From B-St Maurice take the D902 from the N end of town (nearest Val d'Isère) up towards Cormet de Roseland. After about 14km fork L to Les Chapieux. Take the small road up the valley to the end at the hamlet of Ville des Glaciers. Footpath to the crag in 10 mins. (119:E2)

Tamié:
✳ 10.00→19.00
(5 – 7c)(50)   SAVOIE [176]

A 25m limestone crag which has recently been re-equipped with *in situ* gear [2 – 4]. Of the 50 or so routes most are in the grade 6 category. Situated at just under 1,000m.

Dir: 7km W of Albertville. From the W side of town take the D64 to Gémilly, then carry on to Plancherine and Tamié. The crag is obvious. (118:C2)

Les Villards:
✳ 06.00→12.00
(5 – 7a)(20)   SAVOIE [177]

A short 20m crag with a handful of routes, equipped and not bad. Situated at 1,500m and in a skiing area, so a summer crag only, I'm afraid. *In situ* cemented pegs, etc [3 – 4].

Dir: 12km SSE of St Jean-de-Maurienne. From St Jean take the N6 towards St Michel then turn R on to the D902 over the Col du Télégraphe to Valloire. From the village take a road up to Le Villard. From here a track leads around the mountain towards Albanne. Take this to the crag. (132:C1)

Valloire:
(5 – 7a)(50)   SAVOIE [178]

A limestone crag situated at 1,400m with some good routes on. All are single pitch with lower-off points. The easy routes tend to be better protected but I'm sure that the harder routes will become properly bolted [2 – 4] quite soon.

Dir: 14km SSE of St Jean-de-Maurienne. From St Jean take the N6 towards St Michel then turn R on to the D902 over the Col du Télégraphe to Valloire. The crag is very close to the village and quite obvious. (132:C1)

Villarodin:
✳ 9.00→19.00
(3 – 7a)(100)   SAVOIE [179]

A good, well-developed limestone crag with a lot of new bolts [2 – 3], 20 – 30m high and situated at 1,000m. Quite a lot of the routes are in the grade 6 – 7a category.

Dir: 30km N of Briançon, 3km ENE of Modane. From Modane take the N6 E towards Bramans but after 3km turn L to the village of Villarodin-Bourget. The crag is 10 mins' walk from the village on the N side of the river. (133:E1)

Isère – 38

If you are visiting this area then I suggest you buy the local topo guide, *Escalade Autour de Grenoble*, by D. Duhaut, Claude Vigier and B. Lambert.

La Carrière:
✳ 10.00→19.00
(Bouldering)   ISÈRE [180]

Quite a historical limestone bouldering and car break-in area. There are a couple of circuits:

Yellow, easy; Blue, 5–6a; Red, 6b–6c; Black, 7a and harder. Some of the problems are quite awkward and high up off the ground and injuries are quite frequent. A top rope can be useful. Bolts [4].

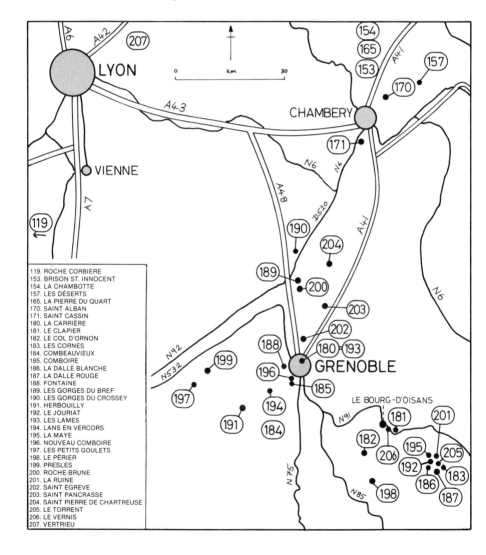

119. ROCHE CORBIERE
153. BRISON ST. INNOCENT
154. LA CHAMBOTTE
157. LES DÉSERTS
165. LA PIERRE DU QUART
170. SAINT ALBAN
171. SAINT CASSIN
180. LA CARRIÈRE
181. LE CLAPIER
182. LE COL D'ORNON
183. LES CORNES
184. COMBEAUVIEUX
185. COMBOIRE
186. LA DALLE BLANCHE
187. LA DALLE ROUGE
188. FONTAINE
189. LES GORGES DU BREF
190. LES GORGES DU CROSSEY
191. HERBOUILLY
192. LE JOURIAT
193. LES LAMES
194. LANS EN VERCORS
195. LA MAYE
196. NOUVEAU COMBOIRE
197. LES PETITS GOULETS
198. LE PÉRIER
199. PRESLES
200. ROCHE-BRUNE
201. LA RUINE
202. SAINT EGREVE
203. SAINT PANCRASSE
204. SAINT PIERRE DE CHARTREUSE
205. LE TORRENT
206. LE VERNIS
207. VERTRIEU

Dir: In Grenoble. At the N end of the centre of town cross over the Isère river (Pont de la Bastille) to the start of the A48 but go straight over towards St Martin. Turn R and go up the hill towards Chambéry (Les Lames on the R). After about 800m a path leads off on the R to the boulders. (131:E1)

Le Clapier:
✳ 11.00→18.00 (5 – 6c)(7)   ISÈRE [181]

A granite crag which reaches up to 110m but only the 1st pitches are equipped with bolts [3 – 4]. Good crag worth visiting for the middle grade climber.

Dir: 34km SE of Grenoble. Take the N91 to Le Bourg-d'Oisans, carry on towards Briançon for 6km to Le Clapier where the crag is obvious. 1 min. (132:B2)

Le Col d'Ornon:
✳ 06.00→12.00 (4 – 6c)(12)   ISÈRE [182]

A granite crag up to 100m with bolts [4 – 6] situated up at 1,300m and only a summer crag really. A bit ancient.

Dir: 24km SE of Grenoble. From town take the D5 then N91 towards Bourg-d'Oisans. 2km before the town at La Paute turn R on to the D526 towards the Col d'Ornon, signposted 'La Mure'. The crag is on the R about 1km before the col and reached in 10 mins. (132:A2)

Les Cornes:
✳ 12.00→21.00 (3 – 6a)(10)   ISÈRE [183]

A granite crag with 2 pitch climbs, *in situ* gear [4] but nuts are useful as well. Situated at 1,800m.

Dir: 52km SE of Grenoble. *See* Le Torrent. (132:C2)

Combeauvieux:
✳ 12.00→21.00 (4 – 7c)(20)   ISÈRE [184]

A mainly undeveloped limestone crag 30 – 60m high but situated at 1,800m and very much a summer crag. Bolts [3 – 4].

Dir: 24km SSW of Grenoble. Take the N532 out of town past Fontaine to the far edge of Sassenage. Here turn L on to the D531 up to Villard-de-Lans. Bypass the town and go straight on to Corrençon and up to Combeauvieux. The crag is obvious near some industrial buildings (132:D2)

Comboire:
✳ 07.00→16.00 (4 – 8a)(80)   ISÈRE [185]

A good limestone crag up to 60m high but with most of the routes being one pitch only and having a good lower-off point; 50m rope necessary. Bolts [3 – 4] with a lot of new replacements. The hard routes here are quite steep and big arms will come in useful.

Dir: 8km SE of Grenoble. Go to the S part of Grenoble then turn to the W off either the *autoroute* or the N85 to the village of Claix. On arriving at the village turn R on to the D106 towards Seyssans. After 1km there is an old fort on the R. Just before this there is a track down to the R to some parking. The crag is in two sections to the L. There is a third section – *see* Nouveau Comboire. (131:E1 – 2)

La Dalle Blanche:
✳ 09.00→14.30 (4 – 7a)(7)   ISÈRE [186]

A good granite crag with *in situ* gear [4]. Situated from 1,850m to 1900m.

Dir: 52km SE of Grenoble. Take the N91 to Le Bourg-d'Oisans, carry on towards Briançon for 6km to Le Clapier, then turn R on to the D530 which winds its way up to La Bérarde after a good 30km. From here ask locally. (132:C2)

La Dalle Rouge:
✳ 12.00→21.00
(4 – 7b)(10)   ISÈRE [187]

A granite crag situated at 1,850m, summer only, and offering very good climbs. Its name means 'Red Slab'. The climbs are up to 50m long and have *in situ* gear [4]. Ideal for a good summer's afternoon and in magnificent scenery.

Dir: 52km SE of Grenoble. Take the N91 to Le Bourg-d'Oisans, carry on towards Briançon for 6km to Le Clapier, then turn R on to the D530 which winds its way up to La Bérarde after a good 30km. From here take the footpath to the R which leads up to the Refuge du Carrelet. After a while go L into the Gorge due Landin and to the crag. 20 mins. (132:C3)

Fontaine:
✳ 06.00→09.30
(4.17.32.21.2)(76)   ISÈRE [188]

This crag is sometimes referred to as STADE DES VOUILLANTS. A sort of black limestone crag with most of the routes being 30−100m high. Bolts [3−4]. The climbing is very varied and good. Cracks, overhangs and fine walls. The view of the industrial estate somewhat tarnishes the stature of the crag. Good on a hot summer's day.

Dir: 5km W of Grenoble. From the town centre take the N532 towards Fontaine and Sassenage. The crag is very near the Fontaine Zone Industrielle to the L. (131:E1)

Les Gorges du Bref:
✳ 10.00→16.00
(5−7b)(17)   ISÈRE [189]

A new limestone crag 60m, which is in the throes of development with lots of new routes coming in the harder grades. Bolts [2] and situated at 700m. A topo guide by Jean-Marc Maljournal can be bought at Sport 2000 in Grenoble.

Dir: 20km NNW of Grenoble, 35km SW of Chambéry. From Grenoble take the A43 towards Lyon and then exit at the Voreppe turn-off. Go into the village then take the D520 towards St Laurent-du-Pont. Pass over the Col du Placette, and shortly after fork L to St Julien-de-Raz. Carry on this road into the Gorge where the crag overhangs the road. A footpath marked in blue leads to the routes. (117:E4)

Les Gorges du Crossey:
✳ 12.00→19.00 (3−7c)(60)   ISÈRE [190]

A 25m limestone crag with routes well spread across the grades and bolts [3−4]. A good place to bring beginners as well and now quite popular.

Dir: 30km SW of Chambéry, 6km ENE of Voiron. From Chambéry take the N6 to Les Echelles, bypass the town and follow the D520 to St Laurent-du-Pont. Stay on the D520 towards Voiron, after 6km enter the Gorge and in a couple of km the crag is on the R (before St Etienne) (117:E4)

Herbouilly:
✳ 12.00→22.00 (Easy)(25)   ISÈRE [191]

The best crag in the area to bring beginners or first-time climbers. Only 15m high but *in situ* bolts [3−4]. Situated at nearly 1,400m but quite bearable in the mid-season afternoons.

Dir: 27m SW of Grenoble. Take the N532 out of town past Fontaine to the far edge of Sassenage. Here turn L on to the D531 up to Villard-de-Lans. From the town take the route Col d'Herbouilly towards St Julien-en-Vercors. The crag is located about 500m to the S of the col. (131:D2)

Le Jouriat:
✳ 09.00→14.30 (4−6b)(6)   ISÈRE [192]

A granite crag up to 75m high and situated at 1,850m. *In situ* gear [4] and good for the lower grade climber.

Dir: 53km SE of Grenoble. Take the N91 to Le Bourg-d'Oisans, carry on towards Briançon for 6km to Le Clapier, then turn R on to the D530 which winds its way up to La Bérarde after a good 30km. From there take the footpath on the R side of the river Vénéon towards the Glacier du Chardon. The crag is reached in 20 mins. (132:C3)

Les Lames:
✳ 10.00→20.00
(6a−8b)(40)   ISÈRE [193]

A very good limestone crag indeed with excellent hard single pitch routes up to 40m long. Bolts [3−4]. Situated at 300m high. The crag has been developed quite recently, especially the overhanging sections which require gymnastic tendencies. There are, however, a good many routes in the 6b−c standard.

Dir: In Grenoble. At the N end of the centre of town cross over the Isère river (Pont de la Bastille) to the start of the A48 but go straight over towards St Martin. Turn R then after a few hundred metres a footpath leads off top the R and the crag below the Bastille. (131:E1)

Lans en Vercors:
✳ 10.00→22.00
(3 – 8b)(70) ISÈRE [194]

A 50m limestone crag which has been very popular with the local climbers for many years. Recently there have been quite a few new hard routes added bringing the crag up to date. A lot of the routes are in the 5 – 6b category. A cold wind blows here in the mid season. Situated at 1,200m, the crag offers good summer climbing with the possibility of climbing in or out of the sun as it faces many ways. Although some of the cracks need nuts there has been quite a lot of equipping, bolts [3 – 4]. Local topo guides can be purchased from the tourist office at Lans.

Dir: 11km SW of Grenoble. Take the N532 out of town past Fontaine to the far edge of Sassenage. Here turn L on to the D531 up towards Villard-de-Lans. After about 16km turn L to Lans-en-Vercors. Go through the village and after a short while the road bends round to the L back towards Grenoble. Take the small road to the R, signposted 'Stade Neige'. After 50m turn L into a parking spot. From here a path leads to the crag in 5 mins. (131:E2)

La Maye:
✳ 10.00→16.00 (3 – 7a)(36) ISÈRE [195]

There are two granite crags here, LA MAYE and SUPER MAYE. The climbs are the quickest to reach when based at La Béréard. Up to 40m high and situated from 1,800 – 1,900m. *In situ* gear [3 – 4] and perfect crags.

Dir: 53km SE of Grenoble. Take the N91 to Le Bourg-d'Oisans, carry on towards Briançon for 6km to Le Clapier, then turn R on to the D530 which winds its way up to La Bérarde after a good 30km. A footpath leads to the crag from the campsite to the crag in 10 mins. (132:C2)

Nouveau Comboire:
✳ 06.00→12.00
(4.8.16.21.2)(51) ISÈRE [196]

The newly developed part of Comboire with hard routes and new bolts [3]. Steep climbing with modern style.

Dir: *See* Comboire.

Les Petits Goulets:
✳ 12.00→20.00 (5 – 6b)(6) ISÈRE [197]

A small limestone crag with a handful of routes in the lower grades but still pleasant. Bolts [4] and situated at around 300m high.

Dir: 38km ENE of Valence, 34km SE of Grenoble. From Valence take the N532 to Romans, N532 to 2km past St Nazaire then turn R to Pont-en-Royans. From here take the road towards La Chapelle-en-Vercors. Pass through the village of Eulalie and carry on for half a km and the crag is before the first of three road tunnels and is obvious. (131:D2)

Le Périer:
✳ 07.00→14.30
(6a – 8b)(20) ISÈRE [198]

A newly developed limestone crag of single pitch routes situated at 1,200m. The crag is sometimes referred to as COL D'ORNON SUD. There are relatively new bolts [2 – 3]. The climbing is good, hard and modern in style. The crag is also very near the road and close to the pleasant village.

Dir: 34km SE of Grenoble. From town take the D5 then N91 towards Bourg-d'Oisans. 2km before the town at La Paute turn R on to the D526 towards the Col d'Ornon, signposted 'La Mure'. Go over the col and on to the village of Le Périer. (132:A2)

Presles:
✳ 10.00→16.00
(5 – 8b +)(150) ISÈRE [199]

One of the great old-fashioned crags of France. There are a few bolts [3 – 6] and I suggest that you bring a rack of gear with you if you are climbing below 7a. A large limestone crag nevertheless. Situated at 1,000m and reaching up to 1,300m. It can be climbed on in winter but I personally can recommend summer and autumn only. Single pitch routes at the bottom are growing.

Dir: 42km ENE from Valence, 30km SE of Grenoble. From Valence take the N532 to Romans, N532 to 2km past St Nazaire then turn R to Pont-en-Royans. From here take the D531 towards the Gorges de la Bourne (1).

After 1.5km turn L up on to the D292 to Presles and at a bend before the town is a fine viewpoint. Park here. (2) Carry on towards Presles but turn R on to the small road towards Rencurel. After 3.5km turn R to the hamlet of Le Charmeil. There is a path to the crag. (131:D2)

Roche-Brune:
✳ 11.00→18.00
(5 – 7b)(20)   ISÈRE [200]

A limestone crag up to 60m high with some good routes in the 6a – 6b category. Bolts [3] but not all the routes are equipped yet so bring some nuts along as well. A local topo guide to the crag can be obtained from the restaurant La Paillote.

Dir: 18km NNW of Grenoble, 35km SW of Chambéry. From Grenoble take the A43 towards Lyon and then exit at the Voreppe turn-off. Go into the village then take the D520 towards St Laurent-du-Pont. After about 5km you arrive at Placette, turn L and take the small road up to Le Grand Raz. Park here and take a footpath to the crag. 30 mins. (117:E4)

La Ruine:
✳ 12.00→20.00 (3 – 5)(6)   ISÈRE [201]

A granite crag which is ideal for introducing beginners into rock climbing from straightforward mountain walking. Up to nearly 100m high with *in situ* gear [4]. Worth a visit.

Dir: 53km SE of Grenoble. Take the N91 to Le Bourg-d'Oisans, carry on towards Briançon for 6km to Le Clapier, then turn R on to the D530 which winds its way up to La Bérarde after a good 30km. From here take the footpath on the L side of the river Vénéon which leads up to the Refuge du Carrelet. The crag is reached in 20 mins. (132:C3)

Saint Egreve:
✳ 10.00→17.00
(4 – 8a)(104)   ISÈRE [202]

A limestone crag which is one of the most important in the area. There is a stack of excellent two pitch routes in the 6 and 7 grades. The crag is up to 90m high but there is ample opportunity to do single pitch routes. Situated at 200m with a lot of new bolts [3 – 4].

A lot of big flat wall climbing with the angle corresponding to the grade.

Dir: 8km NNW of Grenoble. Leave the town and go towards St Egrève on the A48 or N75. Turn off to the R and go up towards St Egrève and the crag is obvious. A path leads up to the crag in 5 mins. (131:E1)

Saint Pancrasse:
✳ 10.00→16.00 (5 – 7c)(60)   ISÈRE [203]

A limestone cliff in two sections with a lot of routes in the 7a – 7c grades. Situated at 1,000m with all climbs being up to 25m high. Bolts [4]. The climbing is quite technical with good footwork paying dividends, and the rock more similar to that of the south than the mountain districts. A lovely setting. Very popular in the summer evenings, at other times very quiet.

Dir: 16km NE of Grenoble. From the town take the N90 towards Chambéry. After 10km pass through St Nazaire and carry on for 1km. Then turn L on to the D30 which winds its way up to St Pancrasse in about 6km. At the end of the village just past a *tabac* there is a track leading off to the R. This leads to the crag in 15 mins. (131:F1)

Saint Pierre de Chartreuse:
✳ 10.00→16.00
(3 – 6b)(35)   ISÈRE [204]

A small limestone crag which in the main has routes in the lower grades with bolts [2 – 3] and ideal rock to teach beginners on. Situated at 1,200m.

Dir: 25km SSW of Chambéry, 2km NE of St. Pierre de Chartreuse. From Chambéry take the N6 and D520 S to St Laurent-du-Pont. From here take the D520b through the Gorges du Guiers Mort to St Pierre. Then take the D512 up the Col du Cucheron but just after 1km turn R on to a track which winds its way up by the ski lift. After several bends a footpath leads off to a viewpoint and the crag. (117:F4)

Le Torrent:
✳ 07.00→13.30
(4 – 6b)(15)   ISÈRE [205]

A small granite crag situated very high at 1,800m and a summer crag only. *In situ* gear

[4]. A pleasant setting. Also nearby is a crag called LES CORNES. A topo may be available at Bérarde.

Dir: 52km SE of Grenoble. Take the N91 to Le Bourg-d'Oisans, carry on towards Briançon for 6km to Le Clapier, then turn R on to the D530 which winds its way up to La Bérarde after a good 30km. From here take the footpath to the L which leads up to the Refuge du Châtelleret. After about 5 mins the crag is seen beside the river on the L. The crag of Les Cornes is nearby to the R. (132:C2)

Le Vernis:
✲ 11.00→19.00 (3–7c)(60) ISÈRE [206]

A volcanic gneiss crag up to 40m high with routes in all grades. Bolts [2–6] with bolts [2] being popular for abseil points. Situated at 750m.

Dir: 31km SE of Grenoble. Take the N91 to Le Bourg-d'Oisans, carry on towards Briançon for a couple of km where the crag is obvious. 1 min. (132:B2)

Vertrieu:
✲ Not a lot (4–6b)(40) ISÈRE [207]

Quite a small, low-level crag of limestone. Bolts [2–4] and a good crag for the beginner. There is a topo for the crag which can be bought in Lyon at the Spélémat.

Dir: 42m ENE of Lyon, 14km ESE of Pérouges. From Lyon take the N84 via Pérouges towards Ambérieu-en-Bugey. Before the town turn R on to the N75 to Lagnieu, carry on towards Montalieu on the N75, pass over the Rhône river, turn L and the crag is obvious. (116:C1)

SOUTH-WEST FRANCE

Aveyron – 12

Canyon de la Jonte:
(5–7)(30) AVEYRON [208]

Some small limestone crags with lots of possibilities and slowly being bolted [2–3] up by the CAF at Millau. Referred to also as CIRQUE DE MADASSE.

Dir: 56km ESE of Rodez, 16km NE of Millau. From Millau take the N9 to Aguessac, then the D907 to Le Rozier. From here the D996 leads into the Gorge. There is climbing on the peak to the SE, CORNICHE DU CAUSSE NOIR, reached by a footpath from a hairpin bend S of the town. (141:EF3)

Hérault – 34

Saint Bauzille:
(2.12.33.6.0)(53) HERAULT [209]

Quite a trendy crag over the past five years, with many routes being added and bolted [2–3].

Dir: 19km NNE of Montpellier. From the Castelneau part of town take the small road D21 off the D65 ring road. Follow this through Teyran and on up to Saint Bauzille. The crag is close by. (156:C2)

Pyrénées-Atlantiques – 64

Arudy:
✲ 06.00→22.00 (3–7a)(150) PYRÉNÉES-ATL [210]

A limestone crag with quite a few different sections which include SESTO, REFUGE, GSIP, DÉFILÉ and PAROI DU TRERON. The cliffs range from 10m up to 60m. Routes are fully bolted [2–3] up and the area is well worth a visit.

Dir: 23km SSW of Pau, 2km W of Arudy. Take the Fonderie Messier (smelting works) road opposite the station in Arudy. After a couple of km turn R to the Anglas farm where there is a small amount of parking available. Take the Bordella path to the crag. (168:A2)

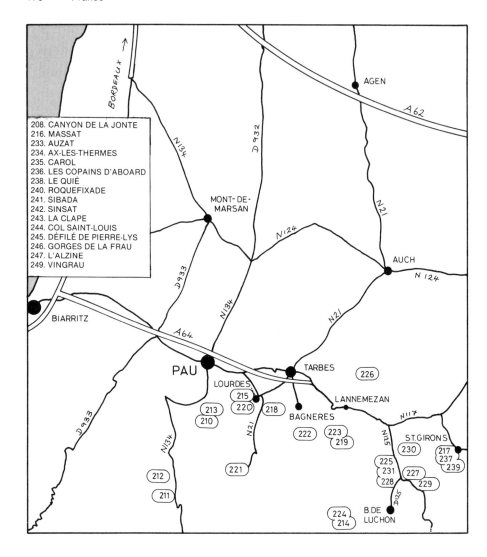

208. CANYON DE LA JONTE
216. MASSAT
233. AUZAT
234. AX-LES-THERMES
235. CAROL
236. LES COPAINS D'ABOARD
238. LE QUIÉ
240. ROQUEFIXADE
241. SIBADA
242. SINSAT
243. LA CLAPE
244. COL SAINT-LOUIS
245. DÉFILÉ DE PIERRE-LYS
246. GORGES DE LA FRAU
247. L'ALZINE
249. VINGRAU

La Mature:
✳ 10.00→16.00
(3 – 7b)(70)   PYRÉNÉES-ATL [211]

A large limestone crag reaching up to 300m high and situated at 1,000m. It is possible to do only the first pitch of many of the routes which are usually 4 pitches. Some of the routes are bolted [3 – 6] and others are not (the easier routes). Bring gear. Good rock and a lot of crack routes.

Dir: 34km S of Oloron-Sainte-Marie, 47km SSW of Pau. From Oloron take the N134 S through Bedous on and past Cette-Eygun (a topo to the crag, *La Goutte d'eau*, can be purchased here), and then to Estaut. Carry on for another 2km then take a road on the R signposted to La Mature. After a short while there is space to park and the crag can be reached in about 15 mins. (167:F4)

Les Orgues de Camplong:
(15) PYRÉNÉES-ATL [212]

Some limestone climbing, 80m high and near the road.

Dir: 28km S of Oloron-Sainte-Marie, 52km SSW of Pau. From Oloron take the N134 S through Bedous then just after L'Estanguet take the road up towards Lescun and the crag is just above the road. (167:F4)

La Pierre-St-Martin:
(20) PYRÉNÉES ATL [213]

Not a lot has been found on this crag but it does sound worth investigating especially if you've come all the way to the particular area. 50m limestone slab routes which tend to be quite smooth.

Dir: Known as 'Dalles de la Pierre-St-Martin.' I suggest you enquire locally at Arudy.

Hautes-Pyrénées – 65

Artiguelongue:
✳ 10.00→20.00 (Bouldering)
(20) HTES-PYRÉNÉES [214]

An average old-fashioned granite crag with routes up to 20m high and situated at 1,100m. Good climbing nevertheless with bolts *in situ*. The area is very beautiful and worth going to for a picnic even if granite is not really your scene. *Bonnes vacances.*

Dir: 60km SSE of Tarbes, 16km SSE of Arreau. From Arreau take the D618 through Bordères-Louron then after 3km turn R on to the D25 to Loudenville. From there take the road up the valley De Louron towards Tramezaygues. At the plateau of Artiguelonge go over the bridge on the R to some good bouldering or carry straight on to the crag. (169:D4)

Col d'Hech:
✳ 13.00→22.00 (1.0.20.10.0)(31)
HAUTES-PYRÉNÉES [215]

A 30m limestone crag offering good, well-protected hard routes in the lower grade 7s. Mostly steep walls. Situated at 750m.

Dir: 4km SW of Lourdes. Leave the town on the D937 towards Pau and Lestelle-Bétharram. After 2km take the road on the R which winds its way up to Omex. Once in the village take the road on the R then 2nd on the L for 200m to a parking spot. A footpath leads to the col. 15 mins. (168:B2)

Massat:
(0.6.7.5.0)(18)
HAUTES-PYRÉNÉES [216]

A very new and recently developed crag. A lot of cleaning has gone on to produce some very good routes around grade 6. There has been access agreed with the locals on the understanding that the crag is kept clean and tidy and no damage is caused to the surrounding area.

Dir: 24km WSW of Foix, 20km SSE of St Girons. Leave St Girons on the D618 and go to Massat. The exact details of the crag are not known but it is only a few minutes from town, which is small anyway. (170:C3)

Montégut:
(20.20.23.3.0)(66)
HAUTES-PYRÉNÉES [217]

Sometimes referred to as MONTAIGUT. A small limestone crag with a lot of bouldering. Problems can be extended to give the above routes. There are often *in situ* pegs at the top [4]. Recently there have been grade 7 routes added.

Dir: 3km W of Saint-Girons, 42km W of Foix. From St Girons take the D618 towards Moulis. Just after leaving town take the D104 off to the R leading to Montégut and the crag is obvious. (170:B3)

Pic du Jer:
✳ 10.00→18.00 (5−7b)(30)
HAUTES-PYRÉNÉES [218]

An excellent limestone crag close to Lourdes at 600m. The routes are 20m and on slabby walls with no shortage of good strong bolts.

Dir: 2km SSE of Lourdes. The N21 to Arglès-Gazost leaves at the far S end of town. Here there is a funicular railway up to the top of Pic du Jer. A footpath leads off to the R from the car park here to the crag. 15 mins. (168:B2)

Pène-Haute:
✳ 10.00→16.00 (4.10.44.41.10)(109)
HAUTES-PYRÉNÉES [219]

One of the great newly developed limestone crags in the Pyrénées. The crag varies in height up to just over 100m and offers all types of fantastic well-equipped climbing. There are some 8b pitches here on which to get exhausted. The French climbing press have quoted it as being a very good crag for SEXtogradistes! Definitely worth a trip. Situated at 1,500m. Topos can be bought locally at Chez Momon bar hotel. There is also a sports shop nearby at Arreau, selling equipment.

Dir: 38km SE of Tarbes, 15km S of Lannemezan. From La-Barthe-de-Neste just to the S of Lannemezan take the D929 S up the Neste valley, pass Hèches on to the village of Sarrancolin. Turn L and cross over the river then take the small road up to the Col d'Estivère. A path leads off to the L and the crag in about 15 mins. There is no water anywhere near here so bring some bottled, but please respect the crag and its site by not leaving any litter. (169:D3)

Pibeste:
(0.0.3.6.1)(10)
HAUTES-PYRÉNÉES [220]

A limestone crag with single pitch routes and popular with the hard climbers in the area. New bolts [3].

Dir: 6km SE of Lourdes. On the slopes of Pic du Pibeste. Seek local advice on exact crag location. (168:B2)

Pont d'Espagne:
✳ 06.00→22.00 (4−7c)(80)
HAUTES-PYRÉNÉES [221]

A granite crag offering climbs 10−40m high and situated at 1,500m, not a winter crag. Good slabby wall climbing with cracks and well equipped. There are several areas: BLOCS;

FALAISE DU CLOT; ROCHER DU BAM; ROCHER BLANC.

Dir: 28km SSW of Lourdes. Take the N21 to Argelès-Gazost, then D921 and D920 to Cauterets, and carry on then to Pont d'Espagne. The area Blocs is next to the parking. Falaise du Clot is just lower down than the military camp (3−7a). Rocher du Bam can be seen from the Chalet du Clot. By carrying on into the forest you reach Rocher Blanc, with about 40 routes up to 7c. (168:B3)

Sainte-Marie-de-Campan:
✳ 12.00→19.00 (4.2.22.20.0)(48)
HAUTES-PYRÉNÉES [222]

A very good mountain limestone crag situated at only 850m. Up to 50m routes but the hard ones are single pitch only. Rock is very good and so are the bolts − yeah. Wall climbing predominates, either side of the vertical. A topo for the crag can be bought locally at the bar Chez Hourcade in Campan; camping just along from Ste-Marie-de-Campan (6km from Campan).

Dir: 31km SSE of Tarbes, 10km NW of Col d'Aspin. Go S from Tarbes to Bagnères-de-Bigorre on the D935, carry on S through Campan, Arrimoula and then just before Ste-Marie turn L by a church. The crag is quite obvious. (169:D3)

Suberpène:
✳ 10.00→16.00 (14.4.12.9.2)(43)
HAUTES-PYRÉNÉES [223]

Another great limestone crag in the region. The crag varies in height from 80 to just over 100m high with routes going up to 3 pitches. There is very good *in situ* gear, mainly new bolts. Typical types of steep wall climbing in water pockets and on the easier routes cracks. The crag is situated at 650m and can offer sport in winter if it is nice and sunny.

Dir: 34km SE of Tarbes, 12km S of Lannemezan. From La Barthe just S of Lannemezan take the D929 S to Hèches. After leaving the town take a track on the R by a quarry then before going under a bridge turn L. Follow this for about 2km and the crag. (169:D3)

Tramezaigues:
(4 – 6b)(10)
HAUTES-PYRÉNÉES [224]

Some small 25m crags which have been recently developed with bolts and moulinette chains.

Dir: 60km SSE of Tarbes, 16km SSE of Arreau. From Arreau take the D618 through Bordères-Louron then after 3km turn R on to the D25 to Loudenville. From there take the road up the valley De Louron towards Tramezaigues. At the plateau of Artiguelonge go over the bridge and up a track past the crag of Artiguelonge. 500m then on the L are some buttresses with the routes on. (169:D4)

Troubat:
✳ 12.00→22.00 (6.6.11.28.8)(59)
HAUTES-PYRÉNÉES [225]

A very good limestone crag with some cracking routes. A lot of the routes here are of very high standard and the crag has been used quite a lot for outdoor competitions. About 60m high with two pitch climbs, big golden walls which tower over the scenery below mountain-type limestone with a rugged appearance and small face holds. Situated at 700m. On summer afternoons it gets quite hot, but also stays dry in the rain. Great for the hard climber. There is now a very hard route here, Répétition de Silence (8b – c).

Dir: 50km SE of Tarbes, 13km S of Montréjeau. Take the N117 E to Montréjeau, then the N125 in a S direction towards St Béat. After 4km pass around the town of Labroquère and over the river and 0.5km later turn R on to the D925 towards Mauléon-Barousse (climbing equipment). In about 7km and 2km before M-B enter the village of Troubat where the crag is signposted. (169:E3)

Haute-Garonne – 31

Montmaurin:
✳ 10.00→19.00
(3 – 5,100)(6 – 7,100)(200)
GARONNE-HTE [226]

This is a pocketed 20m limestone crag set in the Gorge de la Save. The *in situ* gear is a mixture of bolts and cemented pegs but in most cases is good enough. You can buy a topo to the gorge in the Snack Bar des Gorges, which is about 250m from the crag. Worth a visit.

Dir: 47km E of Tarbes, 26km NE of Lannemezan, 6km S of Boulogne-s-Gesse. From Boulogne take the D633 in a S direction to Blajan, carry straight on and to the village of Montmaurin. Carry on to the gorge and after the bridge there is a footpath on the R which leads to the crag beside the river. (169:E1)

Pic du Gard:
✳ 10.00→16.00
(0.0.0.2.0)(2) GARONNE-HTE [227]

A large limestone crag up to 300m high with a couple of quite hard climbs of which the first pitches are 7c. All of the route is not fully geared up so bring nuts. Virtually all of the 6 pitches are at least 7a. 50m abseil so I recommend that you climb with two ropes.

Dir: 60km ESE of Tarbes, 18km S of St Gaudens. From Montréjeau take the N125 S towards St Béat but just before the town turn L on to the D44f to Bezins-Garraux. Park by a small church. Here a path leads to the crag in 1½ hours; ugh! (169:F3)

Rousiet:
✳ 10.00→16.00
(6.3.13.6.1)(29) GARONNE-HTE [228]

An excellent crag with good routes at any grade. Wall climbing with good bolts up to 25m high. Situated at 500m and hot in summer. Watch out for snakes! For local info enquire at the *boulangerie*.

Dir: 59km SE of Tarbes, 14km NNE of Bagnères-de-Luchon. From Montréjeau take the N125 S towards B. de Luchon. After about 20km the road turns L to St Béat. Carry straight on (D125) and the crag is on the R just before the village of Cierp-Gaud. (169:E3)

Saint Béat:
(2.1.9.2.0)(14)   GARONNE-HTE
[229]

A newly developed limestone crag with bolts [3].

Dir: 18km NE of Bagnères-de-Luchon, 24km SSE of Montréjeau. From Montréjeau take the N125 to St Béat. Then take the D44 up towards the ski station of Bout-le-Mourtis. The crag is about 100m before the cross. (167:F3)

Sainte-Pé-d'Ardet:
✳ 10.00→16.00
(0.12.32.6.0)(50)   GARONNE-HTE
[230]

A limestone crag which has single pitch climbs near the side of the road. Good rock and a handy crag to know about. There is also lots of development here. Bolts [1 – 3].

Dir: 56km ESE of Tarbes, 14km SSE of Montréjeau, 14km SSW of St Gaudens. From Montréjeau take the N125 S towards St Béat, after 5km take the D33 in the same direction but on the W side of the river. After 9km at the town of Ore turn L and take the small road towards the Col Bouchet. Pass through the village of Ste-Pé-d'Ardet. The crags are situated near the lake to the L and R. (169:F3)

Thèbes:
✳ 10.00→16.00
(0.0.12.4.0)(6 + 10)   GARONNE-HTE [231]

An excellent small limestone group of two crags situated at 700m. The first is a 10m slabby wall with some grade 6 routes on and the second section as a 25m steep wall with some harder routes on up to 7b. Good bolts.

Dir: 51km SE of Tarbes, 14km S of Montréjeau. From Montréjeau take the N125 in an S direction towards St Béat. After 4km pass around the town of Labroquère and over the river and 0.5km later turn R on to the D925 towards Mauléon-Barousse (climbing equipment). In about 7km enter the village of Troubat, carry straight on (D22) for 2km to Thèbes and the crag. A footpath leads to the first section and then on to the second in about 10 mins. (169:E3)

Ariège – 09

Arabeau:
✳ 10.00→19.00
(Bouldering)   ARIÈGE [232]

No details available.

Auzat:
✳ 17.00→22.00
(5.6.23.4.0)(38)   ARIÈGE [233]

A 30m granite crag offering well-bolted routes up to 30m high and situated at 800m. In the main, friction slabs and in the shade for the hottest part of hot summer days.

Dir: 28km SSW of Foix. Take the N20 S to Tarascon-s-Ariège, then turn R on to the D8 to Auzat. From the village take the D108 towards Mounicou. This passes the foot of the crag. (170:C4)

Ax-les-Thermes:
(4 – 7a, 15)(3 – 6c, 12)   ARIÈGE [234]

There are two separate limestone crags here: ROCHER DE LA PISCINE and ROCHER DU CHRIST. Both are well equipped and offer good slabby wall climbs.

Dir: 32km SSE of Foix at Ax-les-Thermes. Enquire locally for exact details. (171:E4)

Carol:
✳ 10.00→16.00
(1.1.10.13.0)(25)   ARIÈGE [235]

A good limestone crag 10 – 25m high and situated at 800m. The crag is not that high and is shaded well by trees in the hot summer months. All bolted [2 – 3].

Dir: 12km E of Foix. From just N of the centre of Foix on the E side of the river take the D1 towards Roquefort-les-Cascades. After about 17km enter the village of Carol and take the

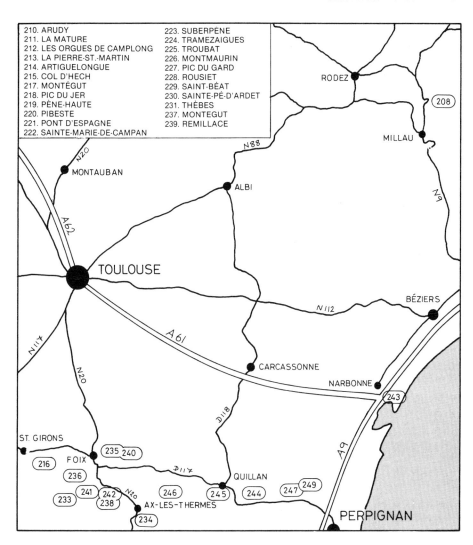

210. ARUDY	223. SUBERPÈNE
211. LA MATURE	224. TRAMEZAIGUES
212. LES ORGUES DE CAMPLONG	225. TROUBAT
213. LA PIERRE-ST.-MARTIN	226. MONTMAURIN
214. ARTIGUELONGUE	227. PIC DU GARD
215. COL D'HECH	228. ROUSIET
217. MONTÉGUT	229. SAINT-BÉAT
218. PIC DU JER	230. SAINTE-PÉ-D'ARDET
219. PÈNE-HAUTE	231. THÈBES
220. PIBESTE	237. MONTEGUT
221. PONT D'ESPAGNE	239. REMILLACE
222. SAINTE-MARIE-DE-CAMPAN	

road Ball-Trap to a relais de télévision. Here a path leads to the crag in about 5 mins. (171:D3)

Les Copains d'Abord:
(3 – 7b)(15) ARIÈGE [236]

A crag which has undergone some recent development and bolting [1 – 3].

Dir: 13km SSW of Foix. Take the N20 to Tarascon-sur-Ariège. Take the D618 towards the Col de Port (Massat). After about 5km enter

the village of Bedeilhac. Park near the church and take a footpath up towards the cliff of Château Calames after 15 mins. (171:D3)

Montégut:
✳ 05.00→10.00 (Bouldering +4) ARIÈGE [237]

A small, well-equipped crag offering some good bouldering and a couple of routes up to 25m. Situated at 500m and good on hot summer afternoons.

Dir: 43km W of Foix. Leave St Girons on the D618 towards Castillon but after 1km turn R on to the D104 which leads to Montégut-en-Couserans. A small footpath leads from the village to the crag. (170:B3)

Le Quié:
✳ 10.00→16.00 (4c−8a, 20)(6a−7c, 20) ARIÈGE [238]

An exceptional limestone crag with clean sweeping walls covered in Verdon-type pockets. There are two crags here: FALAISE ECOLE, which has multi pitch routes up to 400m, and ROCHER ECOLE, a 30m crag with many sectors and 20 routes in the 6a−7c category. There is a climbing ban here 1 Feb till 30 June because of a bird restriction, but this does not cover the smaller crag. Situated at 1,000m.

Dir: 19km SSE of Foix. Take the N20 S to Tarascon, carry on for 8km to Sinsat. Turn L just after the telephone booth and bear L over the bridge. A large sign indicates the way to the crag which is 45 mins' walk away. (Sinsat crag is only 10 mins from here!) (171:D4)

Remillace:
(0.4.9.0.0)(13) ARIÈGE [239]

A very new crag which is in the process of being developed. Bolts [3]. All are single pitch routes.

Dir: 6km SW of St Girons, 42km W of Foix. Take the D619 from St Girons towards Castillon for 5km to Moulis then turn L on to the D137 towards Alos. Follow this to the hamlet of Remillace and park after the bridge, being careful not to block the road. About 100m further on take the footpath on the L. This leads to a hill where there is a small crag on the R. Take the footpath on the R which leads to the crag in about 15 mins. (170:B3)

Roquefixade:
✳ 10.00→22.00
(20.20.10.8.0)(48) ARIÈGE [240]

This limestone crag has two faces which rise up to 80m in parts and in the main are not that steep, offering good climbing in the lower and upper grades. All the routes have very recently been re-bolted. Situated at 800m. Wall and large crack routes.

Dir: 13km ESE of Foix. From Lavelanet take the D117 towards Foix and after about 5km turn R on to the D9 which leads to Roquefixade in 6km. Park in the village; to the L is the Secteur du Château and to the R is the Secteur du Col. (171:D3)

Sibada:
(0.1.4.10.0)(15) ARIÈGE [241]

A newly developed limestone crag with routes up to 25m and moulinettes at the top. A lot of routes at 7a as well as a few desperates. *In situ* gear [1−3]. Worth a visit.

Dir: 17km S of Foix. Take the N20 S to Tarascon-sur-Ariège. From here carry on through Quie then turn R to Niaux. At the village turn L then R towards Miglos. After 1km park near the 1st hairpin bend. The crag is up to the L and reached in 10 mins. (171:D4)

Sinsat:
✳ 10.00→18.00
(10.10.33.15.0)(68) ARIÈGE [242]

A well-bolted and developed crag and very popular. There have been access problems in the past and it is requested that climbers behave in a respectable way to ensure further use of the crag. Limestone up to 50m and situated at 600m which makes it a good winter crag. A topo of the crag can be bought from the bar in Sinsat.

Dir: 19km SSE of Foix. Take the N20 S to Tarascon, carry on for 8km to Sinsat, then turn L just after the telephone booth. Bear L over the new bridge. The crag is 10 mins' walk away. (171:D4)

Aude – 11

La Clape:
✳ 10.00→16.00 (3 – 7c)(23)   AUDE [243]

A small crag not far from the sea with pleasant routes bolted [2 – 4].

Dir: 9km SE of Narbonne. Leave the town going E to the sea, under the *autoroute*, at the end of the dual carriageway turn R towards Gruissan. After 6km turn L on to the small road up to Le Rec d'Argent and then to Notre-Dames-des-Auzils. The crag is nearby, 5 mins. (173:D2)

Col Saint-Louis:
✳ 11.00→18.00 (12.18.33.15.2)(80)   AUDE [244]

One of the best crags in the area. Limestone walls with some good overhanging sections and from 15 – 40m high, situated at 800m. There is camping locally at Cauiès-de-Fenouillèdes with special *grimpeur* rates.

Dir: 42km S of Carcassonne, 14km ESE of Quillan. From Quillan take the D117 S towards St Paul-en-Fenouille. After about 30km turn L on to the D9 at the town of Caudiès. Follow this for 4km towards the Col St Louis to the Pont Escargot (snail bridge). The crag is here. (172:A4)

Défilé de Pierre-Lys:
✳ 07.00→20.00 (3.4.11.4.0)(22)   AUDE [245]

An excellent limestone crag up to 100m high and situated at 450m. A couple of the routes are two pitch 7cs and worth a fling. Bolted [2 – 3] walls and cracks. Apparently the crag can be reached by Tyrolean traverse!

Dir: 43km S of Carcassonne, 50km ESE of Foix, 4km S of Quillan. From Quillan take the D117 S in the direction of Axat. After about 6km and just after Trou du Curé there are a couple of parking spots on the R. (172:A4)

Gorges de la Frau:
✳ 08.00→15.00 (6c, 7a or A1)(1)   AUDE [246]

Only one reported climb here so far. A 200m limestone crag situated at 700m with a seven pitch route. The route is mostly crack climbing, grade 5 – 6a with aid on intermittent pitches. The second pitch is the hardest at 7a. All *in situ* gear [2 – 4].

Dir: 26km SE of Foix. From Lavalenet take the D117 E to Bélesta, at the S end of town take the R fork to Fougax-et-Berrineuf (D5). Turn L near the cemetery towards L'Espine and after 1.5km fork R and go to the end of the valley. Walk to the crag in 10 mins. (171:E4)

Pyrénées-Orientales – 66

L'Alzine:
✳ 06.00→12.00 (0.2.10.4.4)(20)   PYRÉNÉES-OR [247]

A good limestone crag 25 – 40m with walls and good overhangs. Well bolted up and situated very low down at 250m. Good on winter mornings and summer afternoons.

Dir: 20km NW of Perpignan, 6km NNE of Estagel. Take the D117 towards Quillan, after 15km reach Estagel, carry on the D117 in the direction of Maury, after 2km take the D611 then the D9 to Tautavel. From the village take the small road going NW to Col des Alzine and go to the Auberge des Alzine. Take the track which leads down towards the Verdouble river.

The crag can then be seen on the L, 15 mins. Please do not march straight across the vineyards. (172:C4)

Chaos de Targasonne:
✳ 06.00→22.00 (Big bouldering)   PYRÉNÉES-OR [248]

A great collection of at least 150 granite boulders with problems and routes of all standards. Some of the boulders are very large and to finish a climb safely bring a rope. Situated at 1,580m.

Dir: 6km WSW of Font-Romeu. From F-R take the D618 towards Ur and Spain. After about 5km pass through the village of Targassone and the boulders are about 2.5km further on at the side of the road as it starts to wind its way up the pass. (174:C4)

Vingrau:
✶ 11.00→19.00 (4−6, 130)(7−8a, 20)   PYRÉNÉES-OR [249]

A very popular crag which has been steadily developed over the past few years with many more hard routes being added. 20−80m high, limestone which offers climbs of all standards especially in the grade 6 category, slabs and walls. A topo for the crag can be bought in the La Hutte shop at Perpignan. There is camping just to the SW at Tautavel.

Dir: 18km NNW of Perpignan. From Rivesaltes just to the N of Perpignan leave the *autoroute* and take the D12 signposted to Vingrau and Tuchan. About 3km before the town of Vingrau the crags can be seen on the R. You are requested to park at the obvious spot on the bend, so as not to obstruct traffic, and follow the footpaths to the crag, trying to preserve the vegetation. (172:C4)

SOUTH-EAST FRANCE

Haute-Loire − 43

Chamalières:
(2.8.21.2.0)(35)   HTE-LOIRE [250]

A granite crag up to 80m high which has undergone recent development as well as having old established routes. Most of the routes are now fully bolted [2−6]. There are two areas: ROCHER DE COSTAROS and LA PETITE CORBIÈRE, with the former being much larger.

Dir: 18km NNE of Le Puy. From the town take the D103 alongside the Loire river towards Retournac. After about 26km reach the village of Chamalières. Just entering the village turn R on to the D35 towards Blanlhac but after 2km turn L to La Fayolle and the crags are close by. (128:C1)

Lozère − 48

Cévennes:
✶ 07.00→21.00
(Bouldering)   LOZÈRE [251]

There is some very good and quite extensive bouldering here. There are several areas of granite boulders up to 6m high and set at 1,250m, really a summer crag only as they are very exposed. Also nearby there are some small crags of the same rock but I don't know if they have been bolted up. Worth a visit if passing.

Dir: 38km NW of Alès, 15.5km ENE of Florac. From Florac take the N106 N for half a km then turn R on to the D998 to Le Pont-de-Montvert. Then take the D20 towards Finiels. After 4km turn R to Champlong-de-Lozère, then 1km later Montgros. The boulders are over to the L and the road goes straight on to the cliffs in 2km.

Drôme − 26

This area, situated in the Vercors, offers limestone climbing with the exception of the rocks just north of Tournon. It is not an area for the super climber, but very beautiful for the bumblie and super bumblie going well in grade 6. It is often worth organising your camping in the summer as illegal camping here is not approved of. The main club for the area where information can be found is Escalade Club Drômois, No 114, Le Balzac, rue Ninon-Vallin, 26100 Romans (tel: 75 70 51 48). The area has been well equipped with new bolts and if you get fed up with the rain in the Alps it can be reached very easily via the motorway to Grenoble. This is a very pleasant part of France.

Les Aiguilles – Saou:
✲ 08.00→20.00
(5.9.17.2.0)(33)   DRÔME [252]

Some very good sculptured limestone cliffs up to 100m high. Most of the routes have bolts [3 – 5]. There are two sections to the crag situated at 700m and one can either find or keep out of the sun at will. Topos in Saou.

Dir: 10km SE of Crest, 34km SSE of Valence. From Crest take the D538 S to Saou, then take the D136 towards Aouste-sur-Sye. After 2km park on the L side of the road. The two sections are to the R and L and are both reached in about 15 mins. (130:B4)

Abbaye de Valcroissant:
✲ 7.00→12.00
(3.4.8.1.0)(16)   DRÔME [253]

A good 40m limestone crag well situated in the Vercors *massif* and quite close to the town of Die. Not a huge amount of routes but all are equipped with bolts [1 – 3] and if anything all on the easy side. The campsite at Die does become popular in summer and it is advisable to book. Information from Les Ours du Glandasse, 14 rue J. Reynaud, 26150 Die. A lovely spot if the weather is good.

Dir: 46km ESE of Valence, 5km ESE of Die. Take the D93 in the direction of Luc-en-Diors. 1km after leaving the town take the small road on the L to Sallières. Here turn L again and follow the steep road up to Valcroissant. The crag is reached quickly by footpath. (131:D4)

Buis-les-Baronnies:
✲ 9.00→17.00
(Bouldering)   DRÔME [254]

Some good roadside bouldering in the area of Rocher de Saint-Julien. Worth investigating if the weather looks chancy. Up to 10m high and sheltered. A nice spot and easy to rig up a top rope for beginners, bolts in place. Please respect the surrounding countryside.

Dir: 45km ENE of Orange, 21km SE of Nyons. Leave the *autoroute* at Bollène, go E on the D94 to Tulette, then after 4km turn R to Vaison. Go through the town and follow the Ouvèze river via the D54 to Entrechaux then D13 and D5 to Buis-les-Baronnies. Go through the town and after a few hundred metres the road forks.

Go R on the D159 to La Roche-sur-le-Buis. Carry on for about 3km on the way to Les Sias where the boulders can be seen on the R side of the road. (145:D3)

Le Claps:
✲ 10.00→15.00
(Bouldering)   Drôme [255]

Some excellent limestone boulders in a good sunny position at 400m. The blocks in places reach up to 30m so a rope is very useful. Very easy to get to, and worth remembering.

Dir: 3km SSE of Luc-en-Diois, 18km SSE of Die, 56km E of Montélimar. Take the D93 S from Die to Luc-en-Diois. Carry on, under the railway, and continue for a couple of km. The area can be seen from the side of the road and parking is obvious. (131:D4)

Combatier:
✲ 8.00→14.00
(3.4.4.0.0)(10)   DRÔME [256]

Not a large crag but 30m of good limestone and bolted [1 – 3]. Worth a visit, especially for beginners.

Dir: 27km N of Die, 32km SW of Grenoble. Drive to the town of La Chapelle-en-Vercours which is 16km to the SW of Villard-de-Lans. From La Chapelle take the D518 towards the Grands Goulets in a N direction. After 3km the cliff can be seen on the L and is reached by footpath in a few minutes. (131:D2)

Drayas et la Tour:
✲ 8.00→14.00
(0.6.4.3.0)(13)   DRÔME [257]

A large limestone crag up to 250m. In 1987 most of the old bolts were replaced and now the crag is in a better state with *in situ* gear [2 – 4]. A lot of good technical slab climbs. Topos available in Saou and worthwhile on this cliff as it is the largest in the area.

Dir: 10km SE of Crest, 34km SSE of Valence. From Saou take the D136 towards Aouste-sur-Sye. After 1.5km park on the L side of the road, by the big parking sign. To the R of the parking there is a footpath marked in red which leads to the crag in 15 mins. (130:B4)

Omblèze:
✳ 10.00→16.00
(3.8.50.45.4)(110) DRÔME [258]

Sometimes referred to as FALAISE D'ANSE. A very well organised mountain crag with plenty of *in situ* gear [2−4] and a great setting. Limestone, up to seven pitch 220m routes. Very good walls with some good overhangs and eight 7c routes. Abseil descent from the routes. The local authority has plans to bolt up a lot more routes (up to 130 in total), which will make this a fantastic spot to visit. The hike up to the crag is quite exhausting but the views and area easily make it worthwhile. There are also amenities for mountain bikes, canoeing and *parapente*.

Dir: 26km ESE of Valence, 18km NE of Crest. From Crest take the D93 towards Saillans, after 6km turn L on to the D70 to Beaufort-s-Gervanne, carry on to Montrond. Here take the D578 up towards Omblèze, after 4km take the D578a up to Ansage. Just before the village take the road on the R to Chutes de la Druise. Here a footpath leads up to the crag. (130:C3)

La Graville:
✳ 18.1.000→21.00
(23.16.17.1.1)(58) DRÔME [259]

A very good small crag up to 25m high close to the campsite at Saou and well equipped with bolts [2−3]. Faces N so it catches the wind but in summer can be very refreshing and welcome. Good clean rock. Topos available for sale in Saou.

Dir: At Saou, 11km SSE of Crest, 35km SSE of Valance. From Saou take the D136 towards Aouste-sur-Sye. After 1km at the campsite you can park on the R and walk up to the crag in 5 mins (seen from the road). (130:B4)

Paroi de la Vierge:
✳ 12.00→20.00
(1.5.7.1.0)(14) DRÔME [260]

A 100m limestone crag with 3 pitch routes on, situated up at 1,300m. A summer crag really. The *in situ* gear is not very modern with smaller than usual bolts [5−6], watch press for re-equipping. Worth getting a topo from the local club: Club Drômois, No 114, Le Balzac, rue Ninon-Vallin, 26100 Romans (tel. 75 70 51 48).

Dir: 9km SW of Villard-de-Lans, 28km SW of Grenoble. Go to St Martin-en-Vercors (D531, D103 from V. de Lans). Take the D103 N for about 1km then turn R on to the D221; carry on for 1km after the hamlet of La Gratte. park, and the crag is up to the R and reached in 30 mins. (131:D2)

Petits Goulets:
✳ 13.00→16.00 (1.4.1.0.0)(6)
DRÔME [261]

Hardly the biggest crag in the world. 20m limestone in a gorge with bolts [4], reached in seconds from the road. Slabs at not too steep an angle. Situated at 300m.

Dir: 8km ENE of Valence, 34km SE of Grenoble. From Valence take the N532 to Romans, N532 to 2km past St Nazaire then turn R to Pont-en-Royans. From here take the road towards La Chapelle-en-Vercors. Pass through the village of Eulalie and carry on for 0.5 km and the crag is obvious by the first of three road tunnels. (131:D2)

Roche-Colombe et Poupoune:
✳ 10.00→16.00
(10.17.28.9.0)(54) DRÔME [262]

A good, well-organised limestone crag with routes 30−100m long. All bolted [4], slabs, walls and overhangs. Topos available from the Syndicat d'Initiative (75 76 01 72) and at the local store in Saou. Camping available at Saou.

Dir: At Saou, 9km SSE of Crest, 34km SSE of Valance. Take the D538 from Crest to Saou. About 0.5km before the village there is a parking spot by the way to a church. Take the footpath marked in red on the L to the crag in about 20 mins. (130:B4)

Rocher de la Combe-d'Oyans:
✳ 10.00→15.00
(15.13.8.2.0)(38) DRÔME [263]

A limestone crag with some S-facing parts and some N-facing parts. Really a cliff for beginners and children. The cliff stretches up to 100m but the routes are perhaps best left to arranged top-roping. Not a great crag, but a useful one. Camping nearby at Rochefort.

Dir: 22km ENE of Valence, 12km SE of Romans. From Romans take the N532 E, after

3km turn R on to the D124 towards Rochefort-Samson. Just before that village carry straight on to the hamlet of Les Ducs. Park at the farm at the end of the road by a small valley. A footpath leads off to the crag in about 5 mins. (130:C23)

Rocher de Saint-Julien:
✻ 9.00→16.00
(14.20.48.15.0)(97) DRÔME [264]

A large limestone fin offering good quality technical limestone climbing. 3 pitch routes up to 120m. Good wall climbing with *in situ* gear [3−6]. At nearly 800m, but nevertheless protected from the Mistral wind.

Dir: 41km ENE of Orange, 15km SE of Nyons. Leave the *autoroute* at Bollène, via Tulette, Vaison, Entrechaux to Buis-les-Baronnies. Take a small road to the S of the town over a river and up a hill, shortly turning R to go towards La Nible. After 2km the cliff can be seen up to the L. A blue marked footpath leads to the crag in 30 mins. (145:D3)

Rocher du Brudour:
✻ 12.00→19.00
(6.7.2.0.0)(15) DRÔME [264]

Not a very large crag, only 10m high but nevertheless good limestone and an excellent introductory crag for beginners and others to whom climbing is one of many pastimes and not taken very seriously. Can remain damp after rain. Bolts [1−2].

Dir: 34km directly E of Valence, 11km SSE of St Jean-en-Royans by the Grotte du Brudour. Entering the Vercors from Valence take the D68 via Chabeuil, then the D199 which ends at the D76 just S of Lente. Turn R and carry on for about 3km towards Font-d'Urle. The crag is very near the road. (130:C3)

Les Roches Qui Dansent:
✻ 12.00→22.00
(Bouldering) DRÔME [265]

Some good sandstone boulders up to 8m high. There are rings [2] often at the top so it's worth

bringing a rope with you. Some interesting traverses and problems. A good day out with fun for all the family. Not enough for a prolonged stay. Circuits have been worked out up to 6b. Very near the A7, but 12km from any legal exit.

Dir: 25km N of Valence, 6km SE of St Vallier at St Barthélemy-de-Vals. From St Vallier take the N7 S towards Tournon for 2km. At Ponsas turn L on to the D500 which leads to the rocks after 4km and then the village of St Barthélemy. The rocks are adjacent to the road and are signposted. (130:A1)

Romeyer:
✻ 10.00→16.00
(0.2.1.2.0)(5) Drôme [266]

A good limestone crag 30−35m high situated at about 500m. Very quick access and equipped [2−4].

Dir: 4km NNE of Die, 44km ESE of Valence. From the E part of Die take the D742 N for about 4km. The rock face nearby has been bolted to prevent rockfall. (131:D4)

Ubrieux:
✻ 11.00→18.00
(10.10.34.3.0)(57) DRÔME [267]

A great limestone crag for those not suited to the terrors of such places as Volx and Cimai. Routes up to 80m with some in the 30−40m range, so bring a spare rope or a long one to lower off easily without having to split the pitch. Some excellent routes in the lower grades. Bolts [2−3]. A lovely area; look after it.

Dir: 42km ENE of Orange, 3km NNE of Buis-les-Baronnies. *See* Rocher de S-Julien. From Buis take the D546 N to the Gorge du Ubrieux. Park on the L and take a small footpath to the crag in 5 mins. (145:D3)

Hautes-Alpes – 05

Climbing in this area is a pleasure if the weather is very good. Nearly all the crags are at 1,500m, which is about the skiing lower level in winter, so if it's raining at the Calanques don't bother with climbing boots. The mountains of the Ecrins include Mont Pelvoux and many others which offer excellent introductory Alpine-type routes. As a whole the area offers many possibilities for a mix of Alpine and rock romping endeavours. There are many campsites in the area and equipment can be obtained at Loutousport at Briançon. Information about climbing can be found at Amistous Bar Restaurant in St Crépin, and the Bar Central in Guillestre.

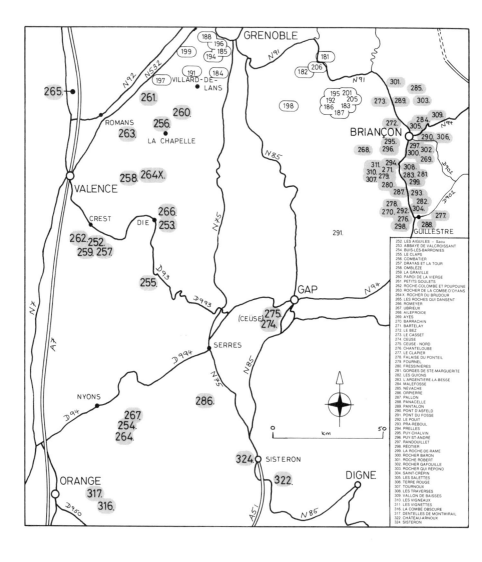

252. LES AIGUILES — Saou
253. ABBAYE DE VALCROISSANT
254. BUIS-LES-BARRONIES
255. LE CLAPS
256. COMBATIER
257. DRAYAS ET LA TOUR
258. OMBLÈZE
259. LA GRAVILLE
260. PAROI DE LA VIERGE
261. PETITS GOULETS
262. ROCHE-COLOMBE ET POUPOUNE
263. ROCHER DE LA COMBE-D'OYANS
264X. ROCHER DU BRUDOUR
265. LES ROCHES QUI DANSENT
266. ROMEYER
267. UBRIEUX
268. AILEFROIDE
269. AYES
270. BARRACHIN
271. BARTELAY
272. LE BEZ
273. LE CASSET
274. CEUSE
275. CEUSE - NORD
276. CHANTELOUBE
277. LE CLAPIER
278. FALAISE DU PONTEIL
279. FOURNEL
280. FRESSINIÈRES
281. GORGES DE STE-MARGUERITE
282. LES GUIONS
283. L'ARGENTIERE-LA BESSE
284. MALEFOSSE
285. NÉVACHE
286. ORPIERRE
287. PALLON
288. PANACELLE
289. PANTALON
290. PONT D'ASFELD
291. PONT DU FOSSE
292. LE POUIT
293. PRA-REBOUL
294. PRELLES
295. PUY-CHALVIN
296. PUY-ST-ANDRE
297. RANDOUILLET
298. RÉOTIER
299. LA ROCHE-DE-RAME
300. ROCHER BARON
301. ROCHE ROBERT
302. ROCHER GAFOUILLE
303. ROCHER QUI RÉPOND
304. SAINT-CRÉPIN
305. LES SALETTES
306. TERRE ROUGE
307. TOURNOUX
308. LES TRAVERSES
309. VALLON DE BAISSES
310. LES VIGNEAUX
311. LES VIGNETTES
316. LA COMBE OBSCURE
317. DENTELLES DE MONTMIRAIL
322. CHÂTEAU-ARNOUX
324. SISTERON

Ailefroide:
✳ 10.00→19.00
(Bouldering) HAUTES-ALPES
[268]

Some really good granite boulders offering plenty of entertainment; one of the top spots in the area. The climbs vary in height but some are up to 50m. There is a lot of *in situ* gear [3−4]. Lots of good pebble problems so bring plenty of skin with you. There are two areas − one E-facing and the other W-facing.

Dir: 15km W of Briançon, 6km NW of Vallouise. From L'Argentière-le-Bessée take the D994 up through Vallouise to Ailefroide. There are two areas − one on the way to Pré de Mme Carle on the R, and the other on the L to Sélé. (133:D3)

Ayes:
✳ 09.00→14.00
(1.3.4.0.0)(8) HAUTES-ALPES
[269]

A mediocre 60m limestone crag at 1,650m elevation. The crag is well equipped with abseil points in *in situ* bolts [3]. The setting is in a very unspoilt valley.

Dir: 6km SSE of Briançon. Drive to Villar-St-Pancrace, then take the D236 up the Ayes valley towards Chalets des Ayes. 1km before the village you can park. Cross over the river to the crag. (133:D3)

Barrachin:
✳ 06.00→10.00
(0.1.12.8.0)(21) HAUTES-ALPES
[270]

A good limestone crag which has been recently well developed and bolted [2−3]. 30m high but best kept for hot afternoons in summer.

Dir: 20km S of Briançon, 9km NW of Guillestre. From St Crépin take the D38 in the direction of Champcella for 4km. Park beside a small cottage. On the R is a footpath which is followed for 150m; then go L and to the bottom of the cliff. (133:D4)

Bartelay:
✳ 10.00→16.00
(1.1.4.0.0)(6) HAUTES-ALPES
[271]

A small 15m limestone crag situated at 1,500m high. A summer spot, well bolted [3−4], walls and cracks.

Dir: 12km SW of Briançon. 4km N of L'Argentière on the D944 is the village of Les Vigneaux. From here take the track to Tête d'Aval. The crag is reached in about 3km. (133:D3)

Le Bez:
✳ 06.00→09.00
(20.7.3.0.0)(30) HAUTES-ALPES
[272]

This 100m quartzite crag has been very well equipped by the local village guides and offers good multi pitch climbing in the lower grades. Handy on very hot summer days. Good belays and abseil points [2−4] and quite easy to get to.

Dir: 8km NW of Briançon. Take the N91 through Chantemerle and on to Villeneuve. Before the bridge take the track on the L which goes towards Le Bez and Fréjus. The crag is situated at the bottom of the forest. (133:D2)

Le Casset:
✳ Not a lot
(Bouldering) HAUTES-ALPES
[273]

Some granite boulders offering excellent entertainment. Climbs in all grades and up to 8m high. Worth a trip on a hot day.

Dir: 17km NW of Briançon. Take the N91 to Le Monêtier-les-Bains. Go W on the N91 and after 1km turn L on to the D300 to Le Casset. The boulders are 5 mins from the road to Le Lauzet. (133:D2)

Ceüse:
✳ 06.00→17.00
(0.19.41.33.13)(104) HAUTES-ALPES [274]

This crag is known universally as the 'crag of the year 2000', simply because it is so futuristic, out there and demanding. For 7c climbing and above there is just about no other crag in the world to rival it. At present it is virtually undeveloped but in time it should give around 300 grade 8 climbs. Is it an impressive crag, indeed it is. Superb limestone, very steep with huge overhanging walls. All bolts [1–3] and I suggest you bring your pilot's licence along too. Now for the big drag — you have to like walking. It's 30 mins for big bulky 7c stompers but a good 60 mins for anorexic limestone weirdos. It gets too hot in summer and snows in winter, it's at 2,000m, you see. For topo *see* Club Omnisport, Gap, or the Syndicat d'Initiative. (Not a great deal of use — they're all very hard.) There are also some good boulders in the forest below the crag known as BLOCS DE CEÜSETTE. There are quite a few circuits here from easy to quite hard indeed, all limestone.

Dir: 12km SW of Gap near Sigoyer. Leave Gap on the D994 and after 5km a road leads off to the L (D247), turning into the D19 which after about 10km leads to the village of Sigoyer. Here take the D219 on the R which leads up to the Col des Guerins. The crag can be seen on the R. Take the footpath to the crag. This is bound to be a popular spot for car break-ins in the future, so come prepared with pet Rottweiler to leave in the car. (146:A1)

CEÜSE, crag shot. (Photo Fred Simpson)

CEÜSE. (Climber Jean-Baptiste Bloggs, Photo Sue Bloggs)

Ceüse — Nord:
✳ 05.00→11.30 (To be developed) HAUTES-ALPES [275]

The size of Ceüse means that it will all eventually become developed and the area to the N is gained by a different route.

Dir: 10km WSW of Gap. Take the D994 for 6km just past the turn-off to the S part. Take the D118 which immediately goes under the railway towards Manteyer. Just before the village a footpath leads off to the S and the Ceüse cliffs. (146:A1)

Chanteloube:
✳ 06.00→09.00 (7.8.3.3.0)(21) HAUTES-ALPES [276]

A grey limestone cliff 15m high, and situated low down in the valley, even so very much a summer crag. Good bolts and moulinettes.

Dir: 22km S of Briançon, 8km NW of Guillestre. From St Crépin cross over the river and take the D38 and 1km after Chanteloube find a parking spot. Take a path for a few hundred metres to the crag. (133:D4)

SUPER MICKY, 7b+, Ceüse. (Climber Nigel Slater, Photo Fred Simpson)

Le Clapier:
✲ Nil (0.0.5.1.0)(6) HAUTES-ALPES [277]

A really good limestone crag which, bolted [2–3] and worth visiting on a hot summer day. For information enquire at Bar Central in Guillestre.

Dir: 26km SSE of Briançon, 5km ENE of Guillestre. From Guillestre take the D902 towards Château Queyras, after 5km turn R on to the D60 to Ceillac. After 500m it is possible to park. The crag can be reached by footpath to the E in 5 mins. (133:E4)

Falaise du Ponteil:
✲ 10.00→16.00 (5.8.10.0.0)(23) HAUTES-ALPES [278]

A 100m limestone crag in desperate need of new bolts, abseil points and belays. Watch press for details, or indeed check it out if climbing at Le Pouit or having some dull weather.

Dir: 21km S of Briançon, 9km NW of Guillestre. Go to St Crépin on the N94. Cross over the river and pass the airport, turning R on to the D38 which leads N towards Le Chambon. Just before the village turn L to Champcella, pass through the village, and take the winding road up the hill towards the village of Ponteil. The crag can be seen on the R side of the road about 15 mins' walk away. (133:D4)

Fournel:
✲ 7.00→22.00 (3.10.16.8.0)(37) HAUTES-ALPES [279]

A well recommended limestone crag up to 100m high. Good water pockets and most of the routes have been re-equipped with bolts [3]. Mainly wall climbing without being too steep. Good abseil points for descent. A crag worth visiting. At 1,500m not a winter crag, and it also gets a lot of drainage. In or out of the sun in summer, very useful.

Dir: 16km SSW of Briançon, 6km W of L'Argentière-la-Bessée. From the town centre of L'Argentière take the road up the Fournel valley which soon becomes the D423. After 6km park on the L and take a footpath to the crag which can be reached in a couple of mins. (133:D3)

Fressinières:
✲ 10.00→17.00 (0.2.30.20.0)(52) HAUTES-ALPES [280]

A huge 200m limestone crag in desperate need of re-bolting and fully equipping. There are about 30 single pitch routes with lower-off points on the LH side. The other routes run up to 8 pitches in length and it would be sensible to take protection along if embarking upon these historical footpaths. The cliff catches the sun for most of the day and is in a fantastic position. There is also a Via Ferrata running across the cliff from L to R which is good fun for a family outing.

Dir: 18km SSW of Briançon, 6km SW of L'Argentière. From La Roche de Rame on the N94 cross over the river and take the D38 downriver to Pallon. Here take the D238 past a campsite to the village of Fressinières. At the village turn L and go up the winding road towards Les Roberts and Col d'Anon for about 2km. The crag can be seen on the R. (133:D3)

Gorges de Ste-Marguerite:
✲ Nil (0.1.5.1.0)(7) HAUTES-ALPES [281]

A summer crag at 1,200m up. Limestone routes up to 25m with very good rock and bolt [2–3] protection. A 50m rope is essential if you are to lower off successfully.

Dir: 12km SSW of Briançon. Take the N94 to the S. At a hairpin bend 1km before L'Argentière-la-Bessée park on the L. Take a path to the gorge. (133:D3)

Les Guions:
✲ 10.00→16.00 (2.2.11.0.0)(15) HAUTES-ALPES [282]

A bolted [3] 30m grey limestone crag. Sometimes referred to as CROIX LUISANTE.

Dir: 20km S of Briançon, 7km NW of Guillestre. Go to St Crépin on the N94. From here take the D738 for 6km towards Guions. At the entrance to the hamlet a footpath leads to the top of the crag. (133:D4)

L'Argentière-la-Bessée:
✶ 12.00→19.00
(0.7.19.0.0)(26)   HAUTES-ALPES
[283]

A newly developed crag with bolts [1−3]. As yet there are no hard routes but I'm sure this is only a matter of time. There are two different sections which can be climbed upon for most of the year but don't expect to get a tan in winter.

Dir: 14km SSW of Briançon. Take the N94 S for 17m to the village and the crag is close to the centre. (133:D3)

Malefosse:
✶ 06.00→12.00
(0.2.10.0.0)(12)   HAUTES-ALPES
[284]

A cool E-facing crag to be reserved for those early mornings or hot, hot summer days. Bolted [3−4], 25m face routes and very quick to get to. Worth remembering.

Dir: 2km NE of Briançon. Take the N94 towards Montgenèvre. About 1km after a petrol station on the R the crag is seen on the L. (133:D3)

Névache:
✶ 05.00→09.00
(0.3.13.1.0)(17)   HAUTES-ALPES
[285]

A 30m limestone crag offering good wall climbing. Most of the climbs are bolted [2−3] up but tend to be on the long side so bring a 55m rope with you. Quite high at 1,600m and definitely not a winter crag. The view from the crag on a hot summer's day is fantastic.

Dir: 13km N of Briançon. Take the N94 towards Montgenèvre, after 3km turn L on to the D994g which after 14km leads to Névache. About 4km before the village of Plampinet, stop and park. A path leads across to the other side of the river across a bridge and to the crag in about 30 mins. (133:D2)

Orpierre:
✶ 06.00→22.00
(24.20.37.5.1)(78)   HAUTES-ALPES
[286]

One of the great French crags with just about everything going for it. Limestone from 30−150m. The rock is superb with plenty of water pockets on the large walls and overhangs. Bolts [3] and a lovely situation. The crag faces many different ways and offers climbing all year round.

Dir: 24km NW of Sisteron, 10km W of Laragne-Montéglin. From that town take the N75 N to Eyguians, turn L on to the D30 which leads to Orpierre after 10km. Park in the village; the crags overlook the village and can be reached in about 15 mins. Please use the proper footpaths which prevent erosion and damage to local property. (145:F2)

ORPIERRE, crag shot. (Photo Fred Simpson)

Pallon:
✶ 10.00→17.00
(0.7.7.1.0)(15) HAUTES-ALPES
[287]

A grey limestone crag with most of the routes being 15m long. There is a second 80m section with 4 pitch routes in the grade 5 area, great for the leisure climbers. *In situ* gear [2−3] and worth a visit.

Dir: 19km SSW of Briançon, 11km NW of Guillestre. Take the N94 to La Roche-des-Rame. Just N of the town cross the river on to the D38 which leads to Pallon; park at point I. The cliff is nearby.

Panacelle:
✶ 10.00→19.00
(0.6.10.16.3)(35) HAUTES-ALPES
[288]

A very good limestone crag with excellent routes up to 70m in the middle and upper grades. The crag is situated at 800m and is very much a spring to autumn playground. New routeing is going on and our thanks to Hatrick hedge cleaner for his fine efforts. Bolts [2−3].

Dir: 30km S of Briançon, 4km SE of Guillestre. From Guillestre take the D902 to the S in the direction of Vars for 2km. At the first hairpin bend a track leads off to the R and the crag in about 5 mins. (133:E4)

Pantalon:
✶ 13.00→19.00
(15.5.1.0.0)(21) HAUTES-ALPES
[289]

A 60m quartzite crag which offers an excellent introduction to multi pitch climbs for the beginner. All are well bolted [3]. The cliff is situated at 1,600m and in a beautiful setting.

Dir: 13km NW of Briançon. Take the N91 to le Monêtier-les-Bains. At the village the crag is about 100m above the road and only takes a few minutes to get to. (133:D2)

Pont d'Asfeld:
✶ 09.00→13.00 (15) HAUTES-ALPES [290]

Some 15m limestone climbing in the centre of Briançon.

Dir: In the town of Briançon. Go to the old part of town and park by the Mairie. A path leads down to the bridge and the cliff. (133:D3)

Pont du Fossé:
✶ 06.00→13.30
(0.0.15.6.1)(22) HAUTES-ALPES
[291]

A limestone crag with routes up to 30m high which have been recently bolt [2−3]-equipped. The crag is popular in summer but not really a winter crag.

Dir: 66km SE of Grenoble, 22km NE of Gap. Take the N85 from Gap going N for a few km then turn R on to the D944 over the Col de Manse. Carry on towards Orcières. After about 12km reach the village of Pont du Fossé. From here the crag is about 2km in a N direction up the valley of Champsaur. (132:C4)

Le Pouit:
✶ 10.00→16.00
(0.7.43.16.0)(66) HAUTE-ALPES
[292]

A great crag for the grade 6 climber. The limestone is the ochre colour of the St Crépin area. The cliff is up to 90m high but a lot of the routes are single pitch only, which can be taken to the top by routes such as crack lines. Watch for future development. A lot of the grade 6 routes are on the L side of the crag, but not on the two big walls on the R. Bolts [2−3].

Dir: 21km S of Briançon, 8km NW of Guillestre. Go to St Crépin on the N94. Cross over the river and pass the airport, turning R on to the D38 which leads N towards Le Chambon. Just before the village turn L to Champcella, pass through the village, after 500m carry straight on instead of following the hairpin bends up the hill. This leads very shortly to parking beneath the crag. (133:D4)

Pra-Reboul:
✶ 10.00→19.00 (Bouldering)
(0.0.4.7.0)(11) HAUTES-ALPES
[293]

A good 20m limestone crag with a handful of middle grade routes and some quite hard ones too. Bolts are good and there is plenty of scope for bouldering. There are two circuits, one easy (Green) and one hard (Red).

Dir: 20km SSW of Briançon, 9km NW of Guillestre. Take the N94 to La Roche-de-Rame. Carry on S towards St Crépin and after 3km Pra-Reboul is reached. The boulders are here beside the road and the cliff has a large diagonal crack in it. (133:D4)

Prelles:
✶ 10.00→16.00
(Bouldering)   HAUTES-ALPES
[294]

Some good granite bouldering to be found here. About 50 routes 5–10m high, in all grades to 7. The rock is very good and offers good technique training. No walk-in and only at 1,000m. Good spot to know about, and very easy to get to. Descents can be awkward from some of the longer routes, so bring a rope along.

Dir: 7km SW of Briançon. Take the N94 S to the village of Prelles. Here take the D4 continuing S for 1km. The boulders can then be seen on the R side of the road. (133:D3)

Puy-Chalvin:
✶ 12.00→19.00
(1.6.16.1.0)(24)   HAUTES-ALPES
[295]

A 20m limestone crag which, although it catches the afternoon sun, has many climbs that are shaded and is good on hot days in the summer. Mainly wall and crack climbs with bolts [3]. Situated at 1,600m.

Dir: 5km SW of Briançon. From the W side of town take the D35 which winds its way up to Puy-St-André. Carry on up the road to Puy-Chalvin and park in the village. From here by a sharp bend a path traverses to the crag in a few minutes. (133:D3)

Puy-St-André:
✶ Not a lot
(5.6.14.0.0)(25)   HAUTES-ALPES
[296]

A limestone and conglomerate crag 20–40m high situated at 1,500m. The gear [3] is quite new but the rock is fragile in places. Situated in a very pleasant pine forest.

Dir: 4km SW of Briançon. From the W side of town take the D35 (Gap) which winds its way up

to Puy-St-André. Go through the village and take a track on a sharp RH bend. Take this for 1km, until the cliff can be seen in the valley. (133:D3)

Randouillet:
✶ 12.00→19.00
(0.6.35.9.0)(50)   HAUTES-ALPES
[297]

A good small 20m limestone crag with fine views. Most of the routes are bolted [2–3], and the crag is great for the ambitious middle grade climber.

Dir: The SE edge of Briançon. Take the D902 road which goes to Cervières. After about half a km after Fontchristiane a track leads to Fort du Randouillet. A path leads along the old canal to the crag in about 5 mins. (133:D3)

Réotier:
✶ 07.00→21.00 (Bouldering)
HAUTES-ALPES [298]

Some good limestone bouldering to be found here up to 20m but the *in situ* gear is not very good at present. Bring a rope anyway, since it may be renewed. There are three circuits, Blue, Red and Black. One of the lowest climbing areas just under 1,000m; dries quickly.

Dir: 26km S of Briançon, 5km W of Guillestre. Take the D94 to St Clément just S of Guillestre. Take the D38 heading upstream towards Les Casses and Réotier. The boulders will easily be seen near the road. (133:D4)

La Roche-de-Rame:
✶ 9.00→16.00
(0.3.15.6.0)(24)   HAUTES-ALPES
[299]

A good 20m limestone crag with some middle grade routes quite low down at 1,000m. A popular evening crag which dries very quickly after rain. Some good route names such as A ma Zone (6b) and Sex à Pile (6c).

Dir: 18km S of Briançon, 12km NNW of Guillestre. Take the N94 to La Roche-de-Rame. From the village take the road on the R to the crag. (133:D34)

Rocher Baron:
✳ 08.00→14.00
(3.7.4.0.0)(14) HAUTES-ALPES
[300]

A quartzite crag up to 80m high with routes appealing to the lower grade climber. Bolts [2 – 3] and abseil points 25m apart so a single rope works out very well. Slabs, walls and cracks. A fine summer spot at nearly 1,500m.

Dir: 5km SSW of Briançon, Go S out of Briançon to the village of Villard-St-Pancrace, pass through and take the D36 on the L side of the river. After 3km a track leads off to the L and the cliff. If you reach Le Villaret you've gone too far. (133:D3)

Roche Robert:
✳ 07.00→12.00
(0.0.3.0.0)(3) HAUTES-ALPES
[301]
✳ 12.00→21.00 (5.4.6.0.0)(15)

Two crags of good limestone. One is small but 100m high, and the other is wide and 30m high. Both are situated at 2,200m and are summer crags only. A 55m rope is very useful here to reach the moulinettes. Bolts [2 – 3].

Dir: 19km NW of Briançon. Take the N91 in the direction of Col du Lautaret. Pass through Le Monêtier and carry on for another 7km to Le Pont-de-l'Alpe. Park here and follow the river up to the R and the crags are on the R. (133:D2)

Rocher Gafouille:
✳ 12.00→19.00
(5.5.2.0.0)(12) HAUTES-ALPES
[302]

A good crag which is easy to get to. *In situ* gear [3] and excellent for beginners or bumblies. Limestone up to 25m and friendly walls and cracks.

Dir: 2km SSE of Briançon. Go to Villard-St-Pancrace. From here take the track up towards Fort de la Croix de Bretagne. After 1km park after the first bend. A footpath on the L leads to the cliff. (133:D3)

Rocher Qui Répond:
✳ 12.00→22.00
(3.3.4.0.0)(10) HAUTES-ALPES
[303]

A 25m limestone crag with much easier access than its neighbour Névache, and well equipped with *in situ* gear on the walls which are not steep at all. A lovely position.

Dir: 13km N of Briançon. Take the N94 towards Montgenèvre, after 3km turn L on to the D994g which after 14km leads to Névache. About 4km before the village of Plampinet, park and walk to the crag on the R. (133:D2)

Saint-Crépin:
✳ 10.00→20.00
(0.7.37.32.3)(79) HAUTES-ALPES
[304]

The major limestone crag in the Briançon area with some very fine routes. The rock is a wonderful colour with an ochre appearance offering steep exposed climbing even though the crag is only up to 40m high. The bolts [3] get well tested. There are three sections – Paroi Jaune is the highest part, up to 40m and about 50m long, with most of the routes double pitch; La Dalle is up to 20m high with the classic and attractively sounding Nuit d'Amour at 8a; Mur du Sept is 20m high but nearly 100m long and offers many grade 6b to 7b climbs. Camping can be found at St Crépin and topos can be bought at the local stores (*Sites du Haut-Val-Durance*). For the chic climber there is a small airport here, so why not come by private plane?

Dir: 21km S of Briançon, 6km NW of Guillestre. Take the N94 to St Crépin, the crag overlooks the valley and village. (133:D4)

Les Salettes:
✳ 10.00→16.00
(2.9.20.0.0)(31) HAUTES-ALPES
[305]

A limestone crag up to 40m high. At the time of writing there is some re-equipping of routes going on, so by 1991 most of the routes should be fully bolted up. Some good overhangs here in the middle grades. A fun crag that is worth a visit.

Dir: At Briançon. From the centre of town, take the road Champs de Mars towards Montgenèvre. Take a small road which leads up opposite a bus shelter for about 100m. Park and walk to the crag in 5 mins. (133:D3)

Terre Rouge:
✶ 12.00→20.00
(0.0.12.2.0)(14)   HAUTES-ALPES [306]

Some good limestone routes to be found here up to 20m high. All are equipped with bolts [2−3] and abseil rings. 1,600m elevation with a great position.

Dir: 5km ESE of Briançon. Take the D902 from Briancon in the direction of Cervières. 4km along the valley bottom there is the hamlet of Terre Rouge; carry straight on and then park. On the L is the crag which is gained by a footpath from the parking. (133:E3)

Tournoux:
✶ 10.00→18.00
(0.0.5.0.0)(5)   HAUTES-ALPES [307]

A 20m limestone crag offering a handful of middle grade routes. Bolted [3] walls and cracks. Please be careful of private property when approaching the cliff.

Dir: 15km SW of Briançon, 4km W of L'Argentière. From that town take the D994 towards Vallouise. Just past Les Vigneaux take the D4 on the L then shortly turn L and follow the track up to the Col de la Pousterle. The cliff can be reached on the R 1km before the actual col through the forest. (133:D3)

Les Traverses:
✶ 13.00→19.00
(0.0.2.11.4)(17)   HAUTES-ALPES [308]

A newly developed limestone crag 25m high in two parts. All new bolts [3], and lots of them. Future possibilities exist here for more grade 8 routes. At 1,200m elevation it is best avoided in the depth of winter. A crag worth visiting when you're going well.

Dir: 11km SSW of Briançon, 2km N of L'Argentière. Take the N94 S from Briancon for 6km, then turn on to the D4 towards Les

Vigneaux. After 4km pass through the hamlet of Villard Meyer, carry on for another km and the crag is on the R. (133:D3)

Vallon de Baisses:
✶ 12.00→18.00
(4.5.14.0.0)(23)   HAUTES-ALPES [309]

A 20m high limestone crag with good wall routes, bolted [3]. The crag is situated at 2,000m so forget it at any time other than summer. A good crag for beginners too.

Dir: 10km NW of Briançon. Drive to Montgenèvre, carry on the N94 towards the Italian border, but before it take the track on the L and go as far as you can by car (about 5km). Walk for a couple of km to the crag, situated on the R side of the Rio Seco gorge. (133:E2)

Les Vigneaux:
✶ Nil (0.0.0.3.0)(3)   HAUTES-ALPES [310]

A 60m limestone summer crag with a couple of 7a routes on. Bolted [3−4] and definitely worth a visit if in the area. Good on very hot summer days.

Dir: 16km SW of Briançon, 2km S of Vallouise. From Briançon take the D94 S and go R to Les Vigneaux on the D4. Carry on the D4 across the large road and go up to Puy-St Vincent. Take the track on the L after 1km. (133:D3)

Les Vignettes:
✶ 07.00→13.00
(0.2.7.6.0)(15)   HAUTES-ALPES [311]

A strata-ed limestone crag with easier 25m routes on than its neighbouring cliff Les Traverses. New bolts [3] and views of the gorge.

Dir: 10km SSW of Briançon, 3km N of L'Argentière. Take the N94 S from Briancon for 6k, then turn on to the D4 towards Les Vigneaux. After 4km pass through the hamlet of Villard Meyer, park just after the village and go down the grassy slope to the crag. (133:D3)

Gard – 30

Castelas:
(1.4.5.1.0)(11)   GARD [312]

A small limestone crag up to 25m with a handful of recently equipped routes [2–3].

Dir: 10km NNW of Nîmes. From the outskirts of town in the NW sector take the D418 to Russan (before the junction of the N106 and D907). Arrive at the town then take a footpath down the L side of the river Gardon to the crag in 10 mins. (157:E1)

Collias:
✷ 10.00→19.00
(14.20.32.16.0)(82)   GARD [313]

Some excellent limestone climbing to be found here on single pitch routes. *In situ* bolts [3–4]. There are quite a few faces on which to climb in the Gorges du Gardon. Notable are FALAISE DU HAUT, GRANDE FALAISE.

Dir: 12km N of Nîmes. From the city take the D979 up towards Uzès. After about 15km enter the Gorges du Gardon where the crags lie. Enquire locally for the exact location of each crag. (157:E1)

Vaucluse – 84

One of the greatest and most famous districts in the world to climb, with a wealth of climbing that could keep anyone happy for years, especially in the upper grades. Buoux is popular, and deservedly so. Camping has always been a sensitive issue and it is wise for all climbers to use organised campsites, otherwise the below areas may be put in jeopardy. The facilities offered for the price are so good that you must have a peculiar sense of hygiene not to want to take full advantage of them.

Climbing shops in the area are Sports Technic, 50 Cours Gambetta, 84300 Cavaillon (tel: 90 78 03 46), and Techniciens du Sport, Route d'Avignon, Apt (tel: 90 74 00 61).

Buoux:
✷ 10.00→17.00
(10.20.64.80.20)(194)   VAUCLUSE [314]

This is one of the best limestone crags in Europe and is always very popular. There is a fantastic concentration of routes here in the upper grades, including 8c. Up to 50m but most people only use a single rope and therefore only do the first pitches of the routes. Overused routes are slowly becoming polished and in future the whole crag will become very polished. Even so the crag is very popular and busy, from Easter till midsummer and autumn. It gets too hot in summer months but is perfect at other times of the year. Climbing is steep on reasonable pockets, with bolts [1–3]. Not as trendy as in the past but still has many of the top European test pieces: Agincourt (8c), Rose et le Vampire (8b+). There is no camping allowed at Buoux, so you must camp at either Apt or Bonnieux.

Dir: 50km ESE of Avignon, 7km S of Apt. From the S part of Apt take the D113. After 6km this crosses the D232 and 2km later Buoux is reached. From the S take the D943 from Cadenet towards Bonnieux and follow signs. The crag is to the S of the village. (159:D1)

Cavaillon:
✷ 11.00→19.00
(13.20.55.16.1)(105)   VAUCLUSE [315]

A good crag with plenty of bolts [1–3]. Good in the lower grades and a nice place if on a rest day from the more strenuous crags in the area. Limestone and very urban. You can see yourself in the holds here.

Dir: West of Cavaillon. Leave the *autoroute* A7 and take the D99 towards the Centre Ville. Take the first L over the river and this leads to the hill of St Jacques and the cliffs beneath. (158:C1)

AGINCOURT, 8c, Buoux. (Climber Ben Moon, Photo Uli Hofsteder)

TABOU, 8a+, Buoux. (Climber Mark Pretty, Photo Sean Myles)

LA ROSE ET LE VAMPIRE, 8b, Buoux. (Climber Ben Moon, Photo Sean Myles)

La Combe Obscure:
✳ 8.00→16.00
(13.14.23.6.0)(56)   VAUCLUSE
[316]

A bit of a quiet backwater. Limestone up to 45m, single pitch and well set up with bolts [1−3] and abseil points. Good mixed climbing and protected from the cold Mistral wind. Up at 500m.

Dir: 28km E of Orange, 14km NE of Carpentras. Take the D974 out of Carpentras to Bédoin. Go through the village then bear L on to the D19 towards Malaucène. After 2.8km you reach the Chapel of St Madeleine. Park after the cottage and take the first footpath which leads up to the R called GR91 and the crag in about 10 mins. (144:C3)

Dentelles de Montmirail:
✳ 10.00→17.00
(60.101.95.40.2)(308)   VAUCLUSE
[317]

A very large limestone 20−80m climbing area with many old-fashioned routes that are ill equipped. However, some of the more modern routes are bolted [2−3] up and the crag will become much more popular in years to come. A superb spot and well worth a visit. Topos are available from Café de la Poste in Gigondas.

Dir: 18km E of Orange, 11km NNW of Carpentras. Take the D7 to Vacqueryras from Carpentras, carry on N for 1.5km then turn R on the D7 almost to Gigondas. Follow the small steep road on the L to Les Florets and Col du Cayron. (144:C3)

Font-Jovalle:
✳ 18.00→22.00
(3.10.16.8.0)(37)   VAUCLUSE [318]

Not a large crag but a very good one. Limestone up to 30m and equipped with modern bolts [2−3]. Definitely not the place to climb in winter. Not for large infantile parties either.

Dir: 11km NNW of Apt, 28km ENE of Cavaillon. 1km to the E of Apt take the D943 towards St Saturnin-d'Apt (from the D100). Go through that town continuing on the D943. After about 7km you reach the few houses called Font-Jovalle on the L. Up and to the L the crag is reached by footpath in about 10 mins. (159:D1)

Ménerbes:
✳ 8.00→14.00
(7.18.70.12.1)(108)   VAUCLUSE
[319]

Access is a delicate issue here and it is requested that school parties climb elsewhere. This also applies to huge rowdy groups of adults with infantile behaviour. A very good molasse limestone crag offering plenty of middle grade climbing of high quality. Good at all times of the year and bolted [1−2] up. The RH side of the face is not bolted and indeed is out of bounds. Plenty of routes to go round though, but it does get busy in the Easter period. Please keep to footpaths and respect the surrounding countryside.

Dir: 14km E of Cavaillon, 8km W of Bonnieux. 1km to the S of Ménebers on the D3 is a small village of La Peyrière. From here a small road leads to the Falaise de Langue d'Aze. After about 1km the crag can be seen and follow the footpath to the crag. (159:D1)

Oppède-le-Vieux:
✳ 12.00→19.00
(0.4.19.0.0)(23)   VAUCLUSE [320]

A good small crag in the molasse limestone similar to most crags in the area. The routes are equipped with bolts [2−3]. Steep pocketed walls. Low-level and warm crag, quite good on sunny winter afternoons.

Dir: 9km E of Cavaillon, 4km W of Ménerbes. Take the D2 in the direction of Apt. 2km after the village of Robion turn R on the D29 towards Maubec. Carry on past keeping L and after 1km turn R on to the D176 to Oppède-le-Vieux. You must park in the village. On the E side of the village is a sign to Oppède. Take the footpath on the R and after a few minutes turn R. A path on the L leads to the crag. (159:D1)

Valloncourt:
✳ 17.00→20.00
(1.4.17.3.0)(25)   VAUCLUSE [321]

A small limestone crag which appeals to the middle grade climber. Steep bolted [2] walls.

Dir: 6km SE of Cavaillon. Take the D973 towards Cadenet from the town, after 4km reach the town of Cheval-Blanc. Turn L at the traffic lights, continue for 1km then just after a bridge turn R on to the road that leads towards the crag. (158:C2)

Alpes-de-Haute-Provence – 04

Château-Arnoux:
✻ 10.00→16.00 (33.16.26.13.0)(88)
ALPES-DE-H-PR [322]

A very good crag for beginners, limestone up to 30m, and out of the prevailing Mistral wind. Quite popular and very polished. Quick to get to and easy to find. Topos available in the Trigano shop near the tourist office.

Dir: 13km SSE of Sisteron. The town of Château-Arnoux is along the D96 from Aix to Gap. A footpath leads to the crag. (146:B4)

Montagne du Teillon:
✻ 12.00→20.00 (12.21.32.12.0)(77)
ALPES-DE-H-PR [323]

A very old traditional limestone crag with many old routes. It is situated at 1,500m and only a pleasant seasonal crag but a lot less popular than Verdon. Bolts [4–6]. Many of the routes are up to 200m high but single pitch climbs are becoming much more popular. Worth a visit, definitely for the middle grade climber.

Dir: 34km WNW of Grasse, 6km ESE of Castellane. From Castellane head S on the N85 for 7km to La Garde. Carry on for 1km where a track leads off the L and the mountain. 15 mins. (163:D1)

Sisteron:
✻ 09.00→16.00 (5.26.31.10.3)(75)
ALPES-DE-H-PR [324]

Also known as ROCHER DE LA BAUME. Another great crag in the area offering a series of excellent limestone walls in the upper grades interspersed by cracks in the lower grades. A very good position, routes up to 100m high. Bolts [3–6] in most places and old ones rapidly being replaced. Definitely worth a visit.

Dir: At Sisteron 80km NNE of Aix-en-Provence on the N96. The cliff is quite obvious above the town with steps leading up. (146:A3)

Verdon:
✻ 08.00→20.00
(30.70.400.200.30)(730)
ALPES-DE-H-PR [325]

The best crag in Europe. The whole of the Verdon Gorge stretches for 30km with cliffs up to 1,000m along both sides. Some of the areas are very popular while others are very undeveloped and quiet. The climbing is on big limestone walls with bolts [1–6]. A lot of re-equipping has gone on but in general the harder the routes the better the bolts. Anybody coming here should buy a guidebook, since many of the routes are approached by abseil from above and are often awkward to locate for the first time. On the older routes the pitches

FALAISE DE L'ESCALES (main area), Verdon. (Photo Nigel Slater)

can be 50m long, so twin 9mm ropes are useful, however, the modern norm is now 55m single rope with 25m pitches. There are 13 major cliffs:

Falaise de L'Escales (main area),
Falaise du Duc,
Falaise du Point Sublime,
Falaise de Malines,
Mirroir du Fou,
Falaise de L'Inbut,
Falaise de Maugue,
Falaise de L'Estelle,
Falaise des Cavaliers,
Falaise de Mayreste,
Falaise de St Maurin.
Falaise de L'Ourbes,
Falaise de Moustiers.

The routes are mainly big walls with cracks for the easy routes and face routes for the harder ones. Many of the routes require you to abseil in so the top pitches become the most polished. Car thieves will watch you carefully so try not to leave valuables in the car and take all precautions. In winter it snows here and in summer it can get very hot, so you must think carefully about where to go. If you abseil into a

MIRROR DU FOU, Verdon. (Photo Nigel Slater)

MAGINOT LINE, 8b+, Volx. (Climber Mark Pretty, Photo Jeff Odds)

300m route without water in summer you are very likely to suffer from a complete sense of humour failure as the sun comes round. Some of the abseil points are dubious; take care.

Dir: 70km NE Aix-en-Provence. Take the *autoroute* A51 to the end near Manosque then turn R on to the D6 to Riez. The D592 leads to Moustiers and eventually La Palud which is the centre for all activity in Le Verdon. Bon grimpe! (162:C2)

Volx:
✻ 09.00→15.00 (2.6.23.11.11)(53)
ALPES-DE-H-PR [326]

This is the latest trendy crag in the south of France. If you like working grade 8 routes then it is the crag for you. Limestone up to 40m with new bolts [1 − 3]. A good winter crag and in the shade on summer afternoons, in fact many of the routes are in the shade anyway because they overhang so much. The cliff is rugged in appearance with holds in abundance, but the rock is very steep, requiring powerful climbing. Altitude 300m. Worth a visit when you're climbing well. I think a lot of the new routes were sponsored by adhesive companies! It is also home to the second 8c climb done in France − Maginot Line, climbed by Le Rasta Anglais, Ben Moon.

Dir: 7km NNE of Manosque on the N96 from Aix to Apt. Take the N96 out of Manosque and after 7km turn L into the village of Volx. There is a campsite just to the S of the crag. (159:F1)

Bouches-du-Rhône − 13
There is good limestone climbing to be found in the area around Marseilles. For up-to-date info and topos go to the Sport à Montagne, Avignon.

Aiguilles d'Aubagne:
✻ 10.00→22.00 (13.19.13.0.0)(45)
B-DU-RHÔNE [327]

Some very good easier climbing to be found on this 25m limestone crag. *In situ* gear [3 − 4] and a spot frequented by families. In the middle of the summer the crag is a real sun trap and a trip to an ice cream parlour is more suitable.

Dir: 2km SE of Aubagne. Take the D559a S out of Aubagne by the *autoroute*. You can park 200m before the quarry Bronzo. A footpath leads off from the bend in the road to the E then the S and the crag is reached in 10 mins. (160:B3)

Bau de Gignac:
✻ 12.00→20.00 (7.15.21.5.0)(48)
B-DU-RHÔNE [328]

A fair limestone crag 20 − 40m offering better climbing in the lower grades. Gear *in situ* [3 − 4]. Mainly easier angled walls.

Dir: 14km NW of Marseilles. Get to the town of Gignac-la-Nerthe, 5km S of Marignane. At the town take the D48a towards Le Rove. In 500m at a warehouse turn L and take the footpath to the crag by the *autoroute*. (159:D4)

Blocs de la Gineste:
✻ 12.00→19.00 (0.10.33.4.0)(47)
B-DU-RHÔNE [329]

A good limestone bouldering area with routes 2 − 5m high. Walls, overhangs with most types of move but nothing out of the ordinary.

Dir: 6km SE of Marseilles. Take the D559 towards Toulon. Go past the few houses at Vaufreges and up to the Col de la Gineste. Park by the second overhang on the R. The blocks can be reached in a couple of minutes. (160:A3)

Chaîne de L'Etoile:
✻ 10.00→16.00 (20.20.60.26.0)(126)
B-DU-RHÔNE [330]

Some quite good limestone climbing in the lower grades. Not very high, only about 15m but well pegged and bolted [2 − 4]. Worth an evening if passing by *en route* to the mysterious quarters of Marseilles. Very near the A7.

Dir: 12km N of Marseilles, 5km NNE of St Antoine. From that town turn off the A8 take the N8 through Septèmes-les-Vallons going N. Carry on for 1km to a road on the R. Take this, it soon turns private (access to the television mast). The crag can be reached in 5 mins by foot. (159:E4)

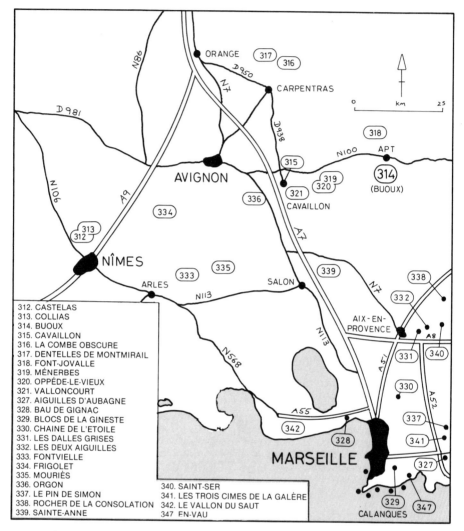

312. CASTELAS
313. COLLIAS
314. BUOUX
315. CAVAILLON
316. LA COMBE OBSCURE
317. DENTELLES DE MONTMIRAIL
318. FONT-JOVALLE
319. MÉNERBES
320. OPPÉDE-LE-VIEUX
321. VALLONCOURT
327. AIGUILLES D'AUBAGNE
328. BAU DE GIGNAC
329. BLOCS DE LA GINESTE
330. CHAINE DE L'ETOILE
331. LES DALLES GRISES
332. LES DEUX AIGUILLES
333. FONTVIELLE
334. FRIGOLET
335. MOURIÈS
336. ORGON
337. LE PIN DE SIMON
338. ROCHER DE LA CONSOLATION
339. SAINTE-ANNE

340. SAINT-SER
341. LES TROIS CIMES DE LA GALÈRE
342. LE VALLON DU SAUT
347. EN-VAU

Les Dalles Grises:
✱ 10.00→16.00 (0.2.13.0.0)(15)
B-DU-RHÔNE [331]

Good technical slab climbing on limestone up to 80m high. A fair position at 400m but can even be quite cold if a strong wind is blowing. *In situ* protection [1–3].

Dir: 10km E of Aix-en-Provence. Go to Le Tholonet via the N7 on the SE corner of Aix. From the village take the D17 towards St Antonon-s-Bayon. Take a footpath on the L near some tight bends before the village up to the Refuge Paul Cézanne. A footpath leads away on the R to the crag in 10 mins. (159:E3)

Les Deux Aiguilles:
✱ 09.00→15.00 (20.20.41.30.1)(112)
B-DU-RHÔNE [332]

Steep good limestone offering very good climbing indeed. The Mistral wind catches the crag and is a blessing in summer. At the moment the cliff is being re-equipped so bring nuts; hopefully it will be bolted up by summer 1991. Worth a visit.

Dir: 12km E of Aix-en-Provence. Go to Le Tholonet via the N7 on the SE corner of Aix. From the village take the D17 E up to St Antonon-s-Bayon. Carry on for 500m to a parking spot. The crag can be seen up to the N and takes about 15 mins to reach on a path with black markers. (159:E3)

Fontvielle:
✳ 09.00→19.00 (15.20.48.23.1)(117) B-DU-RHÔNE [333]

A good hard climbing crag on excellent limestone. Pockets and steep walls. Routes are well geared up [1−3], 10−60m. Definitely worth a visit. Topos can be obtained from the café in Fontville, or by post from Escapades Verticales, 23 rue Henri Fabre, 84300 Cavaillon.

Dir: 10km NE of Arles. Take the D17 from Arles to Fontville. Go through the town, and at the end of the houses take the D82c on the L towards St Jean. After 1km the crags can be seen on the R and the L. (158:B2)

Frigolet:
(5−7a)(40)   B-DU-RHÔNE [334]

A limestone crag with about 40 routes bolted [2−3] up.

Dir: 12km SSW of Avignon. From the town take the N570 over the Durance river towards Arles in the S. Just over the river turn R on to the D35 to Barbentane, then turn L on to the D35 which leads down to St Michel-de-Frigolet. (158:B1)

Mouriès:
✳ 10.00→19.00 (9.26.68.58.7)(169) B-DU-RHÔNE [335]

One of the best crags in the S of France. Up to 25m single pitch routes on bolted [1−3] limestone. Vertical walls − powerful fingers very useful. Most of the very hard climbs are on the two N faces, with other routes on a S face. Le Fluide Enchanté (8b) is a classic testpiece. Well worth a visit and a useful summer crag. You can buy topos locally but they are at present out of date so seek up-to-date info. Worth a visit definitely, near the A7 *autoroute*.

Excellent local campsite which must be used if staying in the area. The access has been delicate in the past so please do not trespass into the olive groves or archaeological sites. Car break-ins have been reported here.

Dir: 20km E of Arles, 20km WNW of Salon-de-Provence. Take the D17 to the town or Mouriès from either town. From the village take the D24 but after 1km instead of going right carry straight on towards Auberge de Servanne. Carry on just past this to a parking spot on the R, then take the track on the R which leads to a footpath and the crag. (158:B2)

Orgon:
✳ 09.00→20.00 (20.23.52.16.0)(120) B-DU-RHÔNE [336]

A good limestone climbing area up to 60m high. Walls, slabs and lots of climbing in the middle grades. Climbing all year round, new protection [1−3]. Worth a visit. Topos can be obtained in Cavaillon.

Dir: 26km SE of Avignon, 5km S of Cavaillon. From Cavaillon go S a few km to the town of Orgon. Find the *camping* in the valley Heureuse, which is signposted. The road runs along a railway line to the campsite where the crags can be seen. Park without obstructing any roads and tracks please. (158:C2)

Le Pin de Simon:
✳ 08.00→13.00 (6.5.8.9.1)(29) B-DU-RHÔNE [337]

A good small 40m limestone crag with easy as well as very hard routes. Quite high at 600m; it gets windy here at times. Harder routes tend to be better equipped.

Dir: 23km E of Marseilles, 8km ENE of Aubagne. Take the D2 from Aubagne to Gémenos. Carry on along the D2 to Parc de Pons, continue for another 7km to just above a forestry conservation area. Park here by the road (the crag cannot be seen). A footpath leads down across to a smaller footpath on the R which goes down to the crag. (160:B3)

Rocher de la Consolation:
✳ 12.00→20.00 (40.25.40.7.0)(112) B-DU-RHÔNE [338]

A very good 25m molasse limestone crag with plenty in all grades. Walls, overhangs on pockets and crack routes also. Typical climbing of the area, bolts [2−4]. Simply a great crag to visit.

Dir: 21km NE of Aix-en-Provence. Take the N96 to Peyrolles. Stay on the N96 in the direction of Manosque. After 2km there is a R turn (D61) to Jouques. Pass this, carry on for 2.2km. Here there is a forest track which leads up to the crag in about 5 mins. (159:F2)

Sainte-Anne:
✳ 08.00→14.00 (21.24.21.2.0)(68)
B-DU-RHÔNE [339]

This crag is sometimes referred to as LAMBESC. Quite a small crag up to 15m high. Molasse limestone, hard on the surface but weak underneath making some of the *in situ* gear unsafe, but it is being re-equipped at present so go for the new bolts [2−3]. Good for beginners.

Dir: 23km NW of Aix-en-Provence. Go into the town of Lambesc and take the D67a (you cannot get off the bypass on to this road) towards La Roque d'Anthéron. After 4km turn L up the steep hill and go to the Monument St Anne and the crag. (159:D2)

Saint-Ser:
✳ 09.00→16.00 (9.23.72.18.2)(124)
B-DU-RHÔNE [340]

This is the best equipped crag at present in the SAINTE VICTOIRE region. Good limestone up to 70m, mainly slab climbing and fun for everyone. Not to be missed. Bring your high-friction boots here, it is slightly polished. Superb views. Topos in Puyloubier, try Relais too.

Dir: 18km E of Aix. From the SE corner of Aix turn off the N7 and go to Le Tholonet. Here take the D17 towards Puyloubier. 2km before the village there is a café, Relais de St Ser. A footpath on the L going N leads up to the crag in 5 mins for the fit, 30 mins for the rest. (159:F3)

Les Trois Cimes de la Galère:
✳ AM (9.16.33.8.0)(62)
B-DU-RHÔNE [341]

This area was known previously as BARTAGNE and is split into many areas, some of which are rarely climbed upon. This is the most popular crag in the immediate area of PIC DE BERTAGNE, centre of the SAINT-BAUME region. Good technical fingery problems to be found on this limestone crag up to 40m. The crag is quite high up at 500m but is out of the cold Mistral wind. The protection is varied [2−4] but in general good. There are longer routes around, but nuts and so on are necessary for these. Don't leave anything in the car, except your cuddly Rottweiler.

Dir: 23km E of Marseilles, 6km E of Aubagne. From Aubagne take the D2 E through Gémenos and up towards the Col de l'Espigoulier. After a couple of km there is a forestry track on the R very near Parc de Pons. This leads to a small school to the L of the Trois Cimes. The crag takes 10 or so mins to reach. (160:B3)

Le Vallon du Saut:
✳ 10.00→16.00 (16.38.99.39.1)(192)
B-DU-RHÔNE [342]

A well bolted [1−2] limestone crag up to 40m high. The crag is on private ground but climbing is permitted.

Dir: 20km WNW of Marseilles. Take the *autoroute* A55 towards Martigues, leave at the exit Mède Est. Just before La Mède turn L near a level crossing, carry straight on but not through the tunnel. At the end turn R on to a track. Take this for 300m where the crag can be seen. (158:C4)

Calanques

Climbing at the Calanques has always been great fun and it is the perfect spot in the colder months. It is quite a popular area and many of the routes have been polished. The protection is open to corrosion from the sea and, although it is replaced from time to time, a full rack of gear should be taken along. Newer and more popular areas have modern bolts which have been painted but much of the charm of the area is to get away from the crowds. A guide to the area is useful and, even if it is sightly out of date, worth buying. There are two major problems in the area. The first is access. All the cliffs are quite a way from car parks so expect a 45-min walk; take plenty of water, and supplies to last you all day. The second problem is that all the car thieves in Marseilles just read the last sentence. There is obviously no real way to beat them, just take the best possible precautions. Make your car look completely unattractive, lock it up, leave a snake on the driver's seat and have a rifle club champion sticker on the window. Perhaps the best way to beat them is to park in Cassis, mingle in the town and then take the ferry around to the crags. The round trip is about a fiver, but it does make a lovely day out. Use official campsites as theft is again a problem, and the police will move you on forcibly anyway.

Alpinodrome:
✳ 09.00→19.00 (Bouldering)
B-DU-RHÔNE [343]

This small area offers some good bouldering and routes up to 15m. Very polished so it becomes tiring very quickly. Quite popular.

Dir: 9km S of Marseilles. *See* Les Gourdes (Calanques). (160:A3)

Crêt de St-Michel:
✳ 11.00→19.00 (10.40.50.5.0)(105)
B-DU-RHÔNE [344]

Some very pleasant slabs here with plenty of routes in the middle grades. 100m routes up to 5 pitches. A very nice setting overlooking the port of Morgiou.

Dir: 7km W of Cassis. From the D559 between Cassis and Marseilles a road leads off to the S just outside Marseilles at Le Redon to Luminy. From here take a path SE to the coast then back along towards Morgiou. About 15 mins to reach the coast. The cliff is seen above on the R. The crag by the sea here is Sugiton, well worth climbing on. (160:A3)

Dalle de Port-Miou:
✳ 12.00→19.00 (2.5.5.1.0)(13)
B-DU-RHÔNE [345]

Some good limestone slabs very close to the town of Cassis. 20−30m.

Dir: At Cassis. A footpath leads from Port-Miou to the cliff. (160:A3)

Devenson:
✳ 09.00→19.00 (30.50.60.20.0)(130)
B-DU-RHÔNE [346]

A really superb part of the Calanques to get away from the crowds. You will need your own protection here more than normal, but the coastline is superb and endless routes can be found. Good 80m limestone with several pitch routes in the middle grades. Easier routes can

also be found. There is a traverse of the coastline here which takes several days; for the enthusiastic.

Dir: 12km SSE of Marseilles. Take the ferry from Cassis to Le Vau, then cut across the headland to the W and locate the crags at will. (160:A3)

En-Vau:
✳ 06.00→20.00 (50.70.70.15.0)(205)
B-DU-RHÔNE [347]

One of the good cliffs in the area. The pro is getting a bit old and needs replacing. Plenty of climbing here.

Dir: 5km SW of Cassis. A ferry can be taken directly here. *See* map. (160:A3)

Les Goudes:
✳ 11.00→19.00
(42.72.106.30.1)(251)
B-DU-RHÔNE [348]

One of the major climbing areas in the Calanques with relatively easy access by road. Lots of climbing in the middle grades, limestone up to 80m high. The gear [2−4] is steadily being replaced. Many of the routes have become very polished, but don't let this put you off. This crag is also well protected from the cold Mistral wind. The nearby crags are all under this heading, including ST MICHEL-D'EAU-DOUCE, TÊTE DE LA MOUNINE and POINTE CALLOT.

Dir: 9km S of Marseilles. From the town drive to the far S peninsula to the small village of Les Goudes, near Cap Croisette. The road carries on to Callelongue. The crags are to the E of here and take about 20−30 mins to reach by well-worn footpaths which are marked green then yellow. Near the village is Alpinodrome. A track off to the R is taken and after a few hundred metres the area is seen on the L. (160:A3)

Crag shot of EN VAU, Calanques. (Photo Simon Carr)

Paroi des Cabanons:
✳ 06.00→08.00 (0.1.7.7.1)(16)
B-DU-RHÔNE [349]

One of the newly developed crags in the *massif*. The hard routes are equipped with new gear [3]. Very steep and in the shade, so a good spot. Two pitch routes up to 70m.

Dir: 7km W of Cassis. From the S end of Marseilles take the road to Les Baumettes. From here a private road leads 3km to the fishing village of Morgiou (I believe it's closed only in summer, but ask locally). Arriving at the village the cliff can be seen on the R behind the cottages. (160:A3)

Pastré:
✳ Rare (5.17.16.4.0)(32)
B-DU-RHÔNE [350]

A small limestone crag up to only 20m, but a very good one with lots of different types of climbing from slabs to overhangs. Better in the middle grades than the harder ones. Good pro and cool in summer; nice by the sea and a pleasant view of the bay, but open to the Mistral wind.

Dir: S part of Marseilles. Go to the S part of town on the coast road past Plage du Prado, to Pointe Rouge. There is a road called Boulevard Piot which leads away opposite the Voile d'Or restaurant. Take this to the end and turn R then L up to the top. Here a path leads off up to the crag in about 15 mins. (160:A3)

Roy d'Espagne
✳ 18.00→20.00 (6.18.36.15.1)(66)
B-DU-RHÔNE [351]

A good urban crag in the southern 8th district of Marseilles. Limestone up to 50m offers some fingery climbing on steep interesting rock. In winter it tends to get blasted by the Mistral wind but in summer the same wind can be a useful cooling asset. New bolts [2–3] and quite a popular spot.

Dir: S area of Marseilles. Go to the S end by the sea and locate the park Roy d'Espagne, and a castle, Andalousie. The crag is beneath it and easy to find. You cannot park beneath the crag so take your valuables with you. (160:A3)

Sormiou
✳ 06.00→22.00 (40.40.40.20.0)(140)
B-DU-RHÔNE [352]

A damn good place to visit in summer or winter. Lots of routes, up to 100m and 3 pitch routes in the medium and lower grades. Right by the sea and a lot of the gear [2–6] has been modernised. Quite simply the place to go.

Dir: 12km SSE of Marseilles. From the Mazarques area in the S of Marseilles a road leads down towards Sormiou. The road is private for 3km and you have to pay (yuk!). The climbing is at the peninsula and only a few minutes from the car. More out-of-the-way places can be found as well. By taking a path by the coast to the E you can reach FALAISE DU CANCEOU with more climbing; this is perhaps more easily reached from Morgiou (*see* Paroi des Cabanons. (160:A3)

Sugiton:
✳ 08.00→22.00 (40.40.40.8.0)(128)
B-DU-RHÔNE [353]

A very good crag by the sea with some marvellous climbing in the middle grades. Bolts [3–4], routes up to 70m and 2 pitches. A good introduction to the area but quite popular and polished.

Dir: 7km W of Cassis. *See* approach for Crêt de St-Michel. (160:A3)

Var – 83

The area around Toulon is very popular and offers very good climbing, but cars left unattended around here are very vulnerable to thieves and precautions should always be taken. Camping in the area is easy enough but in the summer tourist season you will not get a plot by the beach without booking. I would recommend you keep this area mostly for winter entertainment anyway. Camping at Toulon near La Seyne is often popular. Information and topos for the Fréjus area can be obtained from Le Club des Pins, Avenue d'Austerlitz, 83700 St Raphael (tel: 94 40 43 10). Also, in the area around Roquebrune, Perthus snakes (the poisonous ones) live very happily. Don't make them fat! Keep to footpaths and picnic with caution!

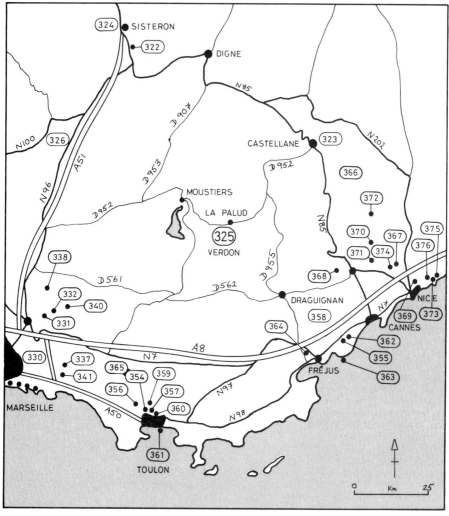

322. CHÂTEAU-ARNOUX
323. MONTAGNE DU TEILLON
324. SISTERON
325. VERDON
326. VOLX
330. CHAÎNE DE L'ETOILE
331. LES DALLES GRISES
332. LES DEUX AIGUILLES
337. LE PIN DE SIMON
338. ROCHER DE LA CONSOLATION
340. SAINT-SER
341. LES TROIS CIMES DE LA GALÈRE
354. BAOU DE QUATRE-OURO

355. BARRE DU ROUSSIVEAU
356. CIMAI
357. COUDON
358. FALAISE DU BLAVET
359. MONT CAUME
360. MONT FARON
361. LA PIADE
362. PIC DU PERTHUS
363. POINTE DE DRAMONT
364. ROQUEBRUNE
365. TOURRIS
366. AIGLUN
367. BAOU DE ST-JEANNET

368. BLOCS DE CABRIS
369. BLOCS DE GAIRAUT
370. COURMES
371. GOURDON
372. GRÉOLIÈRES
373. LA LOUBIÈRE
374. LA SOURCE
375. TÊTE DE CHIEN
376. LA TURBIE

Baou de Quatre-Ouro:
✳ 09.00→20.00 (5.35.76.20.1)(137)
VAR [354]

This crag translates as 'Cliff of the Four Winds'. It is often very windy here, but the crag faces in many directions. It is limestone 40−80m and it is made up of slabs and walls with some good roofs. Climbs in all grades but generally better in the lower grades. Rock quality is good and bolts [2−4]. Worth a visit.

Dir: 6km WNW of Toulon. From the harbour side of Toulon leave directly N on the D62 towards Le Broussan. At the edge of town and before the countryside turn L on to the D262, which winds its way up. After 500m take the steep track on the R which leads up to a parking spot at a reservoir. Walk up to the crag in 15 mins. (160:C4)

Barre du Roussiveau:
✳ 10.00→16.00
(15.17.28.2.0)(62)   VAR [355]

The best crag in the Frèjus-St Raphael area. Red schists with sandstone. Well bolted [3−4] and pegged up, 20−35m. Good rock with interesting steep climbing. A very good winter crag but too hot in summer.

Dir: 9km NE of St Raphael. Take the N98 coast road from St Raphael towards Cannes. Take the D37 on the L at Agay, signposted Valescure. After 1km and a campsite there is a track leading off to the R. Carry straight on for another 2km past another campsite, then take a track off to the R, and after 2km the crag is on the L side of the road. (163:E3)

Cimai:
✳ 08.00→13.00
(8.14.54.58.11)(145)   VAR [356]

One of the great crags in the S of France and known worldwide. Very little here for the beginner and even the middle grade routes tend to be quite hard. Limestone face 70m, superb rock with bolts [2−3]. Many hard grade 8 climbs including the famous Orange Mécanique. The crag is also sheltered from the cold Mistral wind, a fact worth noting in spring. It is in the shade, so summer afternoons are popular, but there are plenty of routes to go around.

Dir: 8km NW of Toulon harbour. Take the N8 towards Le Beausset. Bypass Ollioules, and carry on for 4km to reach Ste Anne d'Evenos. Turn R on to the D462 towards Le Broussan. After 2km, and before the road does a sharp R turn, park, and walk to the crag in 10 mins (seen from the road up to the L). (160:C3)

SAMIZDAT, 8a, Cimai. (Climber Ben Moon, Photo Mark Pretty)

Coudon:
✶ 08.00→13.00
(12.19.38.10.0)(79)   VAR [357]

A friendlier crag than Cimai and a good choice for the middle and low grade climber. Limestone 20 – 70m with slabs as well as walls. Polished holds in places but with bolts [3]. It can get quite windy here, but it is one of the better winter crags.

Dir: 5km NE of Toulon. From La Valette, the NE part of Toulon, take the D46 towards Les Moulins. After a few km there is a road on the R which leads up to Tourris and Le Revest. Take this and after 1.5km take the D446 on the R towards Mont Coudon for about 6km. A sign to the Ecole d'Escalade is seen; park in the car park. You are above the crag, so go to the R and after about 75m the descent is reached. (160:C4)

Crag shot of COUDON. (Photo Nigel Slater)

Falaise du Blavet:
✶ 09.00→12.00
(3.3.33.1.0)(40)   VAR [358]

A spectacular gorge in a very peaceful setting. The rock is a mixture of sandstone and rhyolite but in most places is quite compact and solid. At present the routes are not well bolted so bring nuts and so on along. Approach is by abseil or a path down to the R. Plenty of scope, as yet undeveloped.

Dir: 12km NNW of Fréjus. Take the N7 from Fréjus in the Marseilles direction. After 8km and before going over the *autoroute* turn R on to a small road under the *autoroute*, and opposite the D7 to Roquebrune). This leads up through to the D47 after 6km. Turn R and after a few km the gorge can be seen on the R. (163:E3)

Mont Caume:
✶ 17.00→22.00 (20)   VAR [359]

An old crag which is due for some fine development as a summer crag (most of the other cliffs in the area are winter-based). Limestone and up to 100m, steep. Watch for details.

Dir: 8km NNW of Toulon. From the N of town on the W side head up to Le Revest via the D46. The crag is further up on the L. (160:C3)

Mont Faron:
✶ 10.00→16.00
(8.7.8.5.0)(28)   VAR [360]

In previous years the N face of this peak proved popular, being 100m high. Today the smaller crags on the S side are climbed on and equipped with bolts [2 – 3]. Limestone, single pitch.

Dir: 2km N of Toulon. From the town take the D46 going N towards Le Revest. Before you leave town turn R on to the small road signposted up to Mont Faron. The crags are obvious. (160:C4)

La Piade:
✶ 10.00→16.00
(Bouldering)   VAR [361]

This limestone area by the sea is very good (and indeed famous) for sea-level traversing. The level of difficulty ranges from very easy to

7a. All sorts of slabs and overhangs for almost 1km. The traverse can be done at 5+ in the easiest way but is not recommended for non-swimmers. Bring your sun-tan lotion.

Dir: At the far E end of Toulon on the coast beneath Fort de Ste Marguerite. Take the D42 out of Toulon by the sea, then the N559 to Pradet for 1.5km. There is a small road on the R marked leading to Crossmed. After 1km the sea is reached. Steps lead down to the beach and the crag is about 5 mins' walk. Warning! Do not leave any valuables in the car or at the start of the traverse unless accompanied by a friend. (161:D4)

Pic du Perthus:
✳ 07.00→12.00
(6.4.10.0.0)(20)   VAR [362]

A majestic crag set up on its own with superb views. Climbing is indifferent as is the volcanic rock, but nevertheless there are some very worthwhile routes. Fixed pegs [4] but I would still take gear to the crag as well. 30–70m, 2 pitch routes.

Dir: 10km ENE of St Raphael. Take the N98 coast road from St Raphael towards Cannes. Take the road D37 on the L at Agay signposted Valescure. After 1km and a campsite there is a track leading off to the R. Follow this for 2km, bear L and away from Pic de l'Ours and continue for 1km. The crag can be seen up above. (163:E3)

Pointe de Dramont:
✳ 10.00→16.00
(15.5.12.3.0)(35)   VAR [363]

A bit of an esoteric sea cliff with rock of a dubious nature. However, you may enjoy this sort of thing, so I've jolly well included it. Routes up to 40m on a reddy sort of volcanic yukky rock. The cemented pitons [3–6] may if you wish be trusted. The setting is very nice indeed – a pleasant change from the arid landscape of the region and safe from forest fires.

Dir: 8km E of St Raphael. Take the N98 coast road towards Cannes. After 6km Le Drammont is reached. It is perhaps best to park here and walk to the headland and then descend to sea level. (163:EF3)

Roquebrune:
✳ 12.00→14.00
(8.7.15.0.0)(30)   VAR [364]

Quite a large 60m cliff with 2–4 pitch routes. Sandstone and red schists. One of the best crags in the area. There are pitons [4] in place, but I recommend that you also carry a selection of nuts and Friends at least to make the belays very secure. There is a good bouldering area here as well.

Dir: 11km WNW of Fréjus. Take the N7 towards Marseilles, after about 8km turn L on to the D7 to Roquebrune. Pass under the railway then after 1km the road goes over a river. Take the small road immediately after it on the R. This leads up a steep hill and to the crag. (163:D3)

Tourris:
✳ 10.00→16.00
(5.10.18.8.0)(41)   VAR [365]

A good top-roping crag in the Toulon vicinity where you can work on some good fitness. Quite a popular spot. Limestone 20m high. Not a bad place. Bolts [4–6].

Dir: 5km NE of Toulon. From La Valette, the NE part of Toulon, take the D46 towards Les Moulins. After a few km there is a road on the R which if stayed on bearing L leads up to Tourris. Follow this up and after a couple of km a col is reached. Carry on for 50m to a rubbish tip, where a path leads off to the L, and the crag after 10 mins. (160:C3)

Alpes-Maritimes – 06

A lovely area to climb in France, with many of the crags close to the Riviera; perfect for an evening's climbing after work or a winter visit. In summer it can often be far too hot on many of the crags, however, parts of St Jeannet can nearly always be found in the shade. There is a climbing shop in Nice, Alticoop, 3 rue Caroline (tel: 93 98 58 53) where you can buy topos for most of the crags in the area.

Aiglun:
✳ 12.00→18.00
(0.1.11.6.0)(18)
ALPES-MARITIMES [366]

A good large limestone 200m crag with fantastic views. The crag itself consists of a large reddish wall with bolts [3–6]. Set at 700m and not too hot in winter but catches the sun well and is ideal in May and September.

Dir: 35km NW of Nice, 22km N of Grasse, but takes quite a long time from either town. Take the N202 which runs N out of Nice. A road from the valley D17 leads up to the W and Roquesteron. Carry on up the steep road and after a few km there is a road (D10) on the L which leads up to Aiglun in about 6km. Park in the village (small). The crag is reached in about 15 mins by a path. The descent is on the RH side. (164:C3)

Baou de St-Jeannet:
✳ 08.00→22.00
(30.30.70.60.0)(190)
ALPES-MARITIMES [367]

A good traditional winter crag, limestone 200m. The cliff offers a lot to the grade 6 climber (grade 7 see La Source). The cliff is large but at the sides there are plenty of shorter routes of 30m or so. Bolts [3–6] and re-equipping is going on. Quite polished, especially in the lower grades.

Dir: 13km WNW of Nice, 4km NNE of Vence. From Vence take the D2210 for 6km where a road on the L leads up to St Jeannet. In the town a small road rue du Baou leads up to a winding road and a small reservoir. From here a path leads up to the R and the crag. It is best to park in a small car park in the town on the L side as you drive up. To locate La Source: instead of turning R up to rue du Baou, carry straight on to rue Saint Claude. The road passes a small chapel, Notre Dame des Champs, carry on and eventually a path leads off on the R up to the crag. Total distance about 1.5km. (165:D3)

Blocs de Cabris:
✳ 10.00→19.00
(Bouldering) ALPES-MARITIMES [368]

Some very interestingly shaped limestone boulders. Sandy base so bring a small mat with

you. Problems vary from a few metres up to 10m. Ideal spot if you are finding the restaurants of Cannes too enlarging.

Dir: 18km NW of Cannes, 4km W of Grasse. At Grasse the D13 goes off towards Speracèdes. Take this but after only a few metres take the D4 on the R which leads up to Cabris. Carry on up the D4 towards St Vallier de Thiey. After about 3km the boulders can be seen on both sides of the road. (164:C4)

Blocs de Gairaut:
✳ 12.00→19.00
(Bouldering) ALPES-MARITIMES [369]

A very good limestone bouldering area, with about 12 good 5m boulders. Quick to get to, with some gymnastic climbing. Worth a visit.

Dir: Above the northern outskirts of Nice, to the N side of the autoroute. Exit from the A8 at the Le Ray and Gairaut turn-off. Head N to the D414 towards Falicon and Aspremont. After 2km at a large bend there is parking for a few cars. The boulders only take a couple of mins to reach following a footpath with yellow and green markers. (165:E3)

Courmes:
✳ 16.00→22.00
(0.2.8.10.2)(22)
ALPES-MARITIMES [370]

A small limestone cliff 15–25m of very good quality, bolts [2–3] and no easy routes really. A good summer crag at 600m up. Good hard climbing of different types.

Dir: 12km NNE of Grasse. From Grasse take the D2085 towards Nice, after 5km at Pré-du-Lac turn L on to the D3 towards Gourdon. Carry on along the D3 for 6km past Gourdon and just past the D6 turning on the R is the D503, a small road up to Courmes. Park in the village. Take the first road on the L by the fountain, follow a footpath on the R which crosses a field. Bear L to a gap and then the crag is on the R. (165:D3)

Gourdon:
✳ 09.00→16.00
(8.20.58.24.0)(110)
ALPES-MARITIMES [371]

A very good recently developed crag in the Nice–Cannes area which has helped ease the strain on St Jeannet. Limestone 25m, although at 500m it is very good for winter climbing and far too hot in summer. Worth a visit. There is a huge amount of rock in the area awaiting development, some is quite soft though. Bolts [3].

Dir: 18km N of Cannes, 6km NE of Grasse. From Grasse take the D2085 towards Nice, after 5km at Pré-du-Lac turn L on to the D3 towards Gourdon. The road takes a few bends then after 3.3km passes a quarry on the L. Opposite is a track which leads up to the crag in 10 mins. (164:D3)

Gréolières:
✳ 10.00→16.00
(1.5.17.14.4)(41)
ALPES-MARITIMES [37]

One of the very good recently developed crags in the area. Limestone 16–30m. Good friction, water pockets, excellent steep walls. The crag is situated up at 1,000m and consequently is no good for winter except on a very sunny day. Best in May or September. All new bolts [2–3]. A wonderful view of the Loup valley. Worth a trip, plenty to keep you occupied.

Dir: 16km N of Grasse. From Grasse take the D2085 towards Nice, after 5km at Pré-du-Lac turn L on to the D3 towards Gourdon. Carry on along the D3 past Gourdon and eventually to meet the D2, turn L, go up and through Gréolières. Carry on for about 2km and then park on the L before the first of 4 tunnels. The crag can be seen up on the R. Reached by path in about 15 mins. (164:C3)

La Loubière:
✳ 10.00→17.00
(20.49.119.61.10)(259)
ALPES-MARITIMES [373]

A superb cliff of limestone overlooking Monaco at 400m. Although high above the town it remains a good winter climbing area (well known to the French). Good rock 30–100m with bolts [2–3] on big walls, wonderful view. Too hot in summer, handy for Casino Crag Rats.

LA LOUBIÈRE, climbers en route.
(Photo Nigel Slater)

Dir: 2km NW of Monaco. Take the La Turbie exit off the A8 *autoroute*. From La Turbie go towards Monaco on the Cap d'Ail road D37. Just after leaving La Turbie turn L down a track to the fort and telecommunications station. Follow this for 1km and park at the top of the crag. Looking out to the sea, La Loubière is on the R and Tête de Chien is on the L. (165:E3)

La Source:
✳ 11.00→18.00
(50.50.50.4.1)(155)
ALPES-MARITIMES [374]

This is the sister crag to St Jeannet. Good, steep limestone climbing here and quicker to get to than the higher crag. Also there is some good bouldering to be found at the foot of the crag. Routes up to 30m and all equipped with bolts [2–3]. Very popular with all the climbers in Nice, especially at weekends. Camping can easily be found down at the lower part of St Jeannet. Topos available at the *boulangerie* Nirascou.

Dir: 13km WNW of Nice. *See* Baou de St Jeannet. (165:D3)

PAPPION DIRECT, 7b+, Tête de Chien. (Photo Nigel Slater)

Tête de Chien:
✶ 11.00→18.00 (*See* Loubière)(259)
ALPES-MARITIMES [375]

The classic Champagne 8b is worth having a cruise at, but if you wear glasses or contact lenses get them checked first otherwise you'll never find the holds.

Dir: *See* Loubière.

La Turbie:
✶ 10.00→17.00 (20.30.50.60.4)(164)
ALPES-MARITIMES [376]

Excellent limestone crags in the area to the SW of La Turbie. There are two main sections. There are some very hard routes here up to 8b. Sometimes referred to as Traversées de la Turbie. Bolts [3]. Well worth a visit.

Dir: 3km WNW of Monaco. From La Turbie take the N7 Grande Corniche (high road) towards Nice, after 1.5km park at the road-track on the R (no entry for vehicles). There are two different sections. For the first, take the track for about 5 mins past a couple of hairpin bends, and for the second take the track for about 20 mins to near a tunnel. (165:E3)

Italy

Italian climbing has come a long way since the aid era of the 1960s and early 70s. The sport climbing attitude has been fully adopted and many crags are now fully bolted up. It has been hard to keep track of this new development, and in consequence info here is only just adequate. I suggest that you travel to your chosen area and locate a good climbing shop, then buy the appropriate local climbing topos. The Italians are very good at this and have it well sorted out. Any English literature on different areas is really only suited to the mountaineer, so travel and seek local info on sport climbing.

If imbibing is one of your hobbies, the Italians are the largest wine-makers in the world, so you will never be short of the odd bottle or two, or three. The north-west of Italy has a great many vineyards producing good red wine, but you should not miss the chance to finish off a few glasses of Barolo. A trip 50km to the SE of Torino is worthwhile if you pull any tendons or run out of chalk, while those in the areas of Arco and Lecco will have to hire a lorry and do a quick dash to Verona for supplies of Valpolicella, Soave and Bardolino.

NORTH ITALY

Arco:
✳ 08.00→21.00
(4 – 8b +)(400)   TRENTINO [1]

One of the best areas to climb in Italy. There are numerous crags here offering plenty in all grades and facing both E and W, ideal for a summer trip. There are also other activities such as boating, windsurfing, waterskiing on Lago di Garda. The climbs are on good limestone up to 100m high and with *in situ* gear [1 – 4]. Worth a week. There are six well-known crags near the road from Riva del Garda to Sarche in the N: SPIAGGA DELLE LUCERTOLE (to the S of Torbole near the lakeside), CIMA COLODRI (Arco), SAN PAOLO, NUOVI ORIZZONTI, PLACCHE ZEBRATE, LA GOLA DI TOBLINO (a gorge beside Lago di Toblino). Topos to the crags can be bought from climbing shops locally. There is a good municipal campsite close to Arco.

Dir: 20km SW of Trento, 60km ENE of Milano. From Milano take the *autostrada* towards Bréscia, go up the L side of the lake for the scenic 7-day route or carry on towards Verona (excellent summer opera season) and take the A22 towards Trento. Take the turn-off to Arco and Riva del Garda. The crags are now low down in the valley. (11:F5)

Bardonecchia:
✳ Varied
(5 – 8a)(Unknown)   VALLE DI SUZA [2]

This area has become famous since Italian climbing competitions have been held here. Ironically the crags were over the border in France. There are plenty of crags around, but the best selection is in the Vallée Etroite. For topos enquire locally.

Dir: 75km W of Torino. From the city go W on the No25 which leads all the way to the town. An *autostrada* is being built in the valley at present. Do not go through the tunnel to Modane in France but from the town take the road past Mélezet towards the Col de l'Echelle. Before the hairpins leading up to the col turn R along the Vallée Etroite and there are good crags on the L after a couple of km. (21:B1)(French Michelin 133:D2)

Bismantova:
✳ 10.00→16.00
(4 – 7c +)(35)   EMÍLIA ROMAGNA [3]

A large crag up to 120m but the bolt-protected routes are all single pitch and are at the bottom on the centre of the crag. The rock is a funny type of sandstone. Not bad. A topo is available from the *refugio* at the bottom of the crag.

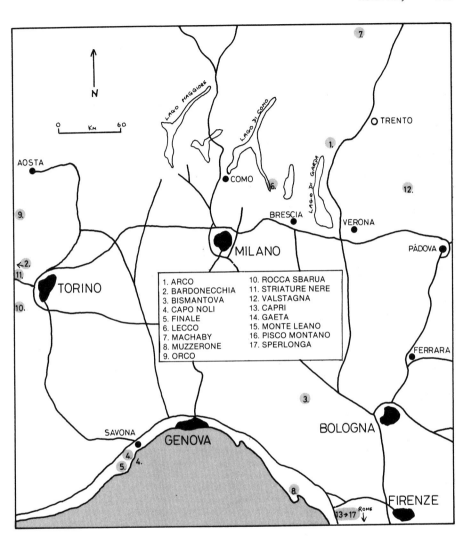

1. ARCO
2. BARDONECCHIA
3. BISMANTOVA
4. CAPO NOLI
5. FINALE
6. LECCO
7. MACHABY
8. MUZZERONE
9. ORCO
10. ROCCA SBARUA
11. STRIATURE NERE
12. VALSTAGNA
13. CAPRI
14. GAETA
15. MONTE LEANO
16. PISCO MONTANO
17. SPERLONGA

Dir: 75km W of Bologna. Take the *autostrada* towards Milano, pass Modena then turn off to Réggio Nell'Emilia. From the town centre take the No63 SW to Vezzano and then Castelnovo ne'Monti. Carry on for 3km to La Pietra di Bismantova. The crag is obvious. (30:D2)

Capo Noli:
✹ 06.00→14.30
(4–7c)(42) LIGÚRIA [4]

A series of sea cliffs which are reasonably short and offer routes as well as good sea-level traversing. A change from Finale and good for a bit of adventurous fun.

Dir: 46km SW of Génova. Take the A10 from Génova towards Nice. Exit just after Savona at Spotorno, go to the town on the coast then head S to Noli, then the point just to the S has the cliffs on. (33:C4)

Finale:
✵ 08.00→22.00
(3 – 8b +)(1000) LIGÚRIA [5]

The best-known crag in Italy and well climbed upon. Good pocketed limestone on 15 crags within close proximity to one another. The crags are almost at sea level and it is possible to climb here all year round. Most face W and in summer climbing in the afternoon is restricted to only 5 of the outcrops. All routes are bolted [1 – 3] and are mostly single pitch. There are routes up to 100m high with good belays or moulinettes. Worth a good long visit. There is an excellent Italian topo guide, *Finale* (ISBN 88-85842-05-4) by Andrea Gallo and Giovanni Massari. This will no doubt be updated but mostly with 8a + routes only. There is a campsite in Finale Ligure. Topo guides can be purchased or browsed through at climbing shops in Finale Ligure and Feglino.

Dir: 54km SW of Génova. Take the A10 from Génova towards Monte Carlo. Go past Savona turn-off, Sportorno, then turn off at Feglino which is due N to Finale Ligure. Take the road towards Finale. Crags are to the L and R. (33:C3)

IL PITTORE, 5 + and ULTIMA VIA, 6b + , Finale. (Climbers Gordon Haines and an unnamed Italian climber, Photo Simon Carr)

Lecco:
✵ 09.30→21.00
(4 – 8a)(78) LOMBARDIA [6]

A fair climbing area close to Lago Como and above the town of Lecco. There are four crags close by of which all have *in situ* gear [1 – 4] and are within 4km of Lecco: MEDALE, ANTIMEDAL, BASTIONATA DEL LAGO and TORRIONE DI VAL REALBA. The routes are up to 200m long but most of the hard routes are single pitch. Limestone.

Dir: 44km NNE of Milano. Take the A4 past Monza then the No36 to Lecco. A topo should be available in the town for the crags which lie above the road running up the E side of the lake towards Sondrio. (10:F3)

Machaby:
✵ 10.00→17.00
(3 – 7c +)(150) AOSTA [7]

A good large climbing area offering a mixture of routes, some to 300m long and other single 30m routes low down. Situated at 200m it offers all year round climbing with the exception of hot summer days, but invariably shade can be found. The long routes tend to be more sporadically bolted [2 – 6] but the shorter single pitch routes have *in situ* gear [1 – 4].

Dir: 35km ESE of Aosta, 64km N of Torino. Take the *autostrada* N from Torino past the town of Ivrea. Carry on towards Aosta for 15km then turn off at the Pont St Martin exit. Continue N on the No26 past Donnas, Bard and then to the village of Machaby. The crag is obvious on the R. A footpath marked with orange paint leads to the crags in 15 mins. (14:B8)

Muzzerone:
✵ 11.00→18.00
(5 – 7c)(75) LIGÚRIA [8]

Some good limestone climbing to be found here Not in the same league as Finale but worth a visit for a couple of days and easy to get to. All single pitch routes up to 50m high. There is plenty of *in situ* gear [2 – 4] and about 4 crags along the coastline.

Dir: 80km ESE of Génova, 5km S of La Spézia. From the town of La Spézia take the road leading towards the southern peninsula and village of Portovénere. Just before the village of La Grázie turn R and follow the road keeping L towards the old fort high up. After the bends there is an obvious parking spot on the R. From here a path leads to the crags in a very nice setting. (34:E6)

Orco:
✳ 10.00→16.00
(4 – 8b)(70)   AOSTA [9]

This area will appeal to some but not others. Big volcanic crags of granite, gneiss, similar to Yosemite (60s climbing), plenty of jamming — yuk! Those with oversize arms, arthritic hands and the brain of an armadillo might like it. Some of the face routes are very good and require superb technique, making a trip here very worthwhile. The crags are big and sunny, routes of 7 pitches and 250m. It is a summer crag and frozen up in winter. *In situ* gear is generally in place but not always brand new! There are about 5 major outcrops here as well as lots of good granite bouldering. Topos and guidebooks to the area are varied and in the process of being updated. Enquire locally.

Dir: 52km NNW of Torino. Take the *auto-strada* A5 towards Aosta but turn off at the junction to Caluso and Rivarolo (one before Ivrea). Go W to Castella Monte, bypass Cuorgnè and continue to Locana. Carry on up the valley forking L after another 4km, to Noasca. The crags are now on the R side (north) of the valley for the next 10km. (14:D5)

Rocca Sbarua:
✳ 10.00→17.00
(3 – 6b)(55)   TORINO [10]

A popular spot for an Italian bumbliano. Lots of routes in the lower grades with *in situ* gear [1 – 5]. Situated at 1,000m with routes up to 120m. Hot in summer but if the sun shines climbing is possible in winter. Volcanic easy-angled rock, a sort of mixture between granite and gneiss. A topo to the crag is unknown.

Dir: 33km WSW of Torino. Take a route going W to Pinerolo. From the town centre take the road towards Perosa and Sestriere. After 300m turn R and take the road N up to Talucco. From here carry on and after a while go L at a fork. The road climbs up then a track leads off to the R signposted 'Casa Darin'. Follow this to a small hamlet, taking care to park out of the way and not obstructing anything. From here a path leads to Colle Ciardonet. From here a path leads down to Rifugio Melano. The crag can be seen from here. 1 hour approach! (21:C5)

Striature Nere:
(6a – 8b)(45)   VALLE DI SUZA [11]

In the opinion of most this is one of the best crags in the valley. All routes are single pitch, bolt protected [2 – 4] with moulinettes. Plenty of good hard climbing here with little below 7a. Worth a visit and very handy from Torino.

Dir: 40km W of Torino. From the *autostrada* going around Torino to the W exit going W on to the No25. Follow this for 25km then turn off into the actual town of Bussoleno. Go through the town, under the railway then after 1km turn R to the village of Foresto. At the village turn R then L after 200m and go to a parking spot 100m further on. A footpath leads off to the R to the top of a crag called LE PARETINE after 400m. Carry on for another couple of mins and the crag will be discovered — big and awesome with black streaks. (21:A4)

Valstagna:
✳ 09.00→17.00
(4 – 7b)(150)   TRENTINO [12]

There are about 5 major crags in the area which are included in a local guidebook. Up-to-date new route info can be found at the La Trattoria Ferronato in Cismon. The two main crags are PARETE DI SON VITO DI ARSII and COVOLO. All the crags are limestone and bolt protected [2 – 4] and close to the road. Some of the crags are single pitch but most are 100m high. Good pocketed rock and worth a visit.

Dir: 50km WSW of Belluno, 34km NNE of Vicenza. From Vicenza go NNE to Bassano. From here take the No47 towards Belluno. After 11km reach Valstagna and the crags are in the valley. (18:A3)

SOUTH ITALY

The info on this area is quite limited unfortunately, but there are coastal cliffs of strong importance that are worth visiting.

Capri:
(Unknown)   NAPLES [13]

All I know is that there is *some* climbing near Capri; good luck!

Gaeta:
✴ 10.00→19.00
(4–7c)(35)   ROME [14]

A good fun 150m limestone sea cliff. All the routes start at the sea and can only be reached by abseil, or, more enjoyably, by boat. This can easily be arranged from the local port of Gaeta. A boat for the day with a picnic, a bottle of Chianti and maybe a route – heaven. Not recommended in high winds or winter.

Dir: 130km SE of Rome. From Rome go SE to Terracina then follow the coast road to Gaeta. The crags are on the peninsula to the S.

Monte Leano:
(4–6c)(15)   ROME [15]

A 65m limestone crag with some excellent routes in grade 6. Some are single pitch and others are double. All have moulinettes for descent and are bolted up [2–4]. Good spot.

Dir: 115km SE of Rome. Take the No7 towards Terracina. 5km before the town the crag is situated on the hill to the L. 10m walk-in.

Pisco Montano:
✴ 10.00→16.00
(4–7b)(25)   ROME [16]

A small 40m limestone crag offering bolted routes [2–4]. Handy and close to the road. Stop if passing.

Dir: 120km SE of Rome. Go SE from Rome to the town of Terracina. From here take the road to the E towards Fondi. Just after the road forks with the other road going towards Gaeta the crag is on the L.

Sperlonga:
✴ 10.00→16.00
(4–8a)(195)   ROME [17]

A good steep limestone crag with no shortage of hard routes on. Popular and well bolted [1–4]. There are several tiers to the crag and therefore a lot of single pitch climbing, although the crag reaches up to 150m high. Worth visiting. Near the sea but not a sea cliff.

Dir: 100km SE of Rome. Go SE from Rome to the town of Terracina. From here continue S along the coast, go past Sperlonga, under 3 bridges in the direction of Gaeta. The crag is soon seen on the L. Access is obvious.

Spain

The climbing in Spain is very good indeed, although it is not in the same league as Verdon or Buoux in France. Unfortunately, the same cannot be said for the protection. The whole of Spain in time will presumably get very well bolted up, but for the time being I would never rely on belays being in place or a route going all the way to the top. A good general rule in Spain is that if the bolts become unreliable or unspottable, retreat.

The weather is very good indeed. In the summer months stay well clear of the low coastal crags, and in winter avoid the high crags like Montserrat or Terradets. There are fewer roads in Spain than in central Europe and you will often have to drive your car over rough ground, or face very long walk-ins.

Spain is a very large country and it takes a long time to drive anywhere. The toll motorways have to be used unless you have a whole year to spare; the other roads with their patchwork tarmac wind up and down mountain passes, leaving you exhausted. However, once you are away from the touristic coastline you cannot fail to have a great trip because of the hospitable Spanish people you will meet.

Much of Spain is pretty backward, so be prepared with supplies when you go away from the cities or coast. Booze is readily available almost everywhere; *dos cervezas por favor* is the phrase to solve any imminent drought crisis.

Petrol stations and shops do not take credit cards in general, so travellers cheques are a must. Banks everywhere have amazing security and are definitely not places to try and rob.

With the lack of development in Spain I wondered whether or not to include half-researched crags. In the end I decided to, on the principle that any info is better than none and the reader will hopefully be pointed in the right direction, and encouraged to climb.

When you visit Spain, take a good pair of very thick trousers and boots. There are many snakes in the bush undergrowth on the walk-ins to crags, and, more important, that undergrowth tends to be made up of very sharp and painful thorns. These will rip your legs apart in no time. You will quickly find that it is worth keeping to footpaths. Never try to descend to the side of the crag, always abseil.

When it comes to imbibing, some of the Spanish wines are excellent, although good wine in Spain is expensive relative to France. Be wary of cheap wine. Some is very good indeed, while the rest tastes almost like a petroleum by-product. There seems to be little control of standards at the lower end of the scale, so I would strongly advise that you quench your thirst on water and beer, then splash out on a single, very good bottle of plonk.

NORTH-WEST SPAIN ─────────────

Galicia:

Faro de Budiño
(60)   GALICIA [1]

A very good granite crag with 100m routes on. The state of *in situ* gear is unknown, so be careful.

Dir: 25km S of Vigo. Seek directions from a climbing shop in Vigo where a topo should be available. (42)

Galiñeiro:
✳ 08.00→20.00
(Bouldering)   Galicia [2]

A very good bouldering area with some routes as well but no real bolting activity yet. Granite and with a wonderful view.

Dir: 12km S of Vigo. From the S part of town take the inland road (550) towards Baiona. After a couple of km turn L towards Gondomar. Pass through Garrida, then 3km later turn L to Arcos. From here a road leads up to the peak of Galineiro. (42.Rb,96)

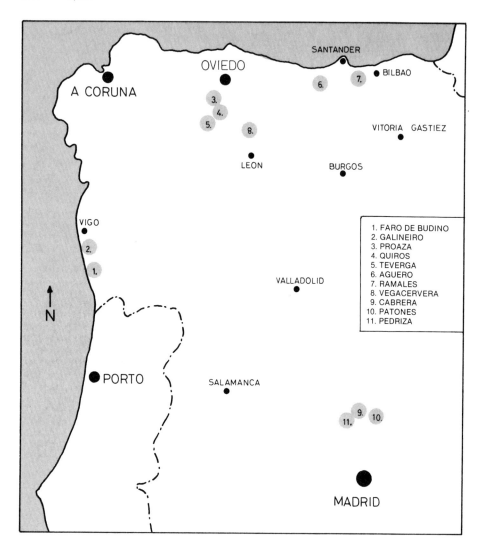

1. FARO DE BUDINO
2. GALINEIRO
3. PROAZA
4. QUIROS
5. TEVERGA
6. AGUERO
7. RAMALES
8. VEGACERVERA
9. CABRERA
10. PATONES
11. PEDRIZA

Asturias

Proaza:
(50)   ASTURIAS [3]

A series of 60m limestone cliffs very near the village of Proaza. Not that well developed but watch press for details.

Dir: 18km SW of Oviedo. From Oviedo take the C634 towards Salas in the W. After 10km at Soto turn L to Trubia, carry on all the way to Proaza. The crags are obvious. (16:Tf,89)

Quiros:
(4 – 8b)(120)   ASTURIAS [4]

A very popular crag. Large, and limestone up to 200m high. The crag is very similar to the limestone of the S of France at the Verdon – big walls with *gouttes d'eau*. *In situ* gear [1 – 4] which is slowly being renewed. Worth a trip. A local topo guide can be seen (if not bought) at a hut just 10 mins from the crag.

Dir: 24km SSW of Oviedo. From Oviedo take the C634 towards Salas in the W. After 10km at Soto turn L to Trubia, carry on all the way to Proaza (reserve crag). Carry on towards Teverga and Puerto de Ventana. This takes you by the Aqueras swamp; turn L and follow the signs to Acicra. From here walk to El Lano where the hut is. The crag is 10 mins away near the village of Bárzana de Quiros. (16:Ua,89)

Teverga:
(3 – 6c)(34)   ASTURIAS [5]

Some very large 200m limestone walls which await full development. There is enough here for a good day at present and if equipping goes ahead, who knows?

Dir: 33km SW of Oviedo. From Oviedo take the C634 towards Salas in the W. After 10km at Soto turn L to Trubia, carry on all the way to Proaza. Carry on to Carranga then turn R and go to San Martin (9km), here follow the signs to La Plaza (1km) where the crags are close by. (16:Tf,90)

Cantabria

Aguero:
(4 – 6c)(26)   CANTABRIA [6]

A very good huge crag with long routes. Limestone up to 400m; really good for a dose of neckache. Some crave this type of crag, others abseil off after the first pitch. *In situ* gear very variable [4 – 6].

Dir: 66km WSW of Santander. Go to the SW and Torrelavega. From here take the C634 W, through Cabezón, San Vincente, then turn L at Molleda on to the C621 signposted Potes. Follow this for about 40km where Lebeña will be signposted to the L. (If you reach Tama you've gone too far.) The crags are near the village. (18:Vc,89)

Ramales:
(40)   CANTABRIA [7]

A very extensive area of big 200m limestone walls awaiting development. *In situ* gear [4 – 6]! Seek adventure climbing here. Local info should be available in Ramales. Worth a visit since there is a lot of climbing in the area. A must for the traditional climber too.

Dir: 45km W of Bilbao, 37km SE of Santander. Take the coast road between the two towns to Laredo. From here a road leads S to the towns of Limpias and then Ampuero. Carry on S to the town of Ramales de la Victoria. The cliffs are on the S edge of town. (20:Wd,89)

Castilla Y León

Vegacervera:
(4 – 7b)(53)   CASTILLA [8]

A limestone crag up to 100m high with a reasonable amount of development. Popular with climbers from León. Climbing shops in León might have info on the whereabouts of a topo for the crag.

Dir: 33km N of León. There are a few ways which might be quicker as roads improve but the old route is as follows. Take the C621 towards Cistierna. After 9km just before Canaleja turn L up the Rio Torro valley, after 10km cross over and turn R to Matueca. Carry on past Pardavé, Matallano to Vegacervera. The road now carries on to Felmin and the cliff is between the new towns.

Madrid

Cabrera:
(4 – 8a)(175)   MADRID [9]

A very similar crag to Pedriza, granite and of good popularity. Worth a detour.

Dir: 48km N of Madrid. Take the *autopista* N1 going N out of Madrid towards Santander. Pass San Sebastian, San Augustín, El Molar and eventually get to La Cabrera. The cliffs are nearby. (85:Wc,103)

Patones:
✳ 10.00→16.00
(5 – 8a +)(170)   MADRID [10]

A very fine limestone area with a lot of crags. The area has become the most popular with climbers from Madrid and in consequence has been well bolted up [1 – 4]. There is a very good mixture of routes here from nice easy-angled walls to technical slabs and steep overhanging routes. It is not that low down and winter cragging is out, but March till Nov is a good time. Very popular at weekends. Local route info can be found at the La Mura bar in town.

Dir: 52km NNE of Madrid. Take the N1 towards Aranda but after 50km turn off to the R to Torrelaguna. Carry on towards Uceda but after 3km follow signs to Patones. At the village cross the river Rio Lozoya (lower cliffs here), and follow the dirt track up to reach the higher crags. (85:Wd,103)

Pedriza:
✳ 09.00→18.00
(4 – 8a)(1000)   MADRID [11]

One of the main areas for the climbers of Madrid. Granite climbing on routes up to 400m high. Double ropes necessary for abseil descents. *In situ* gear is very varied. Bolts [1 – 6]. Plenty of bouldering here. In the shade, which can be very useful. Worth a visit, definitely.

Dir: 40km NW of Madrid. Take the *autopista* out of Madrid to the N in the direction of Colmenar. Pass the town then carry on towards Miraflores. After 8km turn L to Manzanares (campsite). From here La Pedriza is signposted to the R. There is a parking area in front of a bar called Torrero. There is a route book here and a good place to get local info. If there is a topo guide by 1991 it will be available here. (84:Wa,104)

NORTH-EAST SPAIN

País Vasco

Atxarte:
(3 – 7a)(186)   PAÍS VASCO [12]

A very good limestone crag up to 150m high. Bolts [3 – 6]. The most popular in the area and with climbers from Bilbao as it is so quick to get to. Worth a visit.

Dir: 27km ESE of Bilbao. Take the *autopista* to the Durango turn-off. Go into the centre of town then bear to the SE and take the road signposted towards Elorrio. After 2km enter the village of Abadiño Zelaieta. The cliffs are close by. (21:Xc,90)

Eguino:
(4 – 7b)(75)   PAÍS VASCO [13]

Not a lot of info on this one but I hear it is the most popular crag for the climbers in the area and quick to reach in the evening from Vitoria

Gastiez. *In situ* gear unknown, but I would think fair.

Dir: 32km E of Vitoria. Take the N1 going E towards Pamplona. Pass around Salvatierra and carry on to the small village of Eguino about 5km further on (before Alsasua). The crags are close to the village. (29:Uc,91)

Pagassri:
✳ 09.00→19.00
(Bouldering)   PAÍS VASCO [14]

A very good bouldering and climbing area. The crag is up to 40m high so bring a rope, but most use it for training. Quite busy in the evenings.

Dir: 5km S of Bilbao. From the town centre go to the central route leading to the *autopista*. From here go directly S near the outskirts of Larasquito. Here a small road winds its way up

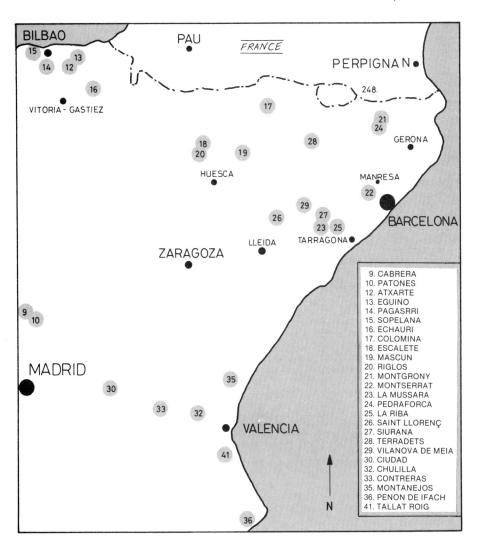

directly S into the hills, after 3km there is a turning on the R which leads up to the Refuge Alpino de Pagassri. The crags are close by. (21:Xa,89)(287)

Sopelana:
✳ 10.00→20.00
(Bouldering)   PAÍS VASCO [15]

Some very good bouldering to be found here on some sandstone outcrops. There is also more nearby at URDULUZ.

Dir: 15km NNW of Bilbao. Go to the N side of the river Nervión to Algorta. From here take the small road leading N to Sopelana. The crags have to be located somehow! (21:Xa,88)

Navarra

Echauri:
(5 − 7c +)(120) NAVARRA [16]

An excellent limestone crag offering a host of new routes in all grades with more development going on. Worth a visit. Car breakins have been a problem here, so be careful.

Dir: 14km W of Pamplona. From the town take a small road going out to the W which passes through Ororbia on the way to Echauri. The crags are near the town. (34:Yb,92)

Aragón − Huesca/Pirineo

Colomina:
✷ 08.00→21.00
(4 − 7c)(70) ARAGÓN [17]

A large granite crag up to 200m and offering plenty of 4 pitch routes in the grade 4 and 5 category as well as harder. There are about 10 different crags in the area and although there is *in situ* gear [3 − 6] I would recommend that you take runners along as well. A fantastic situation, summer climbing only at around 2,000m high. Worth a trip.

Dir: 45km W of Andorra, 23km ENE of Pont du Suert. Take the road 144 going E from Pont du Suert to Senterada. Here turn L and take the road to the end of the valley and the town of Cabdella. Park here and take a footpath bearing N which leads to the crags in 2 hours. (038:AF94)

Escalete:
(6 − 7b)(32) ARAGÓN [18]

A very good limestone gorge which has been developed quite recently. All routes are bolted [2 − 4]. Worth visiting.

Dir: 41km NW of Huesca. Take the C240 to Ayerbe. Carry on through Concilio, then to Murillo de Gállego. Enquire locally for the gorge. (53:Zb,94)

Mascun:
✷ 09.00→16.00
(2.3.24.14.0)(43) ARAGÓN [19]

A crag which has undergone recent development by French and Spanish climbers. The rock is limestone and offers a lot of flat holds and quite technical climbing. All the routes are bolted [2 − 4] and good for the middle and upper grades. The crag is set in the area around Rodellar which has many canyons. There are various sections: VILLAGE, ANDREBOT, CIGARE and PAROI DE LA CHAPELLE. Enquire locally for exact locations, but the most development has gone on in the Village section. The area is sometimes known as SIERRA DE GUARRA.

Dir: 32km NE of Huesca. Take the 240 going E towards Barbastro. Pass Angües, take the next L to Abeigo, then straight N to Rodellar. The crags are very close to the village just below, about 5 mins walk above the river. (054:ZF95)

Riglos:
✷ Sunny
(4 − 7c)(200) ARAGÓN [20]

Quite a famous area with not too sound rock. If you are a lightweight you are fine, but heavyweights should be careful. The rock is conglomerate with cliffs up to 300m high. In summer it is too hot and in winter too cold. Worth a visit.

Dir: 41km NW of Huesca. Take the C240 to Ayerbe. Carry on through Concilio, then just after Murillo de Gállego the village and cliffs of Riglos are to the R. (53:Zb,94)

Catalunya

Montgrony:
✲ Sunny
(15.22.31.6.0)(75) CATALUNYA [21]

A very good crag which is becoming very popular and well bolted [1–4]. Limestone and up to 140m high with mostly two pitch routes. There are five different sections: ZONE DE LA BEAUME, PLA DE FREIXA, PLACE SANT PERE, VENA and COLL ROIG. All offer great climbing and give plenty of entertainment for a few days. Not a winter crag.

Dir: 60km N of Manresa. Take the N1411 from Manresa going N to Berga, bypass the town and carry on in the direction of France. Just before the village of Bagà turn R and go up to La Pobla de Lillet. At the village turn L and go towards Ripoll. Pass through the hamlet of Cassilla then take a track on the L which is marked to a sanctuary. The crags are close by. (57:Bf,95)

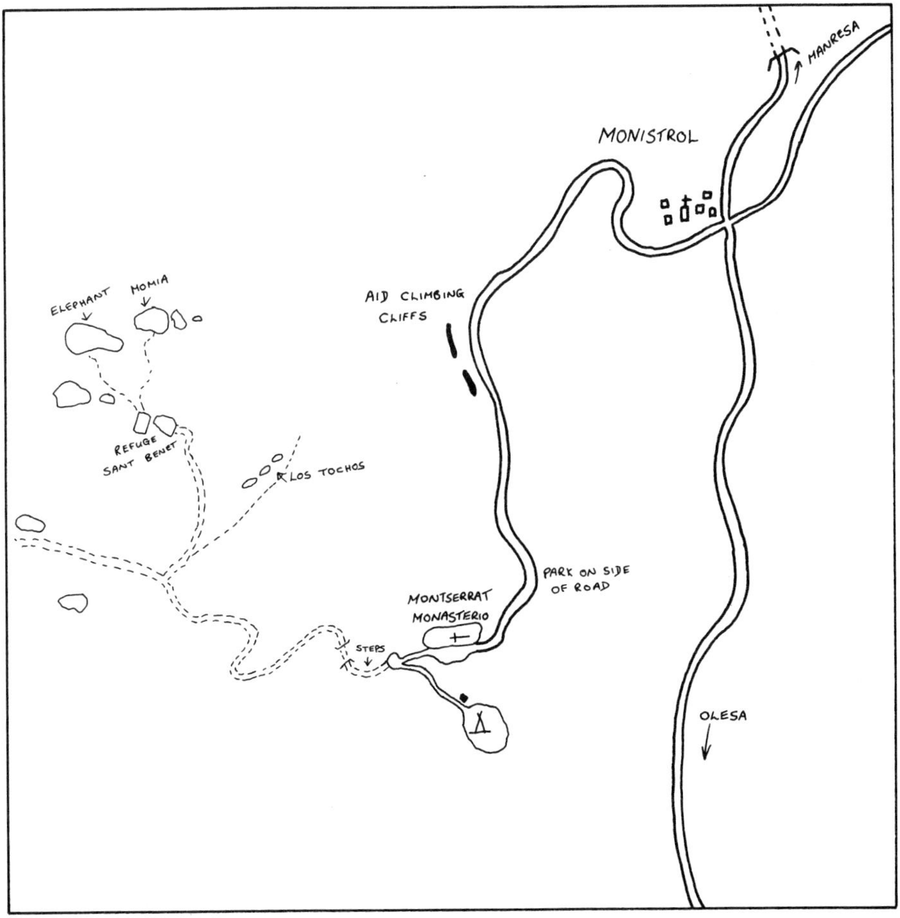

Montserrat:
✲ 07.00→18.00
(20.18.27.32.12)(100)
CATALUNYA [22]

The crags at Montserrat are some of the most impressive in Europe – conglomerate spires which stick up out of the hills to the W of Barcelona. The climbing needs an inspired approach too. There are two main areas. First, the ZONA DEL CAMPING AND TOCHOS. This is an area with short, well-protected climbs for the dogger. Very close to the campsite and in or out of the sun as desired. The second area is ST BENET. This is the higher area, 300m, and takes an exhausting hour to reach. The climbs are longer here, up to 200m, and the easier climbs have most of the bolts missing. Two ropes are better because of the very long abseil descents. There is a refuge though with topos on the walls. If you respect your health I would advise against staying at the refuge – Egon Ronay would not be impressed. The climbing is very similar on the long routes, but even so the positions are incredible. When the sun goes off the spires in the late afternoon it gets extremely cold, especially in shorts. All the other areas around Montserrat have rusted-through bolts and are positively dangerous and a waste of time. In future, with development, Montserrat could become a very important area, but there is still a lot of bolting to be done.

Dir: 40km NW of Barcelona. Take the N2 towards Lleida and after 20km turn R on the C1410 to Manresa. After 10km reach the small village of Monistrol. Buy all your food and drink here, then drive up to Montserrat. The road eventually ends in the monastery 1,300m higher. There is a campsite with almost no grass at the monastery. (57:Be,99)

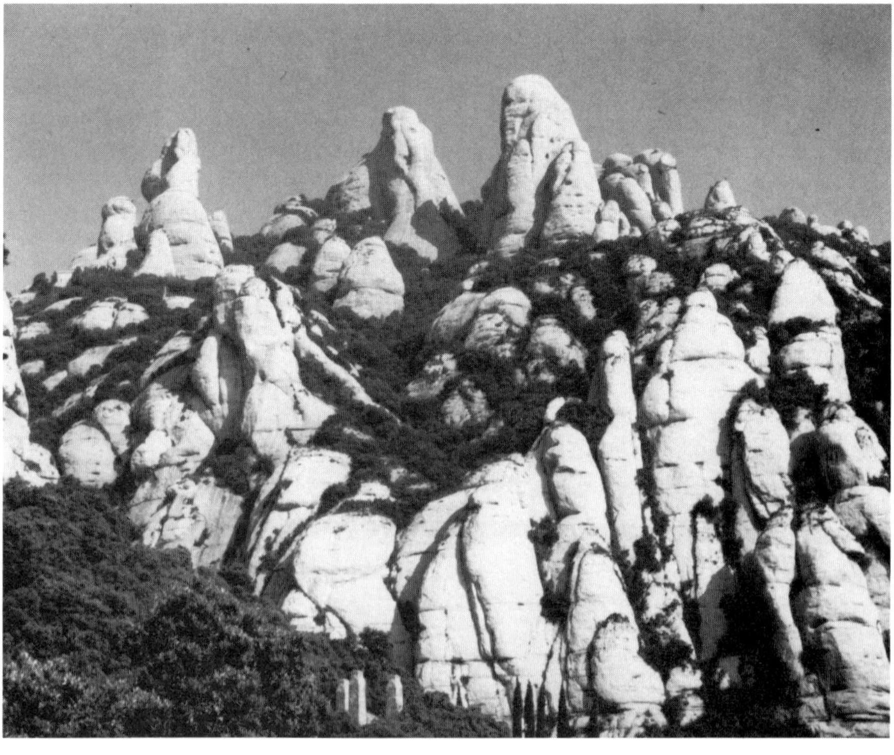

MONTSERRAT, crag shot. (Photo Nigel Slater)

ARRIBABA, 8a, Montserrat. (Climber Jose
Battle, Photo Nigel Slater)

BASTARDO, 7b +, Montserrat.
(Climber Nigel Slater)

La Mussara:
✳ 11.00→17.00
(4 − 7c +)(156)   CATALUNYA [23]

A very good limestone crag in the Siurana
area without such a bad drive-in. Routes up
to 80m high and bolted [2−3]. Excellent
climbing and worth a good trip.

Dir: 24km NW of Tarragona. Take the
autopista to Reus, carry on the N420
towards Falset. After 7km turn R to Alforja.
Carry on in the direction of Cornudella but
after 4km turn R and take this road. Carry on
for 12km then turn R to reach Mussara after
3km. The crag is nearby on the way to the
peak Mussara. (74:Ba,101)

Pedraforca:
(4 − 7c)(240)   CATALUNYA [24]

A famous limestone cliff with routes up to
500m; gosh! In situ gear [3−6] is variable and
I suggest that you bring an adequate supply of
nuts as well. Not a winter crag.

Dir: 57km N of Manresa. Take the C1411 N
from Manresa to Berga, carry on in the same
direction towards Baga but after 15km turn off
L on the road which winds its way up to Saldes
(if you reach Guardiola you've gone too far).
The crag is near the village of Saldes.
(57:Be,95)

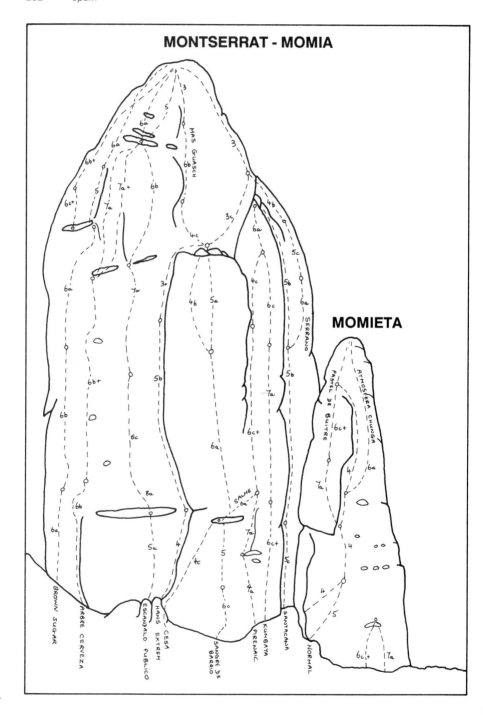

La Riba:
✳ 09.00→14.00
(12.15.25.23.1)(70) CATALUNYA [25]

Not a very large crag but nevertheless a very good one. 5–35m limestone walls with pockets and good protection. There are two areas; to the L is a small buttress with grade 6 and 7 routes, and to the R is the larger crag with routes of all difficulties. Stays in the shade in the afternoon. Plenty of boulders in a very arid setting. Worth a visit.

Dir: 25km N of Tarragona. From Reus drive N on the C240 to Alcover, carry on towards Montblanc and reach the town of La Riba in about 10km. From the village go up the valley in the direction of Farena and shortly a disused house is on the R and the crag is set back on the hill. Cross over the river and walk to the crag. 5 mins. (74:Ba,101)

Sant Llorenc:
(5–7c)(45) CATALUNYA [26]

A good limestone and conglomerate crag.

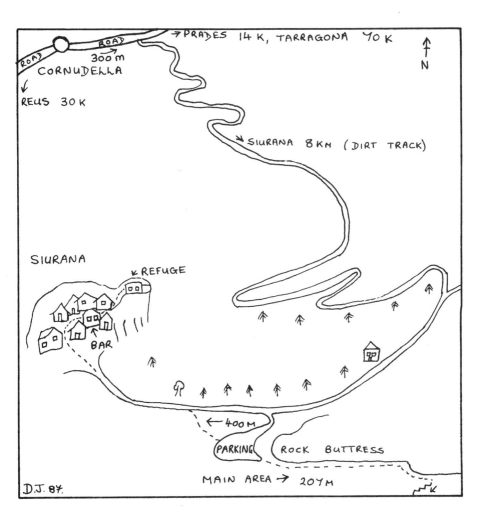

*ESCONDEROS AGUJIDOS, 6c, Siurana. (Climber Marie Agnes Duval,
Photo David Jones)*

Dir: 40km NNE of Lleida. Take the N1313 to the town centre of Balaguer. From here take a small road running N through Gerb and going to Sant Llorenç de Montgay. The crag is beside the road near the town. (56:Af,97)

Siurana:
✶ 07.00→16.00
(5.15.35.22.3)(80) CATALUNYA [27]

One of the best areas in northern Spain. There are many crags in the area but only a few have been fully developed; about 100 still have potential for development. Limestone 5m–25m, natural with all types of route. The holds are often quite small and the routes quite technical. Most of the crags face SE and are a good place in the autumn and spring. The town is a very long way from civilisation so bring all your food with you, and a good supply of mineral water, as the local supply is considered dubious.

PRENDRE LA TÊTE, 7a, Siurana.
(Climber Uwe Gschwendtner, Photo David Jones)

There is a very good refuge but it gets filled up with the Spanish and their dogs at weekends. There is a bar in the town. The 8km track to the town was not designed for your limousine! Bring a hire car or a Renault (both throwaway items).

Dir: 30km WNW of Tarragona. From Reus take the N420 for 10km then turn off R on to the C242 towards Alforja. Carry on all the way to Cornudella ignoring all the thousands of limestone crags around you. Stock up with supplies. Leave town going N towards Albarca but after about 300m turn R on to a track which will lead up to Siurana after 8km. The crags are before the village over the ridge on the L. (74:Af,101)

Terradets:
✶ 11.00→19.00
(4–7c)(80) CATALUNYA [28]

A popular, large, 500m limestone cliff. *In situ* gear [1–6] is varied but there are some climbs fully geared up; nevertheless, be cautious. Not a winter crag and can overheat in the direct summer sun. Lots of thorns on the approach, so wear heavy trousers. Great cliff and worth a trip. Very little in the easier grades but good middle to hard climbing. Becoming increasingly popular with French climbers now that bolting is in full swing.

Dir: 100km WNW of Manresa, 100km NE of Lleida. A very awkward crag to get to, perhaps easiest from France. From Llieda take the N1313 to Balaguer, turn L to the town but do not enter, turn R to Tremp. Eventually, after passing over the hills, drop down to the lake; after passing over the hills, drop down to the lake; after about 10km the crags can be seen (5km before Tremp). (56:Af,96)

Vilanova de Meia:
✶ (Lots) CATALUNYA [29]

A large 250m limestone crag in a wonderful situation which offers some good climbing and is worth visiting.

Dir: 57km NNE of Lleida. Take the N1313 to Térmens, pass Balaguer and continue in the direction of Ponts. 15km before Ponts turn L on to the 1412 which goes to Isona. After 4km turn L to Vilanova. The crag is nearby and referred to as 'La Roca dels Arcs'. (56:Ba,97)

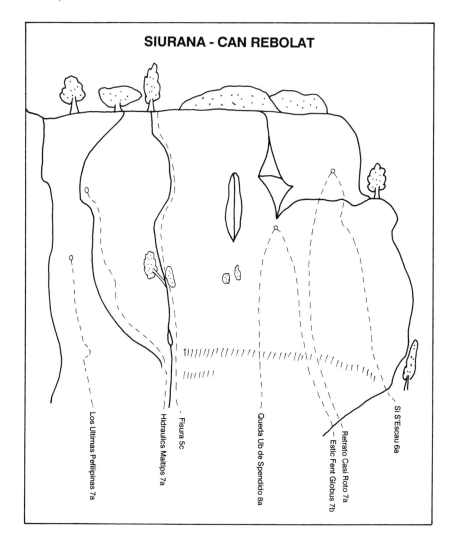

SIURANA - CAN REBOLAT

Los Ultimas Peñlipinas 7a

Hidraulics Maitips 7a

Fisura 5c

Queda Ub de Spendido 8a

Retrato Casi Roto 7a

Estic Fent Globus 7b

SI S'Escau 6a

Cuenca:

Ciudad
✳ 08.00→20.00
(Bouldering) CASTILLA LA MANCHA [30]

A fantastic limestone bouldering area which has been well visited by climbers from afar. Not the place for a week but definitely worth visiting if passing near the area. The rock formations resemble mushrooms and all overhang at the top. Routes to 5m. Great spot.

Dir: 18km NNE of Cuenca. From the town take the small road leading N towards Uña. After 10km there is a L fork to Mariana, bear R and continue for 10km past Villalba de la Sierra. 6km later on the road towards Uña turn R to Ciucad Encantada and the rocks. (102:Xf,107)7

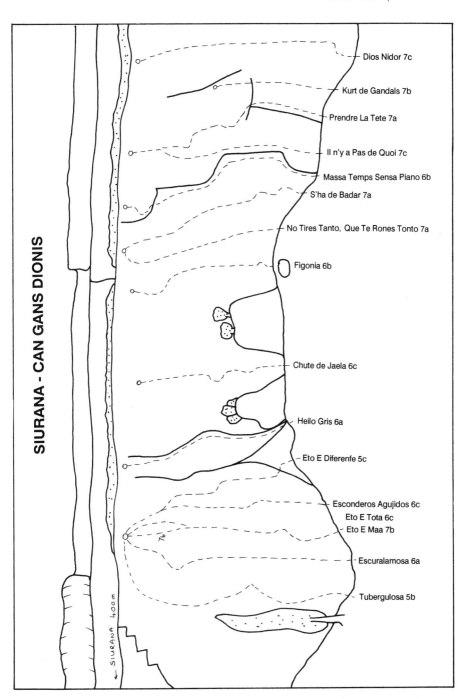

SIURANA - CAN GANS DIONIS

Dios Nidor 7c

Kurt de Gandals 7b

Prendre La Tete 7a

Il n'y a Pas de Quoi 7c

Massa Temps Sensa Piano 6b

S'ha de Badar 7a

No Tires Tanto, Que Te Rones Tonto 7a

Figonia 6b

Chute de Jaela 6c

Heilo Gris 6a

Eto E Diferenfe 5c

Esconderos Agujidos 6c
Eto E Tota 6c
Eto E Maa 7b

Escuralamosa 6a

Tubergulosa 5b

SIURANA 400m

SOUTH-EAST SPAIN

Valencia

Barranco de Mascarat:
✶ 10.00→19.00
(4 – 7c)(15)   VALENCIA [31]

Not one of the world's greatest limestone crags but quite handy and often visited. The spot has become far more famous for bridge-jumping than climbing, nevertheless, there are some routes that are worth doing.

Dir: 57km NE of Alicante. The crag is by the bridges and tunnels on the main road linking Calpe and Altea, NE of Benidorm. (139:Aa,117)

Chulilla:
✶ 12.00→22.00
(3.15.41.8.2)(70)   VALENCIA [32]

A very good area of excellent limestone walls 10 – 50m high. There are 5 cliffs all with a different character. Some have 2 pitches and others only have short single pitches. On Zona de Mas Alla you have to abseil in to the belay which is 35m down a corner, a grade 4 to escape. The hardest climbing is to be found on Zona de los Perros, and for the middle grade climber Peneta offers very good double pitch routes. A warm crag in summer but ideal at other times of the year. There is camping at Fuente de la Pelma.

Dir: 50km WNW of Valencia. From Valencia go NW to Lliria on the 234. Carry on towards Casinos then 9km towards Chelva. Turn R on to the 224 towards Requena. After 12km turn L on to the road that leads to Chulilla after 2km. Locate the Bar de la Juventu where local route info can be obtained. The cliffs are below the town overlooking the river. (123:Za,111)

Contreras:
(4 – 7c)(70)   VALENCIA [33]

An established climbing area. Large 200m limestone cliffs with lots of scope. A guide should be available in Valencia.

Dir: 100km W of Valencia. Take the N111 to Requena, carry on to Utiel, then continue W through Caudete. After 20km arrive at the village of Contreras (before Minglanilla). (122:Yc,111)

La Dalle d'Ola:
✶ 10.00→16.00
(5 – 7a)(18)   VALENCIA [34]

A popular large limestone slab offering excellent middle grade routes. *In situ* gear [2 – 4]. Good finger pockets.

Dir: 56km NE of Alicante. Take the A7 past Benidorm, then turn off at junction 64 to Altea. Carry on towards Calpe on the C332 but after Olla and before Mascarat turn off (signposted 'Residencias Bernia'). Follow this over the road to a road forking R which is usually chained off. This leads to the crag in 15 mins. (139:Zf,117)

Montanejos:
✶ 10.00→21.00
(22.35.160.75.7)(350)   VALENCIA [35]

This is not a crag for the beginner. Steep limestone, 5 – 100m high, offering all middle to hard grade routes. The climbing is very good, warm in the winter, too hot in the summer. Most of the routes are bolted [3 – 6] and 2 – 3 pitches long. The first pitches are often very good so you don't always have to go to the top. There is a campsite with very basic facilities. There is also a climbing hut with finer details of the routes worth climbing. Sun and shade can often be found here and this makes it very much an all-year-round crag. The grading seems to be a bit strange at the moment, so start on a few easy routes to warm up; getting stuck on a two-pitch route is a real pain.

Dir: 66km NNW of Valencia. From Valencia travel N to Sagunto, from here go towards Teruel on the N234. Pass through Segorbe then at Jerica turn R and go to Caudiel. 1km after the village the road forks, go L. This road winds its way slowly for 10km then opens out and goes to Montán and then shortly after Montanejos. There are a few crags near the village but the main ones are about 1km upstream by the river after the first tunnel. (104:Zc,108)

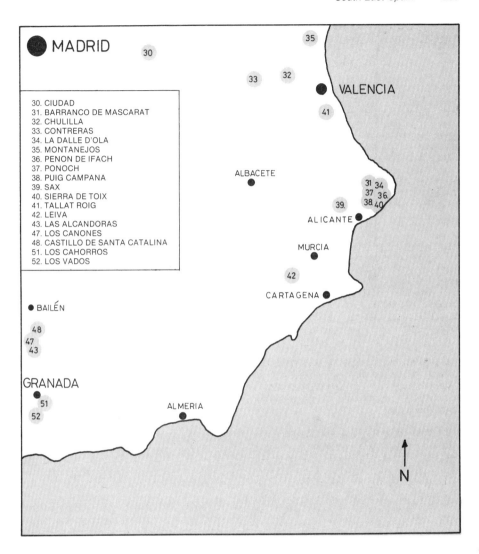

MADRID 30

30. CIUDAD
31. BARRANCO DE MASCARAT
32. CHULILLA
33. CONTRERAS
34. LA DALLE D'OLA
35. MONTANEJOS
36. PENON DE IFACH
37. PONOCH
38. PUIG CAMPANA
39. SAX
40. SIERRA DE TOIX
41. TALLAT ROIG
42. LEIVA
43. LAS ALCANDORAS
47. LOS CANONES
48. CASTILLO DE SANTA CATALINA
51. LOS CAHORROS
52. LOS VADOS

VALENCIA
ALBACETE
ALICANTE
MURCIA
CARTAGENA
BAILÉN
GRANADA
ALMERIA

N

Penon de Ifach:
✴ 10.00→19.00
(4 – 8a)(70)   VALENCIA [36]

A very well-known limestone outcrop by the sea. It is the crag most frequently visited by British climbers in Spain, however, its merit is not great and climbing is only average. Save your effort; there are better crags in the area. The crag is sometimes referred to as CALPE, the name of the nearby village. The crag is over 200m high and offers a great deal of intermittently protected routes. On such a large outcrop a topo is useful, available locally and even in the UK from climbing shops. There is a local climbing club so bolting will no doubt continue at a steady rate. In summer it is far too hot; winter camping is a problem so rent an apartment, and rent a car to get to some of the more distant crags, even if only for a couple of days.

Dir: 60km NE of Alicante. take the *autopista* to the Altea turn-off (64) then follow signs to Calpe to the N. If you can't see the crag I suggest you go to the nearest optician. (139:Aa,117)

Ponoch:
(4 – 7a)(20)   VALENCIA [37]

A well-recommended crag of multi pitch limestone routes. More for the adventurous Himalayan stomper. Best descent is by parapenting. The other crags which are linked to this are TOZAL DE LEVANTE and TORRE DE ENMEDIO. All have similar characteristics. *In situ* gear is very varied and abseil points cannot be guaranteed.

Dir: 42km NE of Alicante. From Benidorm take the C3318 towards Oliva. After 9km reach Polop. The crags are to the W of the town. (139:Zf,117)

Puig Campana:
✶ 10.00→19.00
(3 – 7a)(35)   VALENCIA [38]

A very large 300m crag with real mountaineering (stone-age) traditional climbing. There is *in situ* gear [3 – 6] but a rack of gear is very necessary. Has been popular over the years and the scene of many a happy day's trundling.

Dir: 36km NE of Alicante. From Benidorm go to the motorway junction then go NW to Finestrat, 10km. From here a small road leads off up to the R and the peak. Follow this for a while then turn L by Font de Moli and cross the canal bridge to a parking spot. From here a track leads up to the crags. 30 mins. (139:Ze,117)

Sax:
✶ 07.00→13.00
(4 – 7b)(25)   VALENCIA [39]

A very well recommended crag with lots of easy to middle grade routes. Some of the routes are 100m long so a spare rope to abseil back down can be useful. Limestone with bolts [2 – 4]. Can get quite busy at weekends but is very pleasant midweek. Faces the best way for summer afternoons and winter morning climbing. Worth a visit.

Dir: 36km NW of Alicante, 9km NNW of Elda. From Novelda to the W of Alicante take the N330 towards Villena and Madrid. Bypass Elda then turn off to the L and the town of Sax. Go into the town but bear off to the R rather than carrying on towards Salinas. Here a track leads to some power lines and the crag. (138:Za,117)

Sierra de Toix:
✶ 06.00→22.00
(3 – 7a)(200)   VALENCIA [40]

This is a limestone ridge to the S of Calpe offering good excitement to the lower and middle grade climber. There are harder possibilities but as yet these have not been bolted up. Bring a rack of gear here to supplement some of the bolts [6]. Still a worthy spot to spend a day. There are two cliffs: the west, which is inland and sunny for most of the day, and the east, which is good on hot afternoons. There is also a sea cliff which is below the west cliff.

Dir: 54km NE of Alicante. Take the *autopista* to the Altea turn-off (64) then follow signs to Calpe to the N. The road starts to go up into hills, past Mascarat then through two tunnels. Soon after and before dropping down into Calpe there is a turning on the R. Take this and if you follow it to the R you come to some parking at the W end. By forking L the road leads to Maryvilla and the N end of the ridge, the E section. (139:Aa,117)

Tallat Roig:
(50)   VALENCIA [41]

A good 70 – 80m limestone crag which is popular in the evenings.

Dir: 40km S of Valencia. Go S on the N340 towards Alcoy, or take the *autopista* to Jtn 58 Algemesi turn-off. From here go S to Alzira, 5km. From the town a small road leads off SE which arrives at the cliffs after 9km. The cliffs are in a valley on the S side of the Sierra de la Murta. (123:Zd,114)

Murcia

Leiva:
✳ 10.00→16.00
(4−7b)(85) MURCIA [42]

A very good winter crag provided the wind abates. In summer it is just too hot and unbearable, but never mind − the coast and windsurfing are not that far away. Limestone cliffs up to 160m high with lots of middle grade routes. *In situ* gear varied [2−6]. Can be popular at weekends but there is enough to go round. Worth a visit.

Dir: 40km WSW of Murcia. Take the N340 towards Totana and Almeria. After 30km reach Alhama, turn off to the R on to the C3315 towards Mula. After 2km and just past Los Pavos turn L to Parque Naturel de Sierra Espuña. Pass Moriana, Albergue, then at a junction turn R onto the road which leads to the former Sanatorio Esquela Hogar (turning off the road). The track (going W) forks and by following the R branch you will see the crag up to the R. Walk to the crag. 20 mins. (151:Yc,121)

SOUTH-WEST SPAIN

Las Alcandoras:
(35) ANDALUCIA [43]

A large and steep crag. Limestone up to 200m with multi pitch routes. *In situ* gear state unknown at present.

Dir: 18km S of Jaén. Go to the S part of town then instead of bearing R to Los Villares bear L to Otiñar O Santa Christina. Reach the town and carry on towards the Quiebrajano dam up the valley and the crag is soon reached. (148:Wb,123)

Andújar:
(70) ANDALUCIA [44]

Quite a popular area to climb. There are a few crags locally up to 40m high, some of granite and others of limestone. Seek more local info.

Dir: 67km E of Córdoba. Take the N4 going E through El Carpio, Villa del Rio, then to Andújar. Crags should be close to the town. (147:Vf,120)

Ategua:
(20) ANDALUCIA [45]

Some good sandstone routes and plenty of bouldering, 25m high in places.

Dir: 36km SE of Córdoba. From town take the N432 towards Baena. After 40km arrive at the town of Castro del Rio. The climbing area is nearby. (147:Vd,122)

Benahavis:
(10) ANDALUCIA [46]

A small 25m limestone crag with some middle grade routes. Although there are only a few the quality is very good indeed and worth a trip.

Dir: 61km WSW of Málaga. Take the coast road from Málaga to Marbella, then past San Pedro. On the R is a turn-off to Ronda; pass this and continue for 4km where another road leads off to the R signposted 'Benahavis'. Take this towards the village. About 1km before the village the crag can be seen on the L. (168:Uf,129)

Los Cañones:
(50) ANDALUCIA [47]

Good limestone climbing on some rather large walls. Routes of up to 140m but there are quite a few single pitch routes as well. Worth a trip for the day.

Dir: 9k S of Jaén. Take a small road going S from the town the C3221 which leads to the town of Los Villares. The cliffs are nearby. (148:Wb,122)

Castillo de Santa Catalina
(4−7c)(65) ANDALUCIA [48]

This is a very popular crag at the town of Jaén. Lots of climbs with bolts [1−4]. Routes all single pitch with some up to 40m long. There is also some more climbing to be found locally behind the crag of Catalina, limestone again and referred to as LA MELLA.

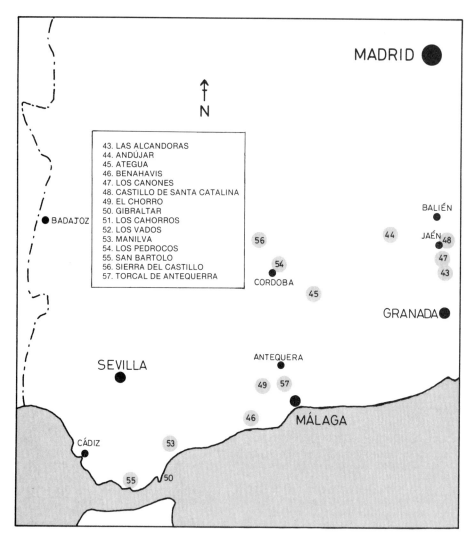

Dir: Overlooking the town of Jaén. (148:Wb,122)

El Chorro:
☆ 09.00→18.00
(4−8c)(300) ANDALUCIA [49]

This is by far the most popular and well-developed climbing area within close reach of Málaga. There is some natural gear at present

but in the main bolts [3−6] predominate. There are climbs of every grade, equally well spread, all up to 200m high. This is a topo guide to the area which can be purchased locally at the small railway station café.

Dir: 40km NW of Málaga. From Málaga take the road going W to Alora. From here El Chorro is signposted and about 12km. (169:Vb,127)

Gibraltar:
✳ A lot (Rubbish) ANDALUCIA [50]

Climbing on the rock is awful in comparison with the other crags in the area; don't bother.

Los Cahorros:
(4 – 7b)(120) ANDALUCIA [51]

A good limestone crag with routes up to 150m high. There are a lot of single pitch routes as well. Popular with climbers from Granada.

Dir: 8km SE of Granada. From the southern part of the town follow signs towards Zubia then fork off to the L to the village of Monachil. The crags are close to the village. (171:Wc,126)

Los Vados:
(Unknown) ANDALUCIA [52]

I hardly know anything of this crag except that it comes by good recommendation. Limestone routes up to 300m high with some very good routes on. Seek and ye shall find heaven, or more Cerveza!

Dir: 48km S of Granada. Just to the E of Almuñécar is the town of Motril. The crags are close by. (171:Wc,128)

Manilva:
✳ 06.00→14.00
(4 – 7b)(45) ANDALUCIA [53]

A very good crag with superb rock and a lovely setting. Limestone up to 100m high. Right in the mainstream development there is good scope for 200 plus routes here. Only above listed are bolted at present. Worth a good visit.

Dir: 30km N of Gibraltar. Take the N340 going N towards Estepona. About 12km before the town turn L at San Suis de Sabinillas. This leads to Manilva. The crags are near here to the E. (175:Ue,130)

Los Pedrocos:
✳ 09.00→18.00
(Bouldering) ANDALUCIA [54]

A well-known bouldering area close to Córdoba. Granite and quite extensive.

Dir: Not exactly sure. Try 4km to the NE of town near the village of Pedroches. (146:Vb,121)

San Bartolo:
(4 – 7b)(24) ANDALUCIA [55]

A 25m crag of very compact sandstone, bolts [2 – 4]. The routes are of good quality and worth a visit.

Dir: 30km W of Gibraltar. Go to the town of Tarifa on the southernmost point then take the road towards Jeréz. The crags are reached after a few km outside Tarifa. (174:Ub,132)

Sierra del Castillo:
(4 – 7b)(90) ANDALUCIA [56]

An important limestone climbing area within easy reach of Córdoba. There are plenty of routes here on walls and pinnacles up to 100m. Gear situation is unknown.

Dir: 40km NNW of Córdoba. Take the N432 which leads N to Espiel. The crags are just to the S of the town. (146;Uf,119)

Torcal de Antequerra:
✳ 07.00→21.00
(4 – 7a)(15) ANDALUCIA [57]

This area will become more busy as climbing gains popularity in southern Spain. The climbing is very good and the aspect is far better than that of El Chorro. However, at present there are few bolts but with a few Bosch frenzies this dilemma should be cured. Not a winter crag as it is quite high.

Dir: 27km NNW of Málaga. From Málaga go N to Antequera. From the S part of town take a road towards Villanueva, and the crags are just about 3km before the town and signposted ('Parador') to the R. (169:Vc,127)

Appendix

English	French	German	Italian	Spanish
About	Environ	Herum	Presso	Cerca
Above	Amont	Über	Sopra	Anterior
Abseil	Rappel	Abseil	Corda Doppia	
Access	Accés	Zutritt	Accesso	Accesso
Approach	Approche	Nähern	Approccio	Entrada
Ban	Ban	Bann	Proibire	Prohibicón
Bear	Aller	Vorgehen	Produrre	Seguir
Beck	P. Rivière	Strom	Ruscello	Riachuelo
Before	Avant			
Beginning	Commencement	Beginnen	Origine	Principo
Belay	Relais	Anker spitze	Sosta	Amarrar
Below	Au dessous de	Unten	Sotto	Abajo
Bend	Courbe	Beugen	Curva	Comba
Birds	Oiseau	Vogel	Uccello	Párajo
Bolts	Verrou	Bolzen	Spit	Flecha
Boulder	Gros galet	Felsblock	M. Roccioso	Peñasco
Bumblie	Bumblière	Bumblicher	Bumbliano	Los Bumblo
Buttress	Contrefort	Strebepfeiler	Pilastro	Murallas
Clean	Nettoyer			
Climb	Grimpeur	Klettern	Via	Subida
Continue	Continuer	Fortsetzen	Continuare	Continuare
Corner	Coin	Winkel	Diedro	Ángulo
Cove	Anse	Kleine Bucht	Piccola Baia	Abra
Crag/Cliff	Falaises	Klippe	Picco	Peña
Crux	Noeud	Schwierigkeit	Furioso	Duropunto
Difficult	Difficile	Schwer	Difficile	Dlfícil
Direction	Direction	Richtung	Direzione	Curso
Double	Double	Doppelgänger	Doppio	Doble
Down	Décent	Flaum	Scendere	Vello
Dozen	Douze	Dutzend	Dodici	Docena
Drive	Auto avance	Fahrweg	Passeggiata	P en Coche
E, East	Est	Osten	Est	Este
Easy/ier	Facile	Leicht	Facile	Fácil
Escape	Evasion	Entweichen	Scappamento	Fuga
Extreme	Extrême	Extrem	Estremo	Extremo
Face	Paroi	Oberfläche	Parete	Cara
Facing	Regard	- Blicken	Viso	Enfrente
Fell	Côte	Hügel	Colle	Cerro
Flash	a vue		a vista	
Follow	Suivre	Folgen	Seguire	Seguir
Footpath	Chemin	Fussweg	P. Senterio	Vereda
Fork	Branche	Wenden	Fenditura	Bifurcación
Further	Nouveau loin	Weiter	Addizionale	Ulterior
Gill	Petit vallée	Klein Tal	Ruscello	Cuenca
Granite	Granit	Granit	Granito	Granito
Gritstone	Roche gravier	Griesstein	Grana Pietra	Arenaroca
Gully	Ravin	Sinkkasten	Canale	Barranca
Half	Demi	Hälfte	Meta	Medio
Hamlet	Hameau	Dörfchen	P. Villagio	Villorio
Hard	Difficile	Schwer	Difficile	Duro
Head, Point	Source, Cap	Spitze	Punta	Punto
Height	Hauteur	Höhe	Alto	
Hill	Côte	Hügel	Colle	Cerro
Hold	Tenir	Schiffsraum	Appiglio	Asidero
Interesting	Intéressant	Interessieren	Interessante	Interesante
Junction	Jonction	Verbindung	Congiunzione	Trabadura
Karabiners	Mousqueton	Karabiners	Moschettone	
Lane	Ruelle	Gasse	Vicolo	Senda
Large	Grande	Gross	Grosso	Grande

Lead	Aller premier	Führen	Fare d guida	Giroprimero
Ledge	Rebord	Sims	Ripiano	Borde
L, left	Gauche	Linke	Sinistra	Izquierdo
Lichen	Lichen	Moos	Lichene	Musgo
Limestone	Calcaire	Kalkfels	Calcare	Calceroca
Loose	Lâche	Lösen	Marcio	Suelto
Map	Carte	Landkarte	Carta	Mapa
Moor	Maure	Vermooren	Burghiera	Páramo
Motorway	Autoroute	Autobahn	Autostrada	Autopista
Mountain	Montagne	Berg	Montagna	Montaña
N, North	Nord	Norden	Nord	Norte
Nuts	Coinceures		Dado	
Opposite	Opposé	Widerstand	Opposto	Opuesto
Outcrop	Fleurement	Tagebau	Rupe a picco	Peña
Overhang	Surplomber	Überhangen	Strapiombo	Colgar
Parallel	Paralèle	Parallel	Paralello	Paralelo
Park	Garer	Parkplatz	Parcheggio	Parqamentio
Pitch	Longueurs	Schneiden	Tiro	Sección
Path	Sentier		Sentiero	
Pocket	Gouttes d'eau	Tasche	Tasca	Bolsillo
Poorly	Pas fort	Schlecht	Povero	Pobre
Protection	Protection	Schutz	Assicuriazione	Protección
Quarry	Proie	Steinbruch	Cava	Canterra
Reached	Atteindre	Reichen	Portata	Alcance
Restriction	Restriction	Einschränkung	Restrizione	Restricción
Ridge	Arête	Rüchen	Cresta	Lomo
R, right	Droit	Recht	Destra	Recto
Ring Road	Rue Cercle	Ringstrasse	Circ. Strada	Circopista
River	Rivière	Fluss	Flume	Fluvial
Road	Route, Rue	Strasse	Strada	Camino
Rope	Corde	Seil	Corda	Cuerda
Routes	Voies	Reise	Via	Ruta
Runner	Protection	Schutz	Protezione	Protección
Safe	Sauf	Sicher	Siccuro	Seguro
Sandstone	Grés	Sandfels	Rena Pietra	Arenaroca
Scar	Rocher	Klippe	Picco	Peña
Score	Vingt	Zwanzig	Venti	Veinte
Scrambling	Escalade	Klettern	Scalata	Trepar
Sea	Mer	See	Mare	Mar
Serious	Sérieux	Ernst	Grave	Serio
Sharp	Tranchant	Scharf	Acuto	Agudo
Side	Bord	Seite	Fianco	Lateral
Single	Seul	Einzig	Singolo	Singular
Situ, in	En cours			
Slab	Dalle	Platte	Placca	Losa
Slate	Ardoise	Schiefer	Ardesia	Slate
Small	Petit	Klein	Piccolo	Chico
Solid	Solide	Fest	Solido	Sólido
S, South	Sud	Süden	Sud	Sud
Start	Sursaut	Anfang	Inizio	Sobresalto
Steep	Raide	Abschüssig	Ripido	Escarpado
Straight	Ligne Droite	Direkt	Diretto	Derecho
Stream	Ruisseau	Wasserlauf	Corrente	Corriente
Summer	Été	Sommer	Estate	Estival
Technical	Technique	Technisch	Technico	Technique
Tides	Marée temps	Ebbe Zeit	Marea. Epoca	De Marea
Tie Off	Dégaines		Rinvii	
Top rope	Hétéroclite			
Towards	Envers	Gegen	Verso	Hacia
Town	Ville	Stadt	Citta	Ciudad
Track	Trace	Feldweg	Cammino	Ruta
Traverse	Traverse	Traverse	Traverso	Atravesar
Tree	Arbre	Baum	Albero	Árbol
Turn	Tour	Umdrehung	Direzione	Vuelta
Until	Jusqu'a, av	Bis	Fino a	Hasta
Up, Upper	En avance	Auf	Piu in Alto	Superior
Various	Varié	Verschieden	Diverso	Vario

Village	Village	Dorf	Villaggio	Pueblo
Volcanic	Volcanique	Vulkanisch	Vulcanico	Volcánico
Walk	Marche	Lauf	Cammino	Paseo
Wall	Dalle	Mauer	Muro	Pared
Way down	Decente	Absteig	Decente	Pasopelo
W, West	Ouest	Westen	Ovest	Oeste
Winter	Hiver	Winter	Inverno	Invierno
Zawn	Caverne-Mer	See-Höhle	Cavernamare	Cueva Mar

Index